# *A*
# LITTLE
# HOUSE
## *Sampler*

The Ingalls family in De Smet in the 1890s. Seated, left to right, are Ma, Pa, and Mary. Standing are Carrie, Laura, and Grace.

# $\mathcal{A}$ LITTLE HOUSE
## *Sampler*

Laura Ingalls Wilder

Rose Wilder Lane

Edited by William T. Anderson

Western Producer Prairie Books

Saskatoon, Saskatchewan

Published in Canada in 1988 by Western Producer Prairie Books,
Saskatoon, Saskatchewan
Published simultaneously in the United States
by the University of Nebraska Press, Lincoln, Nebraska

Printed in the United States of America

Library of Congress Cataloging
in Publication Data

Wilder, Laura Ingalls, 1867–1957.
A Little House sampler.

1. Wilder, Laura Ingalls,
1867–1957—Biography.
2. Authors, American—
20th century—Biography.
3. Children's stories—Authorship.
4. Farm life—United States.
I. Lane, Rose Wilder, 1886–1968.
II. Anderson, William T., 1952–
III. Title.
PS3545.I342Z47 1988   813'.52 [B]   87-19208
ISBN 0-8032-1022-1 (alk. paper)

Available only from
University of Nebraska Press
901 North 17th Street
Lincoln, Nebraska 68588-0520

# Contents

# Illustrations

Key to Main Sources

# Preface

Laura Ingalls Wilder's prairie girlhood was enriched by the beauty and the drama of artful storytelling. Under starry skies beside campfires along the trail or in the flickering firelight at home, her father's tales enlivened her life and stimulated her imagination. Charles Ingalls regularly entertained his womenfolk with spellbinding after-supper storytelling sessions, followed by his one-man fiddle concerts. "It puts heart to a man," Pa Ingalls said of those family evenings of story and song. Laura never forgot those interludes from the rigors of pioneer life; for her, Pa's magical fiddle music and repertoire of stories were integral in the memory of home.

Charles Ingalls learned to weave exciting stories just as he learned to fiddle: by happenstance, on the frontier. And his skills were sharpened by continual demand and use. His fablelike narratives, his accounts of adventurous feats in the forest and on the plains, his humorous anecdotes, and his legendary Indian lore were all repeated and enlarged through years of living in "little houses" all over the heartland of America. When Pa told stories, his girls, especially Laura, listened wide-eyed and intent.

Later, as a wife and mother, Laura Ingalls Wilder continued to practice the family tradition of storytelling. Pa's tales were repeated in Laura's homestead house in South Dakota and later on Rocky Ridge Farm in the Ozarks. To her father's fund of anecdotes Laura added her own; she had lived through and heard of amazing adventures while growing up as a pioneer girl.

Laura's daughter, Rose Wilder Lane, first transferred to the printed word the family talent for description and narrative. By 1915 Rose was a published writer, and she continued her career with great success for another fifty years. It was through Rose's encouragement that Laura first started writing for publication. She originally planned her "Little House" books simply to preserve the stories that Pa Ingalls had first told in the log cabin hidden in the Big Woods of Wisconsin.

During their writing careers, both Laura and Rose jotted extensively, published prolifically, and shared their stories and their skill in telling them with readers of all ages. They were savers; among their personal papers both mother and daughter preserved nearly every manuscript and each draft, along with most of the notes and letters that pertained to their professional writing. Among the reams of yellowing manuscript pages exists a myriad of materials that shed new light on their lives and works.

*A Little House Sampler* is a collection of long-unseen writings of Laura Ingalls Wilder and Rose Wilder Lane. Some of the articles and fictional works appeared in popular magazines of other eras. Many of Laura's essays were published during her association with the *Missouri Ruralist*, years before she thought of writing the "Little House" books. Other material appearing herein is derived from first drafts or abandoned manuscripts that now illuminate some previously untold aspect of the lives of the Ingalls and Wilder families.

The selections in *A Little House Sampler* are not arranged according to their dates of publication, but rather to create a chronological account of the lives of Laura Ingalls Wilder, her husband, Almanzo, and their daughter, Rose. Essentially, Laura's and Rose's writings are reproduced here as they first appeared in print or in their original manuscript form, although they have been lightly edited to regularize spelling, punctuation, and capitalization within selections, and obvious typographical errors have been silently corrected. Available and pertinent background information accompanies each piece.

Most of the material contained in this sampler comes from the extensive Rose Wilder Lane Papers at the Herbert Hoover Presidential Library in West Branch, Iowa. Reproduction here is with the encouragement and consent of Roger Lea MacBride, executor of the estates of Laura Ingalls Wilder and Rose Wilder Lane.

In compiling these writings, I have received assistance from several sources. The staff of the Hoover Library has extended every courtesy to me during my working sessions with the Wilder-Lane Papers. In addition, valuable resource material has come from the collections of the Laura Ingalls Wilder Memorial Society in De Smet, South Dakota, and the Laura Ingalls Wilder Home and Museum in Mansfield, Missouri. Special thanks are due to Phyllis Bell of De Smet for her critique of the manuscript while this book was in the making.

# Prologue

"She had the most beautiful eyes I have ever seen," remarked one of Laura Ingalls's classmates, remembering the small, quiet girl who had diligently studied in the one-room schoolhouse in De Smet, Dakota Territory, during the early 1880s. Those eyes had registered, with clarity and precision, the pioneer childhood images that Laura Ingalls Wilder drew upon when she started writing her autobiographical "Little House" series at the age of sixty-five. These nine books about her childhood, youth, and early adulthood on the American frontier have been read and loved by children around the world.

Hard work had dominated the life she knew and wrote about. She had cooked along the trail when she was so small that she stood on a dry goods box to reach the camp table. She knew the physical labor of making hay under a blazing western sun and then twisting it ceaselessly into fuel to ward off frigid winter blasts. As a teen she had sewn for twelve-hour stints to earn her dollar a day. And she had taught school in an isolated, abandoned claim shanty where three of her pupils were older and taller than she was. Finally, she had spent many years helping a disease-weakened husband build a home and a farm from the grudging, resistant earth.

Laura always saw the beauty of simple things. She found satisfaction in cloud shadows on the green land, swaying wild grasses, singing birds, white-scrubbed board floors, and spots of color and cheer that brightened a crude, primitive house.

Born on February 7, 1867, Laura Elizabeth Ingalls first saw the light of the world in a log cabin hidden in the forests surrounding Pepin, Wisconsin. Her parents, Charles and Caroline Ingalls, were

Laura's pioneering parents, Charles and Caroline Ingalls

products of the frontier. Charles Ingalls was a renowned fiddler and a woodsman, hunter, and farmer; he was a carpenter and a sometime public official. Caroline Quiner Ingalls was descended from Scotch nobility and had roots in New England. She stressed education and the value of stability in the family, whether the home was an unfinished shanty, a sod dugout, or a rowdy railroad camp. Laura's mother instilled in her a sense of propriety and dignity. Her father passed on to her his storytelling ability—a gift that Laura in turn handed down to her daughter.

Charles and Caroline and their four daughters—Mary, Laura, Carrie, and Grace—participated in the last great thrust of the western movement. Lured by the open spaces and the free land of the Homestead Act of 1862, Pa Ingalls led his womenfolk on a ten-year journey throughout the upper Midwest in search of a productive homestead claim. From the Big Woods they traveled by prairie schooner to the Indian Territory of Kansas and back again to Wisconsin. In 1873 they went west to the banks of Plum Creek near Walnut Grove, Minnesota. Then they moved to Burr Oak,

Iowa, in 1876, back-trailers and fugitives from the infamous grass-hopper plagues that stripped the land of every green thing. But the spell of the West led the family back to Walnut Grove. Finally they pushed into Dakota Territory, ahead of the advancing railroads, in 1879. Though he longed to see Oregon and the Pacific coast, Charles Ingalls yielded to his wife's "no further" edict and established a permanent homestead at De Smet, South Dakota.

On the prairie claim, Laura Ingalls first synthesized images into words. For her blind sister, Mary, Laura was the link to light and movement. "Your two eyes are quick enough, and your tongue, if you will use them for Mary," Charles Ingalls had told his daughter (who later recorded it in *By the Shores of Silver Lake*). After Laura had described a flaming Dakota sunset, Mary complimented her in a strangely prophetic way: "And now I see it all," she said. "You make pictures when you talk, Laura."

Laura had little opportunity to develop her word pictures or to set them into prose during her years as a pioneer girl. Books were prized by the Ingalls family, but they were scarce. Reverently, the few volumes the family possessed were carried from place to place on their covered wagon trips; they were read and reread. "I went to 'little red school-houses' all over the west and was never graduated from anything," Laura recalled (*Kansas City Star*, May 25, 1955) as she summed up her formal training. Her high school professor, V. S. L. Owen, had encouraged her to write; he had perceived her natural talent for composition.

Her regular schooling was interrupted three times while she left home to teach at country schools, and after marrying in 1885, she left school, both as a student and as a teacher, permanently behind. Laura Ingalls was eighteen when she married a prosperous young homesteader named Almanzo Wilder. As a young matron in her little gray house near De Smet, she had scanty time to consider writing. Instead, her first years of married life were filled with housekeeping, childbearing, and worrying about crop failures, finances, and disease. Diphtheria left Almanzo permanently impaired with a limp, their infant son died in 1888, and a week after their baby's death a fire consumed their home.

The romanticism of prairie homesteading was tinged with the defeat of repeated crop failures as the lusty fields were ruined by hailstones, hot winds, and drought. Only the waving grass and the masses of wild roses that colored the Wilders' Sunday buggy drives seemed to thrive. It was for those profuse pink blooms that Laura named their only surviving child. With the winter winds whistling around the claim shanty, Rose Wilder was born on December 5, 1886.

In 1894 Laura and Almanzo left De Smet with their seven-year-old daughter, bound for the Ozark Mountains and Mansfield, Missouri. There they set up their final home, marveling that among the trees and hills they could no longer hear the winds howl. Their two hundred acres of thin, stony soil became Rocky Ridge Farm, a productive dairy, fruit, and poultry farm.

When the farm was finally established, Laura Wilder, now middle-aged, found a way to write. Her first published works were for the farm family weekly the *Missouri Ruralist*. For sixteen years, from 1911 to 1927, her columns appeared in the country journal. She discussed agricultural issues, country living, and innovations in rural life; and she sometimes reminisced about her own pioneer girlhood. In her steady flow of poetry, columns, features, and interviews, Mrs. A. J. Wilder became the predominant female voice of the *Ruralist*.

Ironically, Rose had grown dissatisfied with the very life her mother promoted. At seventeen she left the farm for a career in the big city. As a Kansas City telegrapher, she participated in the first Western Union walkout in 1903 and was an ardent suffragist. She was a "bachelor girl," the modern woman who shortened her skirts to clear the dirty sidewalks, cut her hair, and stole the shirt off man's back, making the serviceable shirtwaist a revolution in style.

In 1909 Rose married Gillette Lane in San Francisco. When the couple entered the real estate business, Rose Lane was the first woman to penetrate that field dominated by men. A calculating businesswoman, she sold thousands of acres of the old Spanish-grant ranches in the Santa Clara Valley.

From her real estate career, Rose Wilder Lane gravitated to a literary milieu. By 1914 she was a star reporter for the *San Francisco Call-Bulletin*, and she was urging her mother back in Missouri to write for the "big markets" that paid far more in exposure and cash than the farm journal circuit.

Laura traveled to San Francisco in 1915 to visit the Lanes and to see the Panama-Pacific International Exposition. She went to investigate a possible move for herself and Almanzo, but mostly she sought Rose's secrets for successful publication. Between sightseeing jaunts, Laura conferred with Rose; she hoped "to do some writing that will count." At the end of her trip came assignments and free passes from the *Ruralist;* they were especially interested in Laura Wilder's reports on the Missouri exhibits at the fair.

After observing her daughter at work, Laura confided to Almanzo that she preferred the demands of the henhouse to the high-tension deadlines of a newspaper office. And when she returned to the quietness of Rocky Ridge, satiated with San Francisco sightseeing, she declared that she "would not trade all of California for one Ozark hill."

During World War I, Rose Wilder Lane's writing achieved national prominence. She produced the first biography of Henry Ford; she wrote "Charlie Chaplin's Own Story" and a life of Art Smith, the daredevil aviator, as *Call-Bulletin* series; and she wrote "Life and Jack London" for *Sunset.* Her first work of fiction was the *Sunset* serial "Diverging Roads," later published as her first novel. The romantic tale of a country girl moving to the city was loosely autobiographical; it was based on Rose's marriage to Gillette Lane and their divorce in 1918.

Each in her own realm, Rose Wilder Lane and Laura Ingalls Wilder forged literary careers and gained reader following, the daughter on the West Coast and the mother in the Ozarks. Both wrote in a direct, crisp style about subjects that revealed their lively interest in people, places, and events. And both won staunch reader-friends early in the beginning years of their professional writing. California apricot growers considered Rose Lane their spokeswoman in her series "Soldiers of the Soil," just as the *Missouri Ruralist* audience enthusiastically read Laura Wilder's column "As a Farm Woman Thinks."

The *Missouri Ruralist* and *Sunset* each realized that its readers were curious about the woman behind the byline. In 1918 each

Laura (left) and Rose in the ravine on Rocky Ridge Farm

magazine printed a feature on its celebrated columnist. "Let's Visit Mrs. Wilder" was published in the February 20 issue of the *Ruralist;* the article was written by John F. Case, *Ruralist* editor. "Rose Wilder Lane, by Herself" appeared in the November issue of *Sunset*. Laura was fifty-one and Rose was thirty-one when the pieces were published, but each was just beginning her long writing career.

John F. Case

# Let's Visit Mrs. Wilder

M ISSOURI FARM FOLKS need little introduction before getting acquainted with Mrs. A. J. Wilder of Rocky Ridge Farm.
During the years that she has been connected with this paper—a
greater number of years than any other person on the editorial
staff—she has taken strong hold upon the esteem and affections
of our great family. Mrs. Wilder has lived her life upon a farm. She
knows farm folks and their problems as few women who write
know them. And having sympathy with the folks whom she serves
she writes well.

"Mrs. Wilder is a woman of delightful personality," a neighbor
tells me, "and she is a combination of energy and determination.
She always is cheery, looking on the bright side. She is her husband's partner in every sense and is fully capable of managing the
farm. No woman can make you feel more at home than can Mrs.
Wilder and yet, when the occasion demands, she can be dignity
personified. Mrs. Wilder has held high rank in the Eastern Star.
Then when the Farm Loan association was formed at Mansfield she
was made secretary-treasurer. When her report was sent to the
Land Bank officials they told her the papers were perfect and the
best sent in." As a final tribute Mrs. Wilder's friends said this: "She
gets eggs in the winter when none of her neighbors gets any."

## Born in Wisconsin

"I was born in a log house within 4 miles of the legend-haunted
Lake Pepin in Wisconsin," Mrs. Wilder wrote when I asked her for
information "about" her. "I remember seeing deer that father had
killed hanging in the trees around our forest home. When I was 4
years old we traveled to the Indian Territory—Fort Scott, Kansas,
being our nearest town. My childish memories hold the sound of
the war whoop and I see pictures of painted Indians."

Laura at the time of the "Let's Visit Mrs. Wilder" feature

Looking at the picture of Mrs. Wilder, which was recently taken, we find it difficult to believe that she is old enough to be the pioneer described. But having confided her age to the editor (not for publication) we must be convinced that it is true. Surely Mrs. Wilder, who is the mother of Rose Wilder Lane, talented author and writer, has found a fountain of youth in the Ozark hills. We may well believe that she has a "cheerful disposition" as her friend asserts.

"I was a regular little tomboy," Mrs. Wilder confesses, "and it was fun to walk the 2 miles to school." The folks were living in Minnesota then but it was not long until Father Ingalls, who seems to have had a penchant for moving about, had located in Dakota. It was at De Smet, South Dakota, that Laura Ingalls, then 18 years old, married A. J. Wilder, a farmer boy. "Our daughter, Rose Wilder Lane, was born on the farm," Mrs. Wilder informs us, "and it was there I learned to do all kinds of farm work with machinery. I have ridden the binder, driving six horses. And I could ride. I do not wish to appear conceited, but I broke my own ponies to ride. Of course they were not bad but they were bronchos." Mrs. Wilder had the spirit that brought success to pioneers.

Mr. Wilder's health failed and the Wilders went to Florida. "I was something of a curiosity, being the only 'Yankee girl' the inhabitants had ever seen," Mrs. Wilder relates. The low altitude did not agree with Mrs. Wilder tho and she became ill. It was then that they came to Rocky Ridge Farm near Mansfield, Wright County, and there they have lived for 25 years. Only 40 acres was purchased and the land was all timber except a 4 acre tract that was worn out. "Illness and traveling expenses had taken our surplus cash and we lacked $150 of paying for the 40 acres," Mrs. Wilder writes. "Mr. Wilder was unable to do a full day's work. The garden, my hens and the wood I helped saw and which we sold in town took us thru the first year. It was then I became an expert at the end of a crosscut saw and I still can 'make a hand' in an emergency. Mr. Wilder says he would rather have me help than any man he ever sawed with. And, believe me, I learned how to take care of hens and to make them lay."

Intelligent industry brings its own reward. Mr. and Mrs. Wilder not only paid for the 40 acres but they have added 60 acres more, stocked the farm to capacity and improved it and built a beautiful modern home. "Everything sold by the Wilders brings a good price," their neighbor tells me, "because it is standard goods. It was by following strict business methods that they were enabled to build their beautiful home. Most of the material used was found on the farm. Fortunate indeed are those who are entertained at Rocky Ridge."

One may wonder that so busy a person as Mrs. Wilder has

Almanzo Wilder, the "Man of the Place," making hay on Rocky Ridge

proved to be can find time to write. "I always have been a busy person," she says, "doing my own housework, helping the Man of the Place when help could not be obtained, but I love to work. And it is a pleasure to write for the *Missouri Ruralist*. And oh I do just love to play! The days never have been long enough to do the things I would like to do. Every year has held more of interest than the year before." Folks who possess that kind of spirit get a lot of joy out of life as they travel the long road.

Joined the Family in 1911

Mrs. Wilder has held numerous important offices and her stories about farm life and farm folks have appeared in the best farm papers. Her first article printed in the *Missouri Ruralist* appeared in February, 1911. It was a copy of an address prepared for Farmers' Week. So for seven years she has talked to Missouri women thru these columns; talk that always has carried inspiration and incentive for worthwhile work.

Reading Mrs. Wilder's contributions most folks doubtless have decided that she is a college graduate. But, "my education has been what a girl would get on the frontier," she informs us. "I never graduated from anything and only attended high school two terms." Folks who know Mrs. Wilder, tho, know that she is a cultured, well-educated gentlewoman. Combined with inherent ability, unceasing study of books has provided the necessary education and greater things have been learned from the study of life itself.

As has been asserted before, Mrs. Wilder writes well for farm folks because she knows them. The Wilders can be found ready to enter whole-heartedly into any movement for community betterment and the home folks are proud of the reputation that Mrs. Wilder has established. They know that she has won recognition as a writer and state leader because of ability alone.

# Rose Wilder Lane, by Herself

W RITING ABOUT ONE'S SELF is a most difficult task. It is impossible to do it without appearing egotistic, and since everyone is egotistic, no one likes to appear so. We like to show, by being most modest, how different we are from others, how superior. So, between the delight of being asked to talk about himself, and the hope of concealing that delight, the autobiographer feels frightfully foolish, and can only begin like an after-dinner speaker with his speech carefully prepared, by asking the indulgence of his hearers for these few extemporaneous remarks, "unaccustomed as I am—"

I was born thirty-one years ago, on the snow-buried prairies of South Dakota, in cold December weather. My sagacity was apparent even earlier, for I chose the most wonderful of parents.

They were both of the sturdy American pioneer stock that broke the way for the white race westward across the continent. My mother's father was a hunter and trapper; my mother heard in her childhood the long, blood-chilling screams of panthers in the forest around the log-cabin, and saw brown bears in the woods, and knew the Indians. My father's father "slashed and burned" three hundred acres of good hard-wood timber before he drove the plow through the virgin soil of his Minnesota farm, and my father, as a little boy, saw him shoulder his gun and march away with the men who drove back the Indian raiders.

My mother loves courage and beauty and books; my father loves nature, birds and trees and curious stones, and both of them love the land, the stubborn, grudging, beautiful earth that wears out human lives year by year. They gave me something of all these loves, and whenever I do something that I really can't help sitting down and admiring, I always come plump up against the fact that I never would have done it if I hadn't been wise enough to pick out these particular parents.

When I was three years old I developed another quality. A back-stairway ran up from the big kitchen to the bed-room where I slept in a trundle bed, and at the top of this stairway was a door, and on the door was a handle that I could reach. I suddenly questioned: what would happen if I took hold of that handle, leaned far, far back, and let go?

I tried it, in spite of formless apprehensions; somehow I knew it were wiser not to let go of that handle. But why not? I didn't know that, either. My heart went pit-a-pat, pit-a-pat. I leaned still farther back, and let go. My yells aroused the house.

I can not say that I have altered greatly since that time. Whenever I vaguely perceive something I have not yet experienced, I go headlong into it. The only thing the years have taught me is not to howl.

It follows that I have had a most interesting life. At the moment I think of no life I would rather have had. I have been check girl in a telegraph office, telegraph operator, telegraph manager; I have been an advertising writer, a stenographer, a cub reporter, a newspaper feature writer, a land salesman, a housekeeper, a feminist, and a "parasite." I have never been out of the United States, though I have seen most of them, so there is still three-fifths of the world for me to discover.

Rose as a San Francisco celebrity writer in 1918

I like people—clerks and farmers and highwaymen and tramps and elevator girls and poets and lawyers—all sorts of people. I would like better to write about them if only I could get them down on paper exactly as they really are, and I keep trying and trying to do it. It seems to me that the only reason for writing is the showing of a different angle of life to readers who might not have had the opportunity to see it for themselves. That is what I want a book to

Rose Wilder Lane on assignment for the *San Francisco Call-Bulletin*

give me, and that is what I would like my books to give others.

I enjoy writing, always thinking that this time I am going to capture a bit of life in a network of words; and I hate it, for life is forever uncapturable, and my words are so clumsy. But I never cease to love living.

I love life because it is always, always interesting. Pessimists say that life is bitter and cruel and hard to bear; optimists say that it is bright and joyful and full of hope. I think they are both right. Pain and joy, happiness and suffering, as they enter an individual life, are alike in the one quality of being always a new experience, and therefore interesting. The value of life, to me, is that it is so big, and we are so small, that we can never get hold of all of it: there is forever something more, still unknown.

Laura Ingalls Wilder

# A Bouquet of Wild Flowers

*Though Laura Ingalls was born in the Big Woods of Wisconsin, her first memories were of the treeless expanses of prairie in southern Kansas. Her father, determined to test the plains, was lured in 1869 to the Osage ceded lands, an area south of Independence, Kansas. The early settlers in that region were undaunted by the fact that the land was legally Indian country, promised to the native Americans when they yielded the green hills and streams of their Missouri hunting grounds in 1810.*

*The war chant of the discontented tribesmen brought nighttime terror into the cabin Charles Ingalls had built on the prairie. When word came that the buyer of the Ingalls farm back in Wisconsin could not pay for it, Ingalls decided to take his wife and girls home. At that time there were three daughters—Mary, Laura, and Baby Carrie, who was born on August 3, 1870, in Montgomery County, Kansas.*

*The log house near Pepin once again sheltered the Ingalls family on their return to Wisconsin in 1871. This was the home place Laura lovingly wrote about in* Little House in the Big Woods. *The childhood setting filled her memory with visions of panthers, wild deer in the woods, lush, wooded hills, and the coziness of the snug cabin occupied by Pa, Ma, and the girls.*

*The Barry Corner schoolhouse down the road from Pa's cabin first sparked Laura's lifelong fascination with reading and writing words. Mary was six years old when she proudly trotted down the road to school, leaving Laura bereft. The old school records indicate that Laura Ingalls was a visitor to Anna Barry's classes. When she was five, Laura started to attend school regularly.*

*In 1917, when she was a regular writer for the* Missouri Ruralist, *Laura was reminded of her school days in the Big Woods. Almanzo's proffered bouquet of Sweet Williams from the Rocky Ridge woods brought memories of the little school among the leafy trees. And as she was wont to do, Laura wrought memories into words and shared them with her readers. "A Bouquet of Wild Flowers" appeared in the July 20, 1917, edition of the* Ruralist.

T HE MAN OF THE PLACE brought me a bouquet of wild flowers this morning. It has been a habit of his for years. He never brings me cultivated flowers but always the wild blossoms of field and woodland and I think them much more beautiful.

In my bouquet this morning was a purple flag. Do you remember gathering them down on the flats and in the creek bottoms when you were a barefoot child? There was one marshy corner of the pasture down by the creek, where the grass grew lush and green; where the cows loved to feed and could always be found when it was time to drive them up at night. All thru the tall grass were scattered purple and white flag blossoms and I have stood in that peaceful grassland corner, with the red cow and the spotted cow and the roan taking their goodnight mouthfuls of the sweet grass, and watched the sun setting behind the hilltop and loved the purple flags and the rippling brook and wondered at the beauty of the world, while I wriggled my bare toes down into the soft grass.

The wild Sweet Williams in my bouquet brought a far different picture to my mind. A window had been broken in the schoolhouse at the country crossroads and the pieces of glass lay scattered where they had fallen. Several little girls going to school for their first term had picked handfuls of Sweet Williams and were gathered near the window. Someone discovered that the blossoms could be pulled from the stem and, by wetting their faces, could be stuck to the pieces of glass in whatever fashion they were arranged. They dried on the glass and would stay that way for hours and, looked at thru the glass, were very pretty. I was one of those little girls and tho I have forgotten what it was that I tried to learn out of a book that summer, I never have forgotten the beautiful wreaths and stars and other figures we made on the glass with the Sweet Williams. The delicate fragrance of their blossoms this morning made me feel like a little girl again.

The little white daisies with their hearts of gold grew thickly along the path where we walked to Sunday school. Father and sister and I used to walk the 2$^1$/$_2$ miles every Sunday morning. The horses had worked hard all the week and must rest this one day, and Mother would rather stay at home with baby brother, so with

Anna Barry, Laura's teacher at the Barry Corner school

The Big Woods, near Pepin, Wisconsin, as they appear today

Father and Sister Mary I walked to the church thru the beauties of the sunny spring Sundays. I have forgotten what I was taught on those days also. I was only a little girl, you know. But I can still plainly see the grass and the trees and the path winding ahead, flecked with sunshine and shadow and the beautiful golden-hearted daisies scattered all along the way.

Ah well! That was years ago and there have been so many changes since then that it would seem such simple things should be forgotten, but at the long last, I am beginning to learn that it is the sweet, simple things of life which are the real ones after all.

We heap up around us things that we do not need as the crow makes piles of glittering pebbles. We gabble words like parrots un-til we lose the sense of their meaning; we chase after this new idea and that; we take an old thought and dress it out in so many words that the thought itself is lost in its clothing like a slim woman in a barrel skirt and then we exclaim, "Lo, the wonderful new thought I have found!"

"There is nothing new under the sun," says the proverb. I think the meaning is that there are just so many truths or laws of life and no matter how far we may think we have advanced we cannot get beyond those laws. However complex a structure we build of living we must come back to those truths and so we find we have traveled in a circle.

The Russian revolution has only taken the Russian people back to the democratic form of government they had at the beginning of history in medieval times and so a republic is nothing new. I believe we would be happier to have a personal revolution in our individual lives and go back to simpler living and more direct thinking. It is the simple things of life that make living worth while, the sweet fundamental things such as love and duty, work and rest and living close to nature. There are no hothouse blossoms that can compare in beauty and fragrance with my bouquet of wild flowers.

Mrs. A. J. Wilder

# How Laura Got Even

*Upon returning to Wisconsin after the fruitless Kansas interlude from 1869 to 1871, Charles Ingalls was restless. He disliked seeing smoke curl up from neighbors' chimneys close by, and when he heard someone else's shots among the trees he knew that good hunting in the Big Woods was over. In addition, the woods constantly threatened to usurp his claim on the cleared land, as little saplings rooted in the fields and had to be removed. Pa Ingalls wanted to go west again, to the prairies of western Minnesota. In 1873 he sold the Pepin farm a second time and the Ingalls family again crossed the Mississippi. For weeks the horses plodded on, facing west, leading the covered wagon and the family to a new home.*

*The stopping place was on the banks of Plum Creek, near the new village of Walnut Grove. Home was a dugout in the creek bank until Pa could harvest a bumper wheat crop. A railroad in Walnut Grove could carry grain to the big-city markets and return handsome prices.*

*The railroad pleased Pa, but for Ma Walnut Grove meant having a school and a church. Mary and Laura walked two miles to the schoolhouse. There they met the insufferable Nellie Oleson. Both Laura and the infamous Nellie were strong-minded, and neither wanted a subordinate role among the school friends. Laura never forgot that childhood rival.*

*Occasionally during her* Missouri Ruralist *years, Laura ventured into autobiographical writing in her regular columns. She had not yet discovered that her own life made captivating reading, for the "Little House" books were twenty years in the future. But in one of her columns written before 1920 Laura introduced her readers to Nellie. "How Laura Got Even" features Walnut Grove, Minnesota, in 1874 as its setting. The story corresponds to the chapters "Town Party" and "Country Party" in* On the Banks of Plum Creek, *which Laura wrote in 1936.*

L AURA HAD BEEN to a party but she had not enjoyed herself. She was used to going barefoot and her shoes hurt her feet; then too her dress was not so fine as the dresses of the others. She had never thought much about her clothes for she had been too busy helping her mother and so interested in the calves and colts and chickens, in fishing in the creek and playing along its banks, that she had never noticed that her dresses were much more simple than those of her schoolmates.

The party was for Nellie's birthday and Nellie lived in town, so she missed all the fun of being at home in the big out doors which Laura had, but because her clothes were finer she was rude to her little country guest. She talked about her new dresses and showed her beautiful dolls and nibbled candy when her mother was not looking, which she did not share with the other little girls.

Two of her particular friends did as she did and they were very naughty little girls indeed. They made the country girl feel shabby and slighted.

Walking home thru the fields in the late afternoon Laura planned how to get even. Because three little girls had been rude and unkind she was going to be rude and unkind also.

She did not tell her mother of the unpleasant happenings of the afternoon nor of her plans or she would have felt better and behaved better too. Instead she got her mother's permission to ask Nellie, Maud and Nettie to spend the next Saturday afternoon with her.

They came all nicely dressed with fresh ribbons in their hair and shining shoes and naughty little Laura took them down by the creek to play.

At first they sat daintily on the clean bank and made leaf hats, then they dabbled carefully in the water with long sticks, but finally the sight of Laura, barefooted and bareheaded, wading in the sparkling water, tempted them to take off their shoes and stockings and go into the water too.

This was just what Laura expected and wanted. Nellie, Maud and Nettie held their skirts up carefully at first but soon in the excitement they were dropped and drabbled as the girls followed Laura into the deeper water. Not only were the dresses soaked around the bottom but the water was accidentally (?) splashed over them as the play grew more lively and Laura led them into the pool, with a muddy bottom, where the leeches lived. Knowing the habits of leeches, Laura waded quickly thru to the other side of the pool but kept the others standing in it while she showed them the bird in the tree overhead.

When Nellie, Maud and Nettie at last waded to the bank there were leeches fastened on their feet and legs.

A leech will not brush off, you know. They stick tight and draw the blood thru the skin into their own bodies. The only way to get them off, until they become full and fall away themselves, is to take a firm hold and pull them loose. Then blood will trickle down from the place where they have been. They do not hurt at all, really, but they are rather unpleasant creatures.

When the girls saw them like dark splotches of mud on their feet, they tried to brush them off but could not. Then they became frightened and jumped up and down kicking so fast and furious

Plum Creek, near Walnut Grove, Minnesota, as it appeared in 1947

that Laura could hardly get a chance to pull the leeches off, which she did after she had enjoyed the sight of their antics, and the girls screamed again at sight of the blood.

Of course they did not know that Laura had planned to frighten them so and they went timidly back into the water, where the sun shone and the bottom was gravelly; where Laura assured them there were no "blood-suckers."

She told them the truth but not all of it, for worse than leeches was hiding in the shadow under the large rock. It was there that the cross old crab lived and naughty Laura knew it for she had teased him with a stick many a time until he would rush out at anything that passed and try to pinch it.

She led the girls in, around the rock, and but for sister Mary's cry of warning the old crab would have had Nellie by the toe.

It was a very mussy crowd of little girls that went back to the house to enjoy the treat of good things that Laura's mother had made ready. The pretty dresses were water-soaked and grass stained, shoes and stockings were muddy and torn and the new hair ribbons were lost.

Laura's mother made them as tidy as possible before they went home but Laura thot that when their mothers had settled with them she would be even for the unpleasantness of the birthday party.

It is quite likely that they were punished but—Laura was not invited to the next party.


Editor's Afterword

*The tomboy who frolicked along the banks of Plum Creek was in later years a popular hostess and club member in the little mountain community of Mansfield, Missouri. Laura was active in the Order of Eastern Star; she helped found the Athenians, a group dedicated to establishing a library in Wright County; and she attended Mansfield's Interesting Hour Club and Justamere Club.*

*After a meeting where the Mansfield matrons had sat politely discussing club projects, Laura confided to her* Missouri Ruralist *readers, "My sympathy, just now, is very much with the persons who seem to be unable to say the right thing at the right time. . . .*

*"In spite of oneself there are times when one's mental fingers seem to be all thumbs. At a little gathering not long ago, I differed with the hostess on a question which arose with just a shade more warmth than I intended. I resolved to make it up to her by being a little extra sweet to her before I left. The refreshments served were so dainty and delicious that I thought I would find some pleasant way to tell her so.*

*"But alas! As it was a very hot day, ice water was served after the little luncheon and I found myself looking sweetly into my hostess' face and heard myself say, "Oh, wasn't that water good!*

*"What could one do after that, but murmur the conventional, 'Such a pleasant afternoon,' at leaving and depart feeling like a little girl who has blundered at her first party!"*

Laura Ingalls Wilder

# Burr Oak, a Lovely Place

In 1873 Charles Ingalls had led his family from Wisconsin to the Minnesota prairies, where he had hoped to grow a successful wheat crop. But the wheat he sowed with eager optimism was never harvested. Swarms of grasshoppers, which formed into clouds thick enough to hide the sun, descended on the prairies. In minutes the grasshoppers could strip fields and gardens of foliage and fruitage, and Pa's most valiant efforts could not save his grain. The grasshopper plagues brought anguish to settlers in Walnut Grove and all through the state of Minnesota.

The Ingalls family weathered the misery of the grasshopper years until 1876. There were four children by then: Charles Frederick Ingalls was born on November 1, 1875. Weighted with responsibility, Pa reluctantly decided to take the "back trail" and turn east. Harvesting jobs were available in eastern Minnesota, and friends from Walnut Grove were urging Charles and Caroline to join them in operating a hotel in Burr Oak, Iowa.

In the summer of 1876, Pa drove his covered wagon full of family and possessions over familiar roads. They stopped along the Zumbro River, near South Troy, Minnesota, where they stayed with Uncle Peter and Aunt Eliza Ingalls. Peter was Charles's brother and Eliza was Caroline's sister, so the cousins were double cousins (Laura wrote about these relatives in Little House in the Big Woods). Laura and Mary and Carrie became reacquainted with their cousins, but the summer was overshadowed by the illness and death of Freddie Ingalls. He was nine months old when "one awful day he straightened out his little body and was dead," recalled Laura in a manuscript she entitled "Pioneer Girl." The day was August 27, 1876. Tenderly the little boy was buried, and the family left his lonely grave when they drove on to Burr Oak, Iowa.

The Masters Hotel in Burr Oak was a busy place. The little village was a crossroads for pioneers going west, and sometimes two hundred wagons stopped for the night. Many travelers crowded into the hotel or came in for a hot meal. The Walnut Grove friends, William and Maggie Steadman, were glad to have the Ingallses there to help.

In the fall of 1932, Rose Wilder Lane stopped in Burr Oak en route from

From left to right: Carrie, Mary, Laura

*Mansfield to New York City. Searching for traces of the Ingalls family, she toured the hotel building and emerged, beaming, with an old platter from the hotel china, certain her grandmother must have used it. The Masters Hotel was restored in 1974 and is open to visitors as a memorial to the Ingalls family and their stay in Burr Oak.*

*Laura did not include the Burr Oak era in her "Little House" books. But when she and Rose were both well known in the Midwest, rumors persisted that the family had once been Burr Oak residents. In this reminiscence, published in the* Decorah Public Opinion *in June 1947, Laura verified those claims and described the scenes, people, and experiences she remembered from her family's interlude in the small Iowa town.*

M Y FAMILY DID live in Burr Oak for nearly two years, but I fear my memories of that time will not be very interesting as they are more of the place than the people.

At first we lived in the old Masters hotel. My parents were partners in the business with the new owners, Mr. and Mrs. Steadman.

Their two boys, Jimmy and Reuben, were about the age of my sister Mary and myself and of course we played and quarreled together.

The hotel still stood when Rose saw it a few years ago, as it was then even to the bullet hole in the door between the dining room and kitchen. It was made when the young man of the house, being drunk, shot at his wife who slammed the door between them as she escaped. This had happened some years before, but the bullet hole in the door was thrilling to us children.

Pa used to play his fiddle in the hotel office, and one of the boarders, a Mr. Bisbee, taught me to sing the notes of the musical scale.

We stayed there most of the winter, then moved to rooms over Kimball's grocery.

One night Ma woke Mary and me, telling us to dress quickly. The second building from us, a saloon, was burning and we must be ready to leave quickly if the fire should spread toward us.

Ma and Mary and I stood at the window where we watched the flames and the men in the street carrying buckets of water from the town pump to pour on the fire. Pa was one of them.

The men stood in line. One would fill his bucket and run with it to the fire, while the next man instantly took his place. On returning he took his place at the end of the line, which was constantly moving.

The Masters Hotel in Burr Oak in the 1870s

But they all stood still for some moments, with the same man at the pump. At every stroke of the pump handle he would throw up his head and shout "Fire."

Then someone pushed him away and took his place. The bucket into which he was so frantically pumping water had no bottom in it.

The fire was put out after a while and we all went back to bed.

Mary and I were going to school. It seemed to us a big school, but as I remember there were only two rooms. One began in the downstairs room and when advanced enough was promoted upstairs.

Downstairs we learned to sing the multiplication tables to the tune of "Yankee Doodle."

Next term we went upstairs to the principal, whose name was Reid and who came from Decorah. He was an elocutionist and I have always been grateful to him for the training I was given in reading. I still have the old *Independent Fifth Reader* from which he taught us to give life to "Old Tubal Cain," "The Polish Boy" and "Paul Revere."

We had friends among our school mates. I remember their faces, and occasionally the names escape me.

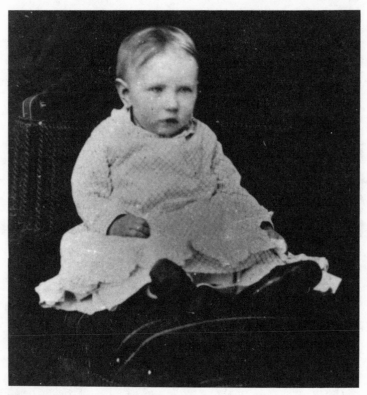

Baby Grace, who was born in Burr Oak in 1877

In the spring we moved to a little brick house at the edge of town. It was a happy summer. I loved to go after the cows in the pasture by the creek where the rushes and the blue flags grew and the grass was so fresh and smelled so sweet. I could see the old stone quarry, but was forbidden to go to it as it was filled with water.

Often on Sunday afternoons my friend, Alice Ward, and I would walk out on the other side of town, past the Sims' rose-covered cottage to the graveyard. We would wander in the shade of the great trees, reading the inscriptions on the tomb stones. The grass was green and short and flowers were everywhere. It was a beautiful, peaceful place.

I spent a great deal of time that summer caring for baby sister, Grace, with the big blue eyes and soft fair hair.

That fall we left Burr Oak and drove in our covered wagon back to Walnut Grove, Minn., and the banks of Plum Creek.

As you see, these are just dim childish memories, but I have thoughts of Burr Oak as a lovely place.


Mrs. A. J. Wilder

# Thanksgiving Time

*Laura wrote, "Everything came at us out of the west . . . storms, blizzards, grasshoppers, burning hot winds and fire . . . yet it seemed that we wanted nothing so much as we wanted to keep on going west" ("Pioneer Girl"). For her father this urge to face west was inherent. The Burr Oak life was too constraining for him, and in 1878, after two years there, the Ingallses returned to Walnut Grove.*

*The family lived in town, where Pa worked as a miller, operated a butcher shop, and did carpentry. But he was torn between wanderlust and responsibility. The burdens increased when Mary was blinded by spinal meningitis in 1879 (scarlet fever is given as the cause in* By the Shores of Silver Lake*). From that time on, Laura was told that she must replace Mary's eyes with her quick tongue and descriptive powers. Laura solemnly assumed the role as Mary's link to color, light, and action.*

*By 1879 the Chicago and Northwestern Railroad had reached Tracy, Minnesota, seven miles west of Walnut Grove. The company then extended its tracks into Dakota Territory. As the railroad was built, new towns sprang up along its tracks, and easterners were encouraged to claim the "free land" of the prairies. Charles Ingalls was anxious to claim a new homestead.*

*During the summer of 1879, Pa worked for the A. L. Wells Company, sellings goods at the company stores in the railroad camps as they progressed west. He served as timekeeper and paymaster for the Big Sioux*

*River camp near present-day Brookings, South Dakota, and then moved*
*on to the Silver Lake camp near De Smet.*

*While Pa worked for wages and saved, his womenfolk prepared to leave*
*Walnut Grove. The family was reunited at the Silver Lake camp, and Pa*
*was satisfied with the rolling, treeless countryside. He promised his wife*
*that this was journey's end; they would travel no more.*

*When the Silver Lake camp closed down for the winter, the railroad*
*surveyor asked Pa Ingalls to remain in the abandoned camp to guard the*
*company tools. The family could live in the surveyors' house on the bank*
*of Silver Lake, rent-free, with provisions to last until spring. They ac-*
*cepted the offer and settled into the comfortable house. And on one of his*
*tramps across the prairie, Pa found the homestead he wanted near the*
*townsite of De Smet.*

*The Ingalls family lived cozily in the surveyors' house during their first*
*winter in Dakota Territory. (The house, the oldest building in De Smet,*
*South Dakota, is now restored and open to visitors as the Surveyors'*
*House. It has been returned to its appearance of the winter of 1879–80 by*
*the Laura Ingalls Wilder Memorial Society.) They were miles from any*
*neighbor, but they celebrated the holidays happily with Mr. and Mrs. Rob-*
*ert A. Boast, who had arrived from Iowa in time for Christmas.*

*On November 20, 1916, thirty-seven years after the holiday season she*
*had experienced by Silver Lake in Dakota Territory, Laura shared these*
*reflections on Thanksgiving with her* Missouri Ruralist *readers.*

A s THANKSGIVING DAY draws near again, I am reminded
of an occurrence of my childhood. To tell the truth, it is a
yearly habit of mine to think of it about this time and to smile at it
once more.

We were living on the frontier in South Dakota then. There's no
more frontier within the boundaries of the United States, more's
the pity, but then we were ahead of the railroad in a new unsettled
country. Our nearest and only neighbor was 12 miles away and the
store was 40 miles distant.

Father had laid in a supply of provisions for the winter and
among them were salt meats, but for fresh meat we depended on
father's gun and the antelope which fed in herds, across the prairie. So we were quite excited, one day near Thanksgiving, when

The pantry of the restored Surveyors' House in De Smet, South Dakota, arranged as Laura described it in *By the Shores of Silver Lake*

father hurried into the house for his gun and then away again to try for a shot at a belated flock of wild geese hurrying south.

We would have roast goose for Thanksgiving dinner! "Roast goose and dressing seasoned with sage," said sister Mary. "No, not sage! I don't like sage and we won't have it in the dressing," I exclaimed. Then we quarreled, sister Mary and I, she insisting that there should be sage in the dressing and I declaring there should not be sage in the dressing, until father returned,—without the goose! I remember saying in a meek voice to sister Mary, "I wish I had let you have the sage," and to this day when I think of it I feel again just as I felt then and realize how thankful I would have been for roast goose and dressing with sage seasoning—with or without any seasoning—I could even have gotten along without the dressing. Just plain goose roasted would have been plenty good enough.

This little happening has helped me to be properly thankful even tho at times the seasoning of my blessings has not been just such as I would have chosen.

"I suppose I should be thankful for what we have, but I can't feel very thankful when I have to pay $2.60 for a little flour and the price still going up," writes a friend, and in the same letter she says, "We are in our usual health." The family are so used to good health that it is not even taken into consideration as a cause of thanksgiving. We are so inclined to take for granted the blessings we possess and to look for something peculiar, some special good luck for which to be thankful.

I read a Thanksgiving story, the other day, in which a woman sent her little boy out to walk around the block and look for something for which to be thankful.

One would think that the fact of his being able to walk around the block and that he had a mother to send him would have been sufficient cause for thankfulness. We are nearly all afflicted with mental farsightedness and so easily overlook the thing which is obvious and near. There are our hands and feet,—who ever thinks of giving thanks for them, until indeed they, or the use of them, are lost. We usually accept them as a matter of course, without a thought, but a year of being crippled has taught me the value of my feet and two perfectly good feet are now among my dearest possessions. Why! There is greater occasion for thankfulness just in the unimpaired possession of one of the five senses than there would be if some one left us a fortune. Indeed, how could the value of one be reckoned? When we have all five in good working condition we surely need not make a search for anything else in order to feel that we should give thanks to Whom thanks are due.

I once remarked upon how happy and cheerful a new acquaintance seemed always to be and the young man to whom I spoke replied, "Oh he's just glad that he is alive." Upon inquiry, I learned that several years before this man had been seriously ill, that there had been no hope of his living, but to everyone's surprise he had made a complete recovery and since then he had always been remarkably happy and cheerful.

So if for nothing else, let's "just be glad that we are alive" and be doubly thankful if, like the Scotch poet, we have a good appetite and the means to gratify it.

Some hae meat that canna eat
And some want meat that lack it.
But I hae meat and I can eat,
And sae the Lord be thanked.


Laura Ingalls Wilder

# According to Experts

*The winter of 1879–80 was an "open" one on the Dakota prairie, and in
the spring the town of De Smet grew up rapidly on the empty land. Charles
Ingalls bought two town lots and constructed store buildings on them. He
also helped to organize Kingsbury County and was active in the formation
of the Congregational church.*

*Although Pa Ingalls gave his time to the establishment of civilization,
he was anxious to get his family away from the town to their homestead
claim a mile away. He built a shanty on his claim and planted cottonwoods
around it, and all summer he broke the prairie acres with his walking plow
and team.*

*As Laura related in* The Long Winter, *an old Indian warned of heavy
snow for the winter of 1880–81. Seven months of winter weather com-
menced with the early blizzard of October 15, 1880, which caught the Ingalls family in their thin-walled claim shanty. Pa moved them into his more
substantial store building on Main Street in De Smet, and there the family
endured the long, bitter winter that went down in history as the "Hard
Winter."*

*Laura eventually wrote about that famous winter of her girlhood, both
in* The Long Winter *and for her* Missouri Ruralist *readers. In this account, published in the* Ruralist *on February 5, 1917, she recalled the
blizzard-bound community of De Smet and the techniques its eighty residents used to survive.*

I N A LATE issue of a St. Louis paper, I find the following: "Experts in the office of home economics of the United States Department of Agriculture have found it is possible to grind whole wheat in an ordinary coffee mill fine enough for use as a breakfast cereal and even fine enough for use in bread making."

If the experts of the Department of Agriculture had asked any one of the 200 people who spent the winter of 1880–81 in De Smet, S. Dak., they might have saved themselves the trouble of experimenting. I think, myself, that it is rather a joke on our experts at Washington to be 36 years behind the times.

That winter, known still among the old residents as "the hard winter," we demonstrated that wheat could be ground in an ordinary coffee mill and used for bread making. Prepared in that way it was the staff of life for the whole community. The grinding at home was not done to reduce the cost of living, but simply to make living possible.

De Smet was built as the railroad went thru, out in the midst of the great Dakota prairies far ahead of the farming settlements, and this first winter of its existence it was isolated from the rest of the world from December 1 until May 10 by the fearful blizzards that piled the snow 40 feet deep on the railroad tracks. The trains could not get thru. It was at the risk of life that anyone went even a mile from shelter, for the storms came up so quickly and were so fierce it was literally impossible to see the hand before the face and men have frozen to death within a few feet of shelter because they did not know they were near safety.

The small supply of provisions in town soon gave out. The last sack of flour sold for $50 and the last of the sugar at $1 a pound. There was some wheat on hand, brought in the fall before for seed in the spring, and two young men dared to drive 15 miles to where a solitary settler had also laid in his supply of seed wheat. They brought it in on sleds. There were no mills in town or country so this wheat was all ground in the homes in coffee mills. Everybody ground wheat, even the children taking their turns, and the resultant whole wheat flour made good bread. It was also a healthful food and there was not a case of sickness in town that winter.

It may be that the generous supply of fresh air had something

A twist, or stick, of hay, like those that kept the Ingalls family from freezing during the famous blizzard winter of 1880–81

to do with the general good health. Air is certainly fresh when the thermometer registers all the way from 15 to 40 degrees below zero with the wind moving at blizzard speed. In the main street of the town, snow drifts in one night were piled as high as the second stories of the houses and packed hard enough to drive over and the next night the wind might sweep the spot bare. As the houses were new and unfinished, so that the snow would blow in and drift across us as we slept, fresh air was not a luxury. The houses were not overheated in daytime either, for the fuel gave out early in the winter and all there was left with which to cook and keep warm was the long prairie hay. A handful of hay was twisted into a rope, then doubled and allowed to twist back on itself, and the two ends came together in a knot, making what we called "a stick of hay."

It was a busy job to keep a supply of these "sticks" ahead of a hungry stove when the storm winds were blowing, but everyone took his turn good naturedly. There is something in living close to the great elemental forces of nature that causes people to rise above small annoyances and discomforts.

A train got thru May 10 and stopped at the station. All the men in town were down at the tracks to meet it, eager for supplies, for even the wheat had come to short rations. They found that what had been sent into the hungry town was a trainload of machinery. Luckily, there were also two emigrant cars well supplied with provisions, which were taken out and divided among the people. Our days of grinding wheat in coffee mills were over, but we had learned without expert aid that it can be done and that the flour so ground will make good bread and mush. Perhaps I would better say that we had all become experts and demonstrated the fact. After all, necessity is the mother of invention and experience is a good old teacher.


Laura Ingalls Wilder

# Home for Christmas

*In 1881, while they were living in De Smet, Dakota Territory, Charles and Caroline Ingalls took their daughter Mary to enroll at the Iowa College for the Blind, in Vinton, where she entered a seven-year course of both academic and manual-arts training. Sending Mary to school culminated a family goal, but the Ingallses were struggling to establish a farm from their prairie homestead, and Mary's school expenses were a hardship. To contribute to the carefully garnered funds for her sister's education, Laura patiently sewed at the dressmaker's in De Smet and gave her earnings to Mary. And though the idea did not appeal to her, Laura planned to teach school as soon as she was sixteen and eligible for a certificate. With so many homesteaders settling in Kingsbury County, schoolhouses were dotting the prairies and qualified teachers were needed.*

*Unexpectedly, Laura started teaching two months before she reached the legal age of sixteen, for the directors of the Bouchie school wanted her to teach a winter term. The school was an abandoned claim shanty twelve miles from De Smet, and Laura had five pupils, some of them older and taller than their young teacher from town.*

*The schoolhouse was drafty and cold, and Laura's living conditions were dreary. She was painfully homesick for Pa and Ma and Carrie and Grace, who were wintering comfortably in Pa's store building in De Smet. But Laura was determined to finish her term and earn the forty dollars for Mary's college fund.*

*To spare her from homesick weekends, a young homesteader named Almanzo Wilder regularly drove out from town with his speedy cutter and matched Morgan team to squire Laura home. Not much was said on those frigid Friday-evening sleigh rides; it was too cold, and sudden blizzards were always a threat. But the clomp of the horses' hooves on the hard-packed snow and the cheery jingle of the sleigh bells broke the ominous winter stillness of the prairie*

*When Laura's first school term ended, she expected her rides behind Almanzo's Morgans to stop; however, he came to Pa's door again in the spring, and they sped under the warm sun over land green with prairie grass and colored with wild flowers. Almanzo came courting for three years and continued to appear at Laura's schools—at the Perry school, close to Pa's homestead, and then at the Wilkin school, north of De Smet—until Laura agreed to marry him. (She later told of Almanzo's drives to fetch her and of their courtship and marriage in* These Happy Golden Years.*)*

*On August 25, 1885, Laura Elizabeth Ingalls and Almanzo James Wilder were married by the Reverend Edward Brown. Their first home was the little gray house on Almanzo's tree claim north of De Smet.*

*At Christmastime in 1924, more than forty years after Almanzo's fearless drives over the bitter-cold prairies, Laura warmly recalled the "man of the place" and his dashing team saving her from a miserable Christmas miles away from Pa, Ma, Carrie, and Grace. In the December 15 edition of the* Missouri Ruralist *she shared the story in her column "As a Farm Woman Thinks."*

T HE SNOW WAS scudding low over the drifts of the white world outside the little claim shanty. It was blowing thru the cracks in its walls and forming little piles and miniature drifts on the floor and even on the desks before which several children sat, trying to study, for this abandoned claim shanty that had served as the summer home of a homesteader on the Dakota prairies was being used as a schoolhouse during the winter.

The walls were made of one thickness of wide boards with cracks between and the enormous stove that stood nearly in the center of the one room could scarcely keep out the frost tho its sides were a glowing red. The children were dressed warmly and had been allowed to gather closely around the stove following the advice of

Laura and Almanzo shortly after their marriage in 1885

the county superintendent of schools, who on a recent visit had said that the only thing he had to say to them was to keep their feet warm.

This was my first school, I'll not say how many years ago, but I was only 16 years old and 12 miles from home during a frontier winter. I walked a mile over the unbroken snow from my boarding place to school every morning and back at night. There were only a few pupils and on this particular snowy afternoon they were restless for it was nearing 4 o'clock and tomorrow was Christmas. "Teacher" was restless, too, tho she tried not to show it, for she was wondering if she could get home for Christmas day.

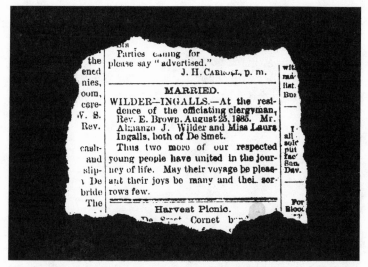

The *De Smet News and Leader* carried this announcement of Laura and Al-manzo's marriage.

It was almost too cold to hope for father to come and a storm was hanging in the northwest which might mean a blizzard at any minute. Still, tomorrow was Christmas—and then there was a jingle of sleigh bells outside. A man in a huge fur coat in a sleigh full of robes passed the window. I was going home after all!

When one thinks of 12 miles now, it is in terms of motor cars and means only a few minutes. It was different then, and I'll never forget that ride. The bells made a merry jingle and the fur robes were warm, but the weather was growing colder and the snow was drifting, so that the horses must break their way thru the drifts.

We were facing the strong wind and every little while he, who later became the "man of the place," must stop the team, get out in the snow, and by putting his hands over each horse's nose in turn, thaw the ice from them where the breath had frozen over their nostrils. Then he would get back into the sleigh and on we'd go until once more the horses could not breathe for the ice.

When we reached the journey's end, it was 40 degrees below zero, the snow was blowing so thickly that we could not see across the street and I was so chilled that I had to be half carried into the house. But I was home for Christmas and cold and danger were forgotten.

Such magic there is in Christmas to draw the absent ones home and if unable to go in the body the thoughts will hover there! Our hearts grow tender with childhood memories and love of kindred and we are better thruout the year for having in spirit become a child again at Christmas time.

Rose Wilder Lane

# Innocence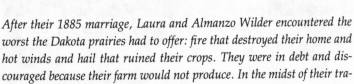

*After their 1885 marriage, Laura and Almanzo Wilder encountered the worst the Dakota prairies had to offer: fire that destroyed their home and hot winds and hail that ruined their crops. They were in debt and discouraged because their farm would not produce. In the midst of their travails they also endured the death of their infant son, and diphtheria left the robust Manly a near-invalid. In 1890, hoping to restore his health, the Wilders went to spend a season on the prosperous farm of Almanzo's parents, near Spring Valley, Minnesota. Three-year-old Rose remembered this, her first covered wagon journey, and the lovely sounds of the syllables Min-ne-so-ta. Her parents, worried and worn, drove east, leaving the dusty, dry Dakota plains behind them.*

*Almanzo, Laura, and Rose were warmly welcomed by the relatives in Spring Valley, but the winter cold hurt Almanzo cruelly, and he was advised to visit the South. They thought of Florida's panhandle, where Laura's cousin Peter Ingalls had settled. He had married a Florida backwoods girl named Molly and was establishing a homestead near the village of Westville when the Wilders arrived in the area by train in 1891.*

*The Florida sojourn was not a happy one for Laura. "We went to live in the piney woods of Florida," she recalled, "where the trees always murmur, where the butterflies are enormous, where plants that eat insects grow in moist places, and alligators inhabit the slowly moving waters of the rivers. But at that time and in that place, a Yankee woman was more of a curiosity than any of these."*

Almanzo and Laura in the piney woods of Florida

*Laura and the local residents did not mix. While Manly worked with Peter, Laura kept Rose protectively by her side, and the neighborhood women dismissed her as a haughty "up-north" gal. Almanzo could see no real hopes for progress in the scrubby pine backwoods, so with relief Laura began to pack for the long train trip back to De Smet. They reached the comforting shelter of Laura's family in August of 1892.*

*Thirty years later, Rose—by then the well-known writer Rose Wilder Lane—ruminated over the Florida stay and used it as the basis for a short story. "Innocence" was published in Harper's magazine in April 1922; it is a poignant piece of fiction prompted by remembered family past. When "Innocence" appeared, Rose was overseas as a foreign correspondent, moving from adventure to adventure in the Albanian highlands, the Soviet Union, Turkey, Greece, and Armenia.*

*Early in 1923 Rose was in Athens and had, she wrote, "replenished a depleted wardrobe after months in the Albanian wilds when the drachma took a tumble which hit [her] expense money with a wallop."*

In the midst of financial distress a letter came containing a check for thousands of drachma without explanation. I decided a bank clerk had made a mistake and returned the check. In a few days, letters began to arrive, hurrahing me over my "award" . . . and finally a letter from *Harper's* which had been trailing me all over Europe, breaking the news that the money I had sent back was really my own: the O. Henry Prize for the best short story of the year had gone to "Innocence"! (*Kansas City Star Magazine*, June 28, 1925.)

*"Innocence," which Rose regarded as the best short fiction she ever produced, became a model of writing craft, and through the years it was continually anthologized. "To think," Rose commented roguishly, "that I should live to be one of the 'Authors' doggedly toiled-at by helpless high school pupils" (letter to Harper and Brothers, October 15, 1928).*

W HEN MARY ALICE came quite awake her mother was rubbing her face with a cold, wet cloth. They were in the little room at the end of the car; the floor was shaking like the skin of a horse that tries to get rid of a fly, and underneath the floor the wheels were talking. Clickety-clack! they said, Clickety-clack!

"Wake up, baby," mother said. "We'll be there in a few minutes." She turned Mary Alice around and began buttoning up. A little light ran along the edge of the shining washbasin; when Mary Alice turned her head the little light ran away very quickly, when she turned her head the other way it stopped suddenly and ran back.

"Stand still dear!" mother said. The best, beautiful pink dress came jerkily down over Mary Alice's head and was buttoned. Then mother turned her around again and pushed into place the thin curved, red comb that held her hair tight. Mother's eyes were clear, like water, and full of happiness. Her two hands gave Mary Alice's face an excited little squeeze.

"We're going to see father and Uncle Charley again. Aren't you glad?" she said.

"Will there be pickaninnies?" Mary Alice asked, anxiously. Pickaninnies were children as black as coal; mother had promised that she would see them in Florida. Mother said yes, there would be pickaninnies.

Mary Alice sat on the chair while mother dressed. When she sat on the edge of the chair her legs disappeared; when she pulled herself back two feet popped up in front of her. That was because her legs bent; her legs had hinges in them, like doors. Mother's hair was very long, and no one could see at once all the lights that scampered through it. Mother's hands were going so fast that they were out of breath, and fluttered. When they came to a snarl they jerked at it, but mother never cried. Her face in the glass smiled at Mary Alice.

"You remember Uncle Charley, don't you?" she said.

Mary Alice remembered Uncle Charley. When they lived at grandfather's he used to put her high on the big backs of the horses at the watering trough. She remembered his legs, going into the pile of hay in the car that had taken father and him down south to Florida. First his arms and head went in, and then one leg and then the other, and that was the last of Uncle Charley. Then there was nothing but hay. She must not tell anyone that Uncle Charley was in the hay, because they were poor, and if people knew that Uncle Charley was going to Florida with father and the horses and the cow they would not let him go. For a long time Mary Alice had not spoken of Uncle Charley, but she remembered him. He was big and strong and always laughing.

When the train stopped they got down the high car steps and were alone in a gray light. Mother looked anxiously this way and that, and her hand hurt Mary Alice's. Then she dropped it, and father was there. "Hello! Here you are!" he said. He and mother looked at each other, and it was as though they were together in a warm little space. Mary Alice was outside, chilly and uncomfortable. She tugged at mother's sleeve and said, "Where are the pickaninnies?" Then they laughed and took her into the warmth.

"Didn't Charley come?" said mother, and father swung Mary Alice into the air and kissed her. His face was suddenly close and big, a brown, prickly face with deep creases in the cheeks.

The horses and wagon waited by the platform. Mary Alice was swung high over the wheel into the seat, father and mother climbed up beside her, and father clucked to the horses. The horses walked quickly, jerking their heads, and little plops of white dust rose from their feet. They passed a store and some low, unpainted houses with wide porches. Strange trees grew in the yards. Their branches grew as though they meant something strange and frightening; their leaves were like flat green hands with wide fingers, and their fruit was black. In one of these trees was a black boy. He sat on a branch and dangled black legs, and with one hand he picked a black fruit. His large mouth was very full of white teeth, and he bit the black fruit with them; he bit it through, and laughed. Mary Alice could not look away from him; her head turned slowly and her eyes stayed fixed on him for a long time.

"Here we are, in the piney woods!" said father. The white road went curving between straight, tall gray trees that had no branches. Far overhead their green-black tops whispered breathlessly, without stopping, telling something terrifying. The gray trunks stood still in a gray light; they knew, but they were silent, and the pale ground looked up at them. A smell of dampness and of wet paint-brushes was in the air.

Father's cheerful voice sounded loud and false. Mother's voice was low and unrelenting, as though she were talking about telling lies. Uncle Charley was her little brother.

"You must tell me what it is," she said.

Mary Alice watched the horses' ears. They turned this way and that, and reminded Mary Alice of birds sitting on a fence.

Suddenly mother cried out, as though some one had struck her. Mary Alice looked up quickly. Mother's face was broken. Mother was crying, and nothing was safe. Terror and strangeness reached out of the gray woods and seized Mary Alice, and she shrieked, and there was nothing anywhere but sobbing and screams. Father was talking to her, but she could not hear him; and he was holding her, but she could not feel that he was near. Then he was putting something into her hand and telling her to taste it. It was sweet and salty. Sugar cane, he said; she was to suck it. It was smooth and green and round, like a large stick of candy. The wagon was still jolting on, and she sat tasting the sugar cane through her sobs until she fell asleep. She fell asleep feeling a blackness of something that had got Uncle Charley and made mother cry.

But when she woke there he was. His big hands were holding her in the air, and he was laughing up at her. His face was red-brown and his eyes were very blue, and beneath the edge of his blue shirt was the strip of pinky-white skin; he had just come in from the fields and was putting her up on the big horse. No, there was the wagon and a strange, zigzag fence and many large, fresh chips scattered around a new house in the piney woods. She was in Florida, and Uncle Charley was here, too, and safe.

"Oh!" she cried, hugging his neck tight. "Mother cried about you, and I was afraid!"

The last sob came unexpectedly out of her throat, and then she felt a queer stillness. She slid to the ground. There was a strange woman, a black-haired, black-eyed, red-cheeked woman in a beautiful, bright-red dress. She was fascinating, like grandfather's big brown horse that lived behind bars and had once killed a man.

"This is your new Aunt Molly, Mary Alice," said mother. Mother's face was smiling, but mother was not smiling. Mary Alice took tight hold of mother's brown skirt and held out a hand.

"How do you do, Aunt Molly?" she said, carefully.

"The other hand, dear," said mother.

Mary Alice saw Aunt Molly's bare feet, bare and brown and dusty with white dust. She looked up the beautiful red skirt to Aunt Molly's hands that were on Aunt Molly's hips, and on up to the bright-colored face. The face tipped back, a thick, white throat came up out of the red collar, and suddenly Aunt Molly laughed a short, queer laugh.

"Well, nyow," she said, "I'm right proud to meet you," and she shook Mary Alice's hand as though she were making fun. But it was the right hand. Aunt Molly's red lips curled and showed her white teeth; she was like the big brown horse laying back his ears, and Mary Alice backed quickly against mother. Everything was wrong and she did not know why; she only wanted to get away, and, turning, she hid her face against mother and shut her eyes.

Then they were all going into the house. The house was made of new yellow boards and smelled good. There was a room with a cook stove and table, and a room with the big bed and Mary Alice's cot. It was a nice house, only Uncle Charley did not live with them any more. He lived in another house with Aunt Molly. Aunt Molly took him away, and at the gate he stopped to look back at mother. Mother and Mary Alice stood in the doorway and waved good-by to Uncle Charley, but Aunt Molly did not look back. She walked fast down the road, and her red skirt switched behind her like a tail.

Mother was very busy and did not say a word. She unpacked the trunk and put on her blue apron and let down the long braid of her hair that stayed in a knot only when she was playing grown-up. For mother was not really grown-up, like father; she liked to sing and dress dolls and play games with toes. Only to-day she did not feel like playing. She bathed Mary Alice sternly in the tin washbasin, and swept, and got supper. Her forehead was pulled into little lumps, and her mouth was queer and tight. When father came in from doing the chores she dished up the potatoes and cut the johnnycake and set Mary Alice on the Bible in the chair without saying anything until father put his arms around her, and then she cuddled her head beside his chin and cried again.

"Oh, how could he? How could he?" she said.

"He didn't do it," said father, bitterly. "He's a Northerner, and she wanted him. She got around him somehow. They say she drugged him."

Mary Alice sat amazed, holding her knife straight up in her fist. "Drugged," she said to herself. "Dragged. I drug; I dragged. She dragged herself around him. She drugged herself around him." It made a song in her mind and she began to sing it, pounding on the table with the handle of the knife, until mother startled her with a sharp, "Stop it, Mary Alice!"

Mary Alice went to sleep every night hearing the piney woods whispering together, and when she woke in her cot they were still whispering. The piney woods had no leaves, only long things like red and brown darning needles. She must not go far from the house—there were snakes in the piney woods. She might go with mother to bring water from the spring. The water came out in the ground and made a little pool that twisted in the middle, then it ran stealthily away into shadows. The air was thick and moldy with smells, and by the water grew a fascinating horrible plant that ate flies.

Uncle Charley came every day to help father dig a well outside the kitchen door. He was busy and did not feel like playing. He dug himself down to the waist and then down to the shoulders, and then he went down into the ground in a bucket on a rope. He sent up the bucket full of red mud, and father dumped it. Mary Alice played with the mud and made things; she set them in a row in the sun and they turned to rock. Mother said she was making mud pies, but they were not pies, they were just shapes she thought of. At noon Uncle Charley came out of the ground and washed and ate dinner. He said it was like old times to eat honest-to-gosh cooking again, and mother looked sad. Uncle Charley should not say honest-to-gosh; it was a bad word.

"Will you stay to supper, Charley?" mother said.

Uncle Charley made marks with his toe in the red mud. "Hang it all! yes," he said.

After supper he sat with father on the doorstep and mother sat near them in the rocking-chair and sang songs to them; they forgot it was bedtime. Aunt Molly came up the road in the moonlight, her face and her arms and her feet were white in the moonlight, and she stood at the edge of the piney woods and called:

"Charley!"

Mother asked her to come in, but she said, "No thanks; I reckon we-all'll be gitting along home."

Uncle Charley did not come any more to dig, and father and mother talked about it. Mother said they must be nice to Aunt Molly. She did not want to, but she pinned up her hair and put on her sunbonnet and she and Mary Alice went up the white road. Sunshine slanted through the piney woods and struck the white road. Lizards lay on the zigzag fence waggling their sleek throats, and ants went across the road in crawling lines, little red lines and big black lines. White dust was on the toes of Mary Alice's little shoes and mother's big shoes.

They came to Uncle Charley's house. It was made of logs, and skins were spread out on the walls. The ground around it was bare and hard and hens were walking about. Large bony dogs with flapping ears stood up and growled, but Aunt Molly came to the door and said:

"Hesh up, you ornery dawgs! I'm right proud to see you-all," she said, looking at mother's calico dress. "We-all ain't fine like Northerners, but sech as we got is good enough for we-uns. Light 'n' come in."

Mother laughed as though she had been running; she said polite things while they went into the house. It was logs on the inside, too, and bits of daylight came through between them. Women and many children were sitting around the fireplace. They were all barefooted and wore queer gray dresses, and they all looked at mother's dress and at Mary Alice's shoes. A woman put out a long skinny arm and pulled Mary Alice close to her. The woman's face was all deep-brown wrinkles and her chewing mouth was somehow like a frog jumping.

"Nyow here's a right peart little girl," she said. "I'd give a pretty for a little girl like you."

Mary Alice shyly said nothing, leaning against the woman's friendly knee.

Aunt Molly sat on her heels by the fireplace, mixing cornmeal and water with her fingers. She took handfuls of it and patted them flat between her hands; she made a print of her hands on each side. Mary Alice admired it very much. Then Aunt Molly laid the yellow cake in the ashes and covered it with ashes and made another.

Each woman had only one or two long yellow teeth, but they never stopped brushing them. They dipped little sticks into boxes of brown dust, and chewed, and spit into the fireplace. Mary Alice had never seen anyone spit so far and so well. There was a box on the knee beside her, and she looked into it, politely. The woman understood; she dipped her stick into the box and twirled it until it was brown, and offered it to Mary Alice. Mary Alice took it eagerly, but mother's eyes opened wide, and then she shook her head.

"She's too little yet, I'm afraid," mother said, and her blue eyes were very blue in her pink face. "Thank the lady nicely, and put it back, Mary Alice," and mother looked around at the faces timidly.

"My childern's dipped snuff sence they was weanlings," said the woman.

Mary Alice wanted to cry, but she let the woman take back the stick. Aunt Molly stood up, and made again that frightening sound like a laugh. Mary Alice felt queer, as though she were big and mother little and something wanted to hurt mother; she went and stood with her back against mother.

The men came tramping in. They were Aunt Molly's brothers—tall, loud men, even bigger than Uncle Charley. They hung their guns on the wall and were noisy; they slapped their big hands on Aunt Molly's shoulders, and she laughed. Aunt Molly's black eyes seemed hot, her black hair was alive. It did not hang limp like the other women's, but each lock of it curled and twisted into the air. She did not look at Uncle Charley, and he did not speak to mother. All the women sat by the fire while the men ate, and Aunt Molly went back and forth with dishes. When her feet touched the floor they seemed to bound. The corn cakes smelled good and Mary Alice was hungry, but she was afraid of the big men, and even mother seemed strange.

Uncle Charley was the last of the men to go. He stood in the doorway turning his hat in his fingers and not looking at anybody. Then he went away and all the women got up and began putting the children on the benches by the table and finding places themselves. Some one filled Mary Alice's tin dish with grease and meat and corn cake; there was a confusing noise of voices and tin cups rattling, a woman slapped a boy and he howled, and suddenly Mary Alice cried:

"I don't want nasty black things to eat with! Why aren't they white, mother, like ours?"

Everybody looked at her, and mother reached down and took her under one arm and carried her out of the house; Mary Alice did not know why. Mother did not listen to anything she said; mother set her down hard and held her head under one arm and lifted up her skirts and struck her from behind. Mary Alice yelled with amazement and terror. Mother struck her more than once, and then said:

"Now come in this house, and eat, and don't let me hear another word out of you!"

Mary Alice sat bowed on the bench and swallowed as much as she could. She was most miserable. Afterward they went home, and all down the white road Mary Alice did not say anything, only she looked up at mother now and then and felt confused. When they got home she hurried into the house and sat alone in a corner, holding her rag doll.

The days were forlorn. Uncle Charley did not come, father did not laugh, and mother never tickled toes any more when she pulled the covers off the cot in the mornings. Father had finished the well; there was no more red clay, and in the yard there were only lizards and ants to watch.

One night Mary Alice had a dream. She dreamed that some one came tapping at the door in the night. Father said, "Who's there?" and Uncle Charley's voice answered, very low. Father got up and lighted the lamp in the kitchen, and mother got up. Mary Alice thought she sat up in bed and looked through the door into the kitchen.

Mother's long braid hung down her wrapper, and mother said to father: "No! I won't do it, Howard. Everything we own in the world is in this farm. You won't be driven off it while I have anything to say about it."

Father's wrinkles were deep black marks on his face above the lamp. He said, "Well, but Mary—"

"I don't believe it, anyway!" mother said. "She couldn't hate us like that. What have we ever done to her?"

Uncle Charley's voice was there, but Mary Alice could not see Uncle Charley. Mother turned quickly and spoke toward the voice.

"Well, why don't you?" she said. "You don't belong with such people. You used to be the finest boy in Webster County, and what's she doing to you? You know it isn't true; you know I've never said a word to turn you against her, but I say it now. Yes, leave her! Married or not married, there's some things wrong in the sight of God. If you'll come with us, Charley, we'll go. We'll go back home."

Then Mary Alice heard the piney woods whispering, and she was frightened and cold and wanted to call to mother, but did not dare.

Uncle Charley said, "It's too late, Mary."

Mother said: "It isn't too late. Yes, I say it. I don't care if you'd married her twenty times—"

Then Uncle Charley said a strange thing. He said: "Mary, you don't know—you don't know what she'd do. The moon's shining." Mother's face went all still and hard in the lamplight. Then she was out of sight, and Mary Alice heard her crying voice, "Oh, Charley, don't! don't!" and a terrible, hoarse, gasping sound. Father coughed, and then he grew very large and very small and the terrible sounds went on and on, until Mary Alice opened her eyes. The sounds were only the whispering of the piney woods and mother was combing her hair in the morning.

"Where is Uncle Charley?" said Mary Alice. "Mother, is the moon shining?"

"What do you mean?" mother exclaimed. "You've been dreaming, Mary Alice. Nobody's been here. Moonshining is a bad word. You must never say it again." Mary Alice's bewilderment opened her mouth, but mother was so stern that she closed it again.

After breakfast mother took Mary Alice between her knees and spoke to her seriously. "I want you to listen to me, Mary Alice," she said. "You must never eat anything that anyone gives you. Never eat anything until I give it to you, or father. Do you understand?"

"Oh, mother," said Mary Alice, "aren't you ever going to tickle my toes again, ever, ever, any more?"

Mother scrunched her up tight in her warm, clean-smelling calico lap and arms, laughing and catching her breath. But in a minute she was stern again. "Listen, dear. You must never, never eat anything until I say you may. Do you understand? Tell me, Mary Alice."

"I must never eat anything until you say I may," said Mary Alice, remembering hard. And next morning mother tickled her toes, but it was not as it used to be, and Mary Alice did not want mother to do it because she was asked.

One could play in the garden, putting the peanut blossoms to bed. Mary Alice had carefully picked up the peanut blossoms and dusted them, until father found her doing it. He laughed then, and called mother to laugh, too. Peanut blossoms must dig down into the ground to make peanuts. So now she put them in little holes and buried them—the peanut blossoms were glad because she was helping them.

"Well, I guess we'll have to live on the peanuts," father said. The cow was dead. He had found her in the piney woods with her legs cut, so he had had to kill her, and there would not be any little calf. Mother looked sick. She said: "How can human beings do such things! But I won't back down for them," she said; "it's like going away and leaving Charley."

There were no more peanut blossoms. Under the ground there were peanuts, and father was digging them up; some day mother would roast them. The banana plant in the yard had grown taller than Mary Alice; its broad leaves hung limp and warm in the sun. Beneath it on the ground a moth fluttered; it was alive, but it was covered with ants. The ants were eating it. Mary Alice got a grass stem and fought them. She poked them off as fast as she could, but they kept coming, and the poor moth fluttered. She must not touch moths, a touch brushed the weeny little feathers off their wings, and hurt them. Mary Alice fought the ants as fast as she could, but in a moment the moth jerked, twisted up its legs, and died. Mary Alice stood up. Aunt Molly was leaning on the fence, watching her from the shadows of a sunbonnet. She did not speak, but beckoned with her hand.

"See what I've fetched you honey," she said, like a secret. She uncurled her fingers, and on her palm was a little red ball. "It's spruce gum," she said. "It grows in the piney woods. Your Aunt Molly's fetched it and chawed it all soft for you."

She felt warm and grateful toward Aunt Molly. But Aunt Molly's eyes were strange; their look came out of them and pushed Mary Alice's gaze down. She could not look at Aunt Molly. She turned the red ball over in her hand.

"Chaw it," said Aunt Molly. "Chaw it."

It was only to chaw; it was not something to eat. Mary Alice lifted it to her mouth, and then took it down and looked at it again. But it was not to eat. The screen door slammed, and she looked up guiltily.

"Mother, see!" she said. "See what Aunt Molly gave me! Mother, can I eat it? It's gum."

Mother looked at Aunt Molly. Aunt Molly stood up straight, and the sunbonnet fell back; her face came out hard and bright, and she smiled at mother.

"Yes, Mary Alice, you may have it," said mother, and just as joy leaped in Mary Alice, mother's hand came down quickly and took the red ball. "After supper," she said.

Mary Alice looked up, protesting, and was struck silent. Something vast and terrible was there, in the air, invisible, coming out of the eyes of Aunt Molly and mother. Mary Alice's legs stumbled as mother led her by the hand into the house.

Mother sat down and took Mary Alice into her lap. She rocked her for a while and then said:

"Mary Alice, I promised you the gum, and mother always keeps her promises. The gum is yours. Will you give it to me for a pan of peanuts?"

Mary Alice thought. She thought of the red ball, how good it looked, and she thought of hot, crackling peanuts.

"A large pan?" she asked.

"The black baking pan," said mother.

"All right," said Mary Alice. Mother got the black baking pan and filled it with peanuts. She put the pan in the oven and shut the oven door. Then she went out. Mary Alice sat on a stool and waited. She looked at the sunshine on the floor and at the ironing board laid on the backs of the two chairs; she heard the piney woods whispering, and the safe sound of the teakettle. Now and then she sniffed. She smelled the peanuts. She smelled them very loud. She began to smell them anxiously; they smelled burning. She was trying to open the oven door when suddenly some one seized her. Mother had her tight; mother was shaking and sobbing and laughing, her face was wet and twisted against Mary Alice's. Mary Alice shrieked aloud and struggled, screaming.

Father came in, running, the hoe in his hand. Mother cried: "She died! She's dead!" and laughed horribly.

Father shook them both. "O my God! O my God! What is it?" he said. "Answer me!"

Mother stumbled across the floor, carrying Mary Alice to the doorway. Outside, on the stain of red mud, the Plymouth Rock hen lay dead with her head on.

"I threw it to her, and she swallowed it, and died," said mother.

And Mary Alice sincerely wept, because she had liked the hen, too. Father and mother comforted her, and talked over her head.

There was no supper that night. Mary Alice was given a piece of bread and butter, and she was not to be put to bed. Father had hitched up the horses, and they were going back to grandfather's. Trunks and boxes were packed and piled in the wagon, with the stove and table and chairs and the sacks of peanuts. As soon as it was dark they started.

The piney woods were shadowy in the moonlight and things without shapes moved through them; the horses' feet made dull thudding sounds and the wagon creaked, the harness jingled. They had gone a long way, but Mary Alice was still awake when the horses shied and some one was holding on to the wheel and looking upward.

"Good-by!" Uncle Charley panted. "I just made it in time across the hill way. I thought I'd get there and fight 'em with you. But it's better for you this way. Don't stop. Keep going. They'll be at the house in half an hour. Good-by."

Mother leaned down to him. "Get in and come with us," she said. "Oh, Charley, how'll I ever stand it? We'll get you off, somehow, Charley. I can't go away and leave you here."

The piney woods were still, listening.

"God! Mary, I can't," Uncle Charley said. "You don't know her. She's got me. She'd have the revenuers after me to-morrow. I—I 'ain't got the nerve, any more. You better hurry on. Good-by. I—Good-by, Mary!"

Then he was gone, and father put his arm around mother and clucked to the horses. Mary Alice thought at first that mother was crying, but she was not; she was quite still.

"Aren't we going to see Uncle Charley again?" Mary Alice asked.

"Hush, Mary Alice!" said father.

The piney woods were filled with strangeness; the gray, straight trunks moved stealthily, and the road was a glimmer that went out in darkness ahead. But Mary Alice slipped away from all vague wonderings into the coziness of sleep.

Rose Wilder Lane

# Memories of Grandma's House

In 1892, after a year in Florida, Laura and Almanzo were lured back to
De Smet by the thought of home. The sinister, ominous Florida backwoods
with its muggy, humid weather had not helped Almanzo's health, and
Laura was restive and unhappy in the South. They knew that drought still
gripped Dakota, for letters from Laura's family spoke of dust storms, rain-
less springs, hot summers, and withered crops. Nonetheless, De Smet offered the security of familiarity, and the Wilders knew there were friends
and family to welcome them. In August 1892, Laura, Almanzo, and Rose
stiffly stepped off the train, walked the length of Main Street, turned down
Third Street, and stopped at Pa's house. They were home.

While they found a place to live—Almanzo and Laura eventually bought
a little house just a block from the Ingalls home—they stayed with Pa and
Ma. Friends stopped in to welcome them back. Laura's old schoolmate Neva
Whaley was as curious as she was happy to see the Wilders back. "I had a
feeling that it wasn't quite civilized to travel around in a covered wagon
the way they did," Neva admitted, "so I asked Laura about it" (interview
with the editor, ca. 1973).

"We want to see the world!" Laura exclaimed.

When they were settled in their own house, Laura went to work for the
dressmaker. Almanzo worked at whatever odd jobs he could find. With her
parents both working, Rose started school a year early; the sympathetic
school board made an exception and allowed her to enter Miss Minnie M.
Barrows's primary class. In school Rose became so enchanted with writing
letters and words and sentences that she would not stop experimenting with
pencil and paper. When she developed writer's cramp, the doctor advised
that she leave school. So while her parents worked, Rose spent the long
days with her Grandma Ingalls and the blind Aunt Mary.

Each morning Rose took the footpath from the Wilder house to the Ingalls house, the home Pa—Rose's grandpa—had built in 1887. Those days
spent with her mother's family made deep impressions on Rose. From them
she learned about patience, acceptance, kindliness, and thankfulness for
small comforts and securities.

*Late in her life, Rose Wilder Lane liked to think of those long-ago days in De Smet. Somehow, to her, it seemed to have always been summer in De Smet. "I hope ice cream still tastes as good to De Smet youngsters as it did to me in the hot summers," she wrote to a De Smet woman who had given her a friendly update on the town (letter to Mrs. I. P. Myers, 1968). And to a class of blind children who loved her mother's "Little House" books, Rose wrote of the days she had spent with her grandmother and her Aunt Mary.*

I STAYED WITH MY mother's family in De Smet for (it seemed to me) a long time, while my father and mother were very sick with diphtheria in the Little Gray Home described in my mother's last book (*These Happy Golden Years*). Her Pa and Ma and sisters lived in a white house on a street shaded by tall poplar trees. Carrie was studying to be a teacher; Grace was a big girl in the highest class in school; so I saw more of Aunt Mary and knew her best. She was always busy, sweeping and dusting and making beds and taking care of the house-plants in the mornings. Strangers never guessed that she was blind, she knew so well where everything was and did everything so confidently. After dinner at noon she helped do the dishes and then combed her hair again and changed her morning apron for a white one trimmed with crocheted lace, and then she wrote letters and did her fancywork. She had a wonderful work-basket, a big one, fitted inside with needles and thread and scissors and shuttles and everything. She taught me to knit and to crochet and to sew a little.

Well, actually all I sewed was carpet-rags. Aunt Mary made her clothes and Carrie's and Grace's, and from the worn-out things she cut narrow strips and sewed them together, end to end, to make carpets. She did not have a loom, so someone else wove the carpets; the whole house except the kitchen was carpeted with them. In those days, almost everyone had rag carpets. Aunt Mary pieced quilts, too; and strung thousands of tiny beads on thread and then crocheted them into purses and bracelets and bookmarks; she strung beads on wire and made little baskets. She had all sizes of shuttles, wee ones for tatting and big ones for netting; with middle-sized ones she netted hair-nets (Grandma and all the aunts wore them to keep their hair neat) and with the biggest one she

Aunt Mary as Rose remembered her

netted two hammocks. One hammock hung between two trees in the yard beside the house; on summer afternoons we could swing in it, or lie in it and watch the birds and sky. The other hammock she made for my mother and gave it to her when we left De Smet and went to the Ozarks in Missouri after my father and mother were well again.

I can almost read Braille, because when I was a little girl, six years old, I used to watch Aunt Mary write it. She had a kind of slate with a ruler attached to it which moved up and down, and a stylus, and she wrote beautifully. She sent and received many letters, her college classmates always writing to each other.

My Aunt Mary was busy and cheerful always; she used to hum

The Ingalls home in De Smet, built by Charles Ingalls in 1887

and softly sing to herself while she did the housework and on Sundays she played her organ and we all sang hymns. I never saw her after we left De Smet, but I wrote to her for years. Once she sent me a doll made of cotton batting, the only one like it that I ever saw; maybe it was the only one ever made. I named her Mary. She was made of a roll of fine white cotton batting, so she had no feet. She had arms of little rolls of the white batting. Her face was embroidered; little red mouth and blue eyes and brown eyebrows and brown curls; and she wore a bonnet and a dress and a little apron, all made of a single thin layer of the batting and embroidered around the edges.

When I was five years old, sitting one day in my grandmother's parlor on a footstool beside her rocking chair, and helping her sew carpet rags, after a long meditative silence I said dreamily, "I wish I had been there when Christ was crucified." My sincerely, deeply pious grandmother was (I now realize) deeply touched by this tender, young piety; I can recall the tone of her voice saying softly, "Why, dear?" I replied, "So I could have cursed him and been the Wandering Jew."

I'm sure I recall the incident because of the inexplicable effect, upon my grandmother, of these candidly innocent words. It was like an earthquake, a silent one. She said nothing. Somehow the air sort of crashed, terrifically.

But for most of my life it seemed ideal to be that mythical Wanderer. Imagine having been thirty-five years old—the perfect age; vigorously young yet somewhat recovering from being a total fool—since the year One, when Rome's Golden Age was beginning and Hellenic not yet wholly ended. Imagine being able to remember 1900 years, to be able to speak all languages, and to anticipate seeing all the rest of human history to the final destruction of this planet.

Only lately I've decided against that youthful ambition. Here I'm not yet ninety, and far from knowing all languages, I don't even know my own. Words I've relied upon all my life are quicksand under my feet. Just think of "square" for example.

And hep, hip, hippie change so rapidly that they escape a grasp. And as for understanding people—Once I thought I had begun to, but now I give up. . .

Rose Wilder Lane

# Grandpa's Fiddle

*Dry years persisted in Dakota; 1893 and 1894 gave farmers no hope that the parched land would again be green. Losing their drought-stricken land, many farm families packed their remaining possessions and left the prairies. Lines of wagons passed through De Smet, filled with the same homesteaders who had so hopefully flocked in to claim the free land of the 1880s.*

*Laura and Almanzo earned dollars from day labor, and from their earnings they saved for a new start somewhere. They spoke of emigrating to New Zealand; they had to go where the cruel cold would not cause Almanzo's crippled feet so much pain.*

*Many of the covered wagon folks were southbound, heading for Missouri. The Gilberts from De Smet were already there, and Mr. Cooley and Mr. Sherwin had made a trip by train to look over the Ozark country. When*

Mr. Sherwin returned, he brought Laura an apple, the biggest, reddest apple she had ever seen. Laura set it on the windowsill, not to eat, but to look at and think about. A country that grew apples like that had to be good.

"Missouri fever" was what the De Smet Leader called the enthusiasm for and exodus to the "Land of the Big Red Apple" in the Ozark Mountains. Glossy real estate literature described the lush fruit that grew there and the long autumns, short winters, early springs, and bountiful summers. A man could live in plenty on a small plot of Ozark land by raising fruit, poultry, and cattle. "Good homes, good farms, good life!" shouted those real estate folders.

Almanzo and Laura caught Missouri fever. They had saved enough for a new start in the new country, so early on a July Monday in 1894, Almanzo, Laura, and Rose said their farewells to their family. The Wilders turned south, to the promise of a new home and a new life in Mansfield, Missouri.

In this previously unpublished account, Rose graphically recalled her childish memories of her family's preparations and trip during the summer of her seventh year.

Grandpa's Fiddle I

I only remember hearing him play it once, the night before we left Dakota. Of course I was only a little girl, I was just seven years old then, and I hardly remember Grandpa Ingalls. I remember Grandma better.

She was a real sweet, patient old lady, with brown hair parted in the middle and a shell comb standing up from the knot in back. Even at the washtub, or ironing over a hot stove on a blistering hot day, Grandma was always neat. In the afternoons she'd change her apron to a white one and sit in her rocker in the sitting room, mending or knitting or sewing carpet rags. She took care of me patiently when Mama had to leave me with her all day.

That was after we had lost the homestead and even the tree claim on the mortgages, and Papa was not able to work. He had diphtheria and it left him partially paralyzed for some years, so all he could do was hunt for odd jobs. Mama was working at the dressmaker's, she worked from six in the morning to six at night and she was getting a dollar a day and saving up to make a fresh start. Mama always hated to sew, but could do it when she had to, and I remember how proud she was once when she cut and worked forty buttonholes in sixty minutes.

Those afternoons I sat on a stool by Grandma's chair, and she taught me to knit and crochet and to piece my first patchwork quilt. When I finished a day's stint, I could help her sew carpet rags. Grandma did not talk much, but she was pleasant. We'd just sit there working together, and her gentle voice seemed to murmur in with the sounds of the leaves and wind and insects outside, if it was summer, or with the teakettle's humming on the heating stove, if it was winter.

Aunt Mary was blind. Strangers never knew it, because her eyes were beautiful, clear and blue, and in the house she knew her way around as well as anybody. She'd had scarlet fever as a child, and it left her blind. Grandpa and Grandma never quite got over it. She was their oldest, and so beautiful and so smart. They'd had great hopes for her. They wanted her to be a school teacher. She was the smartest of the family, everyone said so, she loved books and studying and even as a little child she had great ambitions and they were all ambitious for her. But she went blind, and that ended everything. In a way, it was an ending for Grandpa and Grandma, too. Mama told me once that they were never quite the same after Mary went blind.

There were two other children, both girls, besides Mama and Aunt Mary. Aunt Carrie set type at the newspaper office and Aunt Grace was still in school when we left Dakota. They had a brother, he would have been my uncle, but he died early. He died as a baby, in Minnesota. They never knew what he died of; he just sickened and wasted away and died. Of course there were no doctors there then. And it seems after that they pinned all their hopes on Aunt Mary and then she went blind.

That was in Minnesota, after they came back from Indian Territory. You see, they went to Indian Territory from the Big Woods of Wisconsin, and they fixed up a nice little home there, a log cabin with glass windows that Grandpa brought all the way from Independence, Kansas, without breaking it. But it seems, being

Caroline Quiner Ingalls as Rose knew her in the early 1890s

white, they had no right to be in Indian Territory. All the white settlers were driven out by soldiers. Grandpa wouldn't wait to be
pushed out like an ornery hound.

So they had to leave all they had worked for in Indian Territory,
their nice, comfortable home with the two glass windows, the sods
broken and crops in and the barn built and all. It hurt Grandpa, to
think of leaving those glass windows.

Charles Philip Ingalls

Mama has told me so much about that wild country, but after all, there's really nothing to say about it, that most everybody hasn't heard from their own folks. Nothing out of the ordinary ever happened to any of us Ingallses, we've always been ordinary folks like everybody else.

Grandpa drove them back across Kansas and Missouri and Iowa and they'd settled down along Plum Creek in Minnesota. But those were the grasshopper years, and it seemed they could never get ahead in Minnesota. But Grandpa was able to get them out of the dugout and into a frame house; he was proud of that. But then they'd all had scarlet fever and Aunt Mary lost her sight.

It sounds, to tell it, as if they'd known nothing but calamities, but the truth is they didn't expect much in this world and they just shed thankfulness around them for what they had. You'll never see a more cheerful home as the one I remember in De Smet. There they had a snug house, two little bedrooms downstairs, and the lean-to kitchen and that sunny sitting room with a rag carpet and lace curtains. They'd been the first settlers in De Smet and had helped to found the church; everybody respected them. Grandpa was Justice of the Peace and made a little something from fees, and besides he was hired to do most of the carpentry work that was hired in town. With the garden and the hens and what little he made, they didn't really want for anything.

Seems to me I can hear Grandma saying, when she was lighting the lamp to get supper by, and a wild stormy night was starting outside, "My, I am thankful for a good roof over our heads!" And when she was chopping the warmed-up potatoes in the frying pan and they'd begin to brown, Aunt Mary's face would light up and she'd say, "Mm, that smells good!" On winter nights they cooked on the heater and ate in the sitting room instead of the kitchen, to save a fire in the cookstove. Coal cost a lot on those Dakota prairies and there wasn't any wood to burn.

Aunt Grace would come home from school, and she'd change from her school dress and shoes, and wrap up in an old shawl to bring in a pail of water, and Grandpa would come in for a minute and then go out to do the chores. But all I can remember about him is patched shoes, and a long beard, and bright blue eyes.

Then Mama'd come hurrying in to take me home, and she'd tell them about the dresses she was working on, who they were for and how they were trimmed, and sometimes she'd say she had to hurry back after supper and work till all hours to get some dress done before morning, and her quick hands would be bundling me into my wraps just any way to get me into them. But she never failed to ask Grandma a little anxiously, "Has she been a good girl, Ma?"

I tried all day to be good but I dreaded that question. I knew how much Mama hated to impose on Grandma by leaving me there, but what else could she do when Papa was out looking for odd jobs, because how could we get along without that dollar she earned every day?

Grandma was kind, but she must be truthful. Sometimes she had to answer, "I don't want to tell you, Laura, but I've got to. She has not been very diligent." And there would be my nine-patch block, not finished.

There it was, and nothing could change it now. I could never get back the hour I'd dawdled away. Or perhaps, all afternoon long, the thread knotted and the needle had slipped or I'd sewed the wrong pieces together, and I'd had to do the seams over and over again. But there it was, my day's stint not done. A little sigh, no more than a sad breath, would come from Mama's chest. She didn't know she made that little sound, and that was why it made me feel worse, in a way, than a spanking would have.

Mama was always advanced for her time. She told me once that she made up her mind before I was born that she wouldn't whip me; she did not believe in breaking a child's will. She had to change back to "Spare the rod and spoil the child" before I can remember, because I told a lie. And if she warned me to keep my dress clean or not lose my hair ribbon or something like that, or I'd get a spanking, then she had to keep her word. But she never actually spanked me for not being diligent.

Sometimes she'd try to be cheerful. "Well, she'll do better tomorrow!" And sometimes, I suppose when she was tireder than usual, she'd say desperately, "Oh Ma, whatever am I going to do with her?" Grandma would not advise her as to that, because of course raising me was Mama's responsibility.

Then Mama'd take a firm grip on my hand and hurry me home. We lived then in a tall old house behind the other houses in town, between their barns and the railroad tracks. In spring the low, wet land there was covered with violets. We had no furniture because it had been chattel-mortgaged. In the whole big house there was only a cookstove and a big box for a table, Papa's and Mama's trunks, and their big bed and my little bed lying on the bare floors. At night there was lamplight only in the kitchen. The blank window seemed to stare at us, and through the empty rooms there were breathings and crawlings and creakings in the dark. And the wind had a different sound around that house, it sounded mean and jeering.

We lived there until I was seven years old, and then at last we were going away. We had a team again and a covered wagon, Mama had saved up one hundred dollars. We were going to the Land of the Big Red Apple. Papa showed me pictures of it printed on shiny-smooth paper, pictures of hills and woods and orchards, and I was able to spell out the words myself, the Land of the Big Red Apple. Mama's voice was singing when she spoke about living in the woods again, like the Big Woods of Wisconsin. She said to me, "Just wait till you see trees!"

We were ready to start early next day, before sun-up, and that evening we went to Grandma's to say good-by. We were all bathed, as if the next day were Sunday. I was big enough then to take my turn and wash myself all over, in the washtub in a corner behind a blanket that Mama pinned up, and not waste the soap by leaving the wet washcloth on it. Papa blacked all our shoes, and he had put on his Sunday clothes and combed his hair and mustache carefully. Mama wore her black merino wedding dress, with the jet buttons twinkling all down the front of the bodice. We walked slowly along and were careful of our clean shoes as the sun was just setting and new grass was coming up along the edges of the board sidewalks.

Grandma said, when she saw us, "You aren't going to travel in your good clothes, are you!" And Mama answered softly, "No, Ma, we put them on because we were asked to supper and this is our last evening."

"You needn't have dressed up for that, child," Grandma said. But she had put the white tablecloth on the table, and baked a dried-apple pie, and when she saw me watching her pour out the tea, she told Mama it wouldn't hurt me for once, and gave me a grown-up cup of cambric tea. I had always wanted one, but when I tasted the hot milky water then, I felt as if I were drinking tears. We all sat there eating around the white tablecloth in the kitchen and it was an ending, we would never be in Grandma's house anymore.

After they had washed the dishes, Mama and Grandma came out to the porch. It was a narrow little porch in the ell of the house between the front parlor and the sitting room, and there was hardly room on it for more than two chairs.

Aunt Carrie and I sat in the doorway. Papa got up to give Grandma his chair and Mama stood a minute in the doorway to the dark sitting room. They had blown out the lamp, and there was just a faint star-shine that seemed to be more in the summer air than in the sky. Then, Mama said, "Pa, would you play the fiddle just one more time?"

"Why yes, if you want I should," Grandpa said. And then he said, "Run get me my fiddle-box, Laura," and somehow I knew that he had said those words in just that way, many times, and his voice sounded as if he were speaking to a little girl, not Mama at all.

She brought it out to him, the fiddle-box, and he took the fiddle out of it and twanged the strings with his thumb, tightening them up. In the dark there by the house wall you could see only a glimmer in his eyes and the long beard on his shirtfront, and his arm lifting the bow. And then out of the shadows came the sound. It was—I can't tell you. It was gay and strong and reaching, wanting, trying to get to something beyond, and it just lifted up the heart and filled it so full of happiness and pain and longing that it broke your heart open like a bud.

Nobody said anything. We just sat there in the dimness and stillness, and Grandpa tightened up a string and said, "Well, what shall I play? You first, Mary." And from the sitting room where she sat in her rocker just inside the doorway, Aunt Mary said, "'Ye banks and braes of Bonnie Doon,' please Pa."

So Grandpa played. He went on playing his fiddle there in the warm July evening, and we listened. In all my life I never heard anything like it. You hardly ever hear anymore the tunes that Grandpa played.

Once he said, "You folks are starting pretty early in the morning," and Papa answered, "We've got till sun-up, and we only live once." Two or three times, Mama asked softly if I'd gone to sleep and I spoke up, "No, Mama."

Finally Grandpa played the last tune. It was "Camping Tonight on the Old Tent Ground." He laid the fiddle in its box and put the bow in, and Mama came to take it from him, and he said, "Laura, you've always stood by us, from the time you was a little girl knee-high to a grasshopper. Your Ma and I never have been able to do as much for you girls as we'd like to. But there'll be a little something left when we're gone, and I hope, and I want to say now, I want you all to witness, when the time comes, Laura, I want you to have the fiddle."

"Oh, Pa," Mama just managed to say. Then Grandpa got up and said to Papa he'd try to be around to see us off in the morning, thought it was pretty near morning already, by that moon. The moon was coming up and the grass was all silvery with dew, and the very air had that queer dead feeling of deep in the night.

On the way home Papa put his arm around Mama and said, "Don't cry, Laura."

"I'm not crying," Mama said, as if she hated the thought.

"We're going to get a new start," Papa said. "It's the only thing to do."

"To think, Manly, he gave me the fiddle," Mama said. "It's the first thing I remember, Pa's playing us to sleep when we were little, in the Big Woods of Wisconsin. And by the campfires, all through that awful mud, across Kansas and Missouri, all the way down to Indian Territory and back, and all the way out here, across the whole of Minnesota and beyond the Big Sioux river clear to Silver Lake. He played the fiddle by the campfire at night. We never could—I see it now, though I didn't then—we never could have gotten through it all without Pa's fiddle."

"I see what you mean," Papa said, hobbling along. His left leg always dragged, after that diphtheria. "It puts heart into a fellow. Well, we're making a fresh start, and maybe this time next year—who knows?"

I can remember all that so well, the sounds of their voices and the words they said, the sound of our feet on the hollow wooden sidewalk, Papa's clumping and dragging, and the tiny grating sound of Mama's merino skirt, gathered up full in her hand to clear the dew-damp boards, but still just touching them on the other side, and I remember the moonlight, the whole curve of the sky full of moonlight over the dark earth and dark houses. You'd think I'd have been sleepy, but I wasn't.

Next morning, early, we were loaded up and ready to leave for Missouri, the Land of the Big Red Apple. Grandma and Grandpa and the aunts all stood around to watch us go. I never saw them again, never sat around the table in that cozy little house of theirs.

I rode on the high spring-seat of the wagon, between Papa and Mama. The wagon-top curved over our heads and a pale light came through it. The horses plodded ahead, their heads bobbing in time with their steps and the harness-straps moving a little over their rumps and along their backs, the check-reins lifting and falling above their manes. In the fresh mornings, Papa and Mama often sang, and I sang with them:

Oh Dakota land, sweet Dakota land!
As on thy burning soil I stand
And look away across the plains,
I wonder why it never rains!
Till Gabriel blows his trumpet sound
And says the rain has gone around.
We don't live here we only stay,
'Cause we're too poor to get away!

We sang "The Little Old Sod Shanty on the Claim," too:

Oh, the hinges are of leather,
The windows have no glass
And the roof it lets the howling blizzard in,
And I hear the hungry coyotes
As they sneak up through the grass,
Round my little old sod shanty on the claim!

Then Papa and Mama sang the songs they had learned in singing school, gay, dashing, new songs, a little naughty somehow . . .

So if ever you're caught in any such scrap,
Through being too timid or bold,
Recollect my friends, whose fault it is,
And blame yourself if you're sold!

I remember the songs, though probably I really learned the words later, and I remember our singing and that feeling of going onward, always moving onward into something unknown, far in front of the horses' patiently bobbing heads, and I remember the hardtack. Mama had baked a whole sack of flour into hardtack, enough to last us for the journey to Missouri.

The pieces of hardtack were white and flat and round, as large and as hard as a plate. You could not possibly bite or chew them. At mealtimes Mama boiled tea over a little fire of dead grass and weed-stalks and Papa cracked the hardtack into bits with a hammer. We could eat a piece slowly, by soaking it in tea. There was plenty of hardtack, and as long as it lasted, we'd never go hungry.

"Hardtack beats crackers all hollow," Papa said. "You can starve to death on crackers." And he told us how, when he and his brother Royal were driving west to Dakota from eastern Minnesota, they had come to a cracker factory, running by waterpower, not far downstream from a ford. They were dashing young men then, full of ginger and go and money to jingle. They were always ready to try anything once. And when they saw that cracker factory they both had the same thought, Why not have all the crackers they wanted to eat, for once, and hang the expense! They figured at that, they'd save the cost of dinner. Well, they asked the price, and it was less than you'd suppose. Being at the factory, they got pretty near half a bushel of crackers, fresh and hot from the oven, for twenty-five cents. They set that big sackful of crackers between them in the buckboard and just dived into it. Well, sir, the more they ate of those crackers, the hungrier they got. They drove on that whole afternoon, eating those crackers and getting hungrier and not coming to any town or any house, and they drove on far into the night hoping to come to some place where they could get something to eat. Finally, they had to finish up those crackers and camp for the night and they all but starved to death before morning. They were so hungry they could hardly sleep. It was past noon next day before they came to a homesteader's shanty, and they bought him out of bread and beans. Crackers are things for a tasty treat, but they don't stick to a man's ribs, like good solid hardtack does.

I began to know Papa then, sitting beside him all day long. His hands were strong and capable on the lines, and when he spoke to the horses they knew he was their friend. Horses would always do anything for Papa. He did not look like a cripple, sitting there; his arms were firm with easy muscles and his chest and shoulders were deep and broad, not twisted then as they were later by his hobbling lameness. He had a gay mouth under the neatly clipped brown mustache, and little laughter-wrinkles, as well as sun-wrinkles, around his blue eyes. Papa was a capable man, I felt it even then; he knew how to handle anything, and how to meet people and circumstances, and in those days he had a kind of gaiety in his independence.

He'd say, "I'm not licked yet, not by a damn sight!" and he'd say it gayly. I guess that was because, in those days, he was young. And both he and Mama were happy together, as young folks are, just starting out. Though they'd had so many setbacks, with drought and crop-failures and hard times and sickness and all, ever since they were married, still now they were making a fresh start.

We were going to the Land of the Big Red Apple, and we had one hundred dollars, put away, hidden, in Mama's polished wooden writing case Papa had made for her. I knew that hundred dollars was in the writing case, and I must never tell anybody it was there, not *anybody, never*. I must not speak of it even to Mama and Papa. But if anything should happen to them, I must hang on to that writing desk.

"Remember that, Rose," Mama said to me, and I remembered it.

It must have been our first day out that we began to see other covered wagons. I remember Papa standing by the sorrel's haunches; he was going to unhitch, and he'd put a hand on the horse to stroke him as he always did before he unhooked the traces, and he stopped, just stood there, looking back past the wagon cover that hid everything but the road ahead, from Mama and me.

"By George," Papa said slowly. "Here they come. It looks like the whole of Dakota's moving."

It was near sunset. The day must have been hot, for the horses smelled sweaty and Papa's face was grimed with dust and sweat, his mustache was gray with dust and his blue-checked shirt was

Laura at the time of the Wilders' move to Missouri in 1894

wet at the arm-pits. A tired smell of heat and dust came from the green roadside. And all along the road behind us, straight over those low curves of the prairie, covered wagons were coming. In groups of three or four, then a little space and maybe six or eight, then a long line, they were coming on us as far as the eye could see. The wind blew away from them a gaze of dust that looked a thin gold mist in the slanting sunshine.

"I guess hard times are driving them out too," Mama said. "I

Almanzo, circa 1894

wish we'd known it before and taken another road." She did not want to camp among other people camping, strangers, covered wagon folks.

"I don't know why you feel that way," Papa said, just simply not knowing. "Those folks'll be company for us, likely pretty good company, some of 'em. We're traveling in a covered wagon ourselves. And your folks always did, with your Pa."

"Maybe we did, but we're not covered wagon folks!" Mama

cried. "We got above that," she said. "Pa and Ma've got a home of their own, and we had one, and we're going to have one again. We're not just traveling!" she told him. "We know where we're going and what we're going to do." And we had the one hundred dollars in the writing desk, but she would not speak of it out loud, even to Papa. She only said, "You *know* we're not covered wagon folks!"

When Mama felt like that, her forehead twisted all over into tiny knobs, not wrinkles exactly. Her high forehead curved out, not bulging, but curving innocently, like a baby's, and at that time she cut her brown hair in bangs, curled into a little mat above that babyish forehead, for the straight brim of her sailor hat to rest on. Every night, no matter how tired she was, she combed out those bangs with a wet comb and did them up in a row of curl-papers, twisted bits of newspaper that she kept carefully from day-to-day, and she fastened little knot with a pin. And every morning, before she even started breakfast, she undid the curl-papers and combed out the bangs and matted them down neatly, and combed and braided her long, fine brown hair. Mama had beautiful hair. She told me once that when she was married, the thick braids touched the floor when she was sitting down. Of course most of it was gone before I knew her, still the mass of those braids at the back of her head was so heavy that it used to make her head ache.

So she stood there, that evening, in the grass by the dusty road, looking at those covered wagons crawling toward us through the hazy dust, and her forehead wrinkled into little knobs. She looked at Papa with that look her blue eyes never had except when she had her dander up, to cross him, a desperate, cornered, scared look that wouldn't give up without fighting.

"We're not covered wagon folks, and we're not going to be!" she told him. "I don't want us to have anything to do with them. I want us to keep ourselves to ourselves."

Then she thought of what to say to him, and she said, "Besides, there's Rose to think of. Goodness knows what she'd see and hear."

"Well, it's too late for tonight," Papa said. "I can't take another mile out of the horses. Tomorrow we'll turn off onto another road."

So the covered wagons came crawling on, up to us, and they

pulled out all around us, there on the wild grass, and made camp for the night.

We were traveling with another family, but Mama knew they were not covered wagon folks, either. The Cooleys were friends of ours from De Smet; I had always known the two boys, Paul and George. Mr. Cooley had caught what was called in De Smet the "Missouri fever." The railroad company had given him a trip to the Land of the Big Red Apple, just to look it over. And when Mr. Cooley came back to De Smet, he came with stories of the rich countryside, the shady woods, the huge fruit that grew there, and the good farmland, just waiting for folks from the burned-out prairie. When we decided to move to Missouri, the Cooleys said they'd like to travel along with us. Mama hadn't minded that a bit.

Our wagons turned off on a different road the next morning, but as I heard them say afterwards, all roads were the same. It was, as Mama said later, as if the whole country was turned loose and drifting. As soon as we crossed the Missouri, we began to meet long strings of covered wagons coming north, with folks hoping to find some sort of living where we couldn't find one, because they couldn't find any way to live where we were going. And at all crossroads it was the same thing, long lines of covered wagons coming from the east, going west, and coming from the west and going east. From all over the country everybody that Papa met had the same story to tell—factories shut down, mortgages foreclosed, banks busted, no work to be had anywhere and no chance for a man to get back on the land.

We came down to the bank of the Missouri just at sunset. We had been standing in line a long time, the Cooleys right behind us, all afternoon. As far back as I could see, the covered wagons were standing, inching up little by little to the ferry. The ferry could take only two wagons at a time. The sun was hot and the dust was blowing, and there wasn't a thing to do but sit there.

Grandpa's Fiddle II

Since the Cooleys had two wagons, they let Paul drive one of them. I could see Paul and George, bare-legged on the seat of the first wagon. They were about the same size and age, not more than a year apart between them, and Paul wasn't much older than I was. They never turned around; all we could see of them was their big straw hats, the overall straps crossing on the sweaty backs of their gray shirts, and their bare legs hanging down. It scared me a little to think of Paul driving, all by himself, and yet I envied him, too.

Once, as the wagons crept up a bit, Papa said, "That little shaver knows how to drive. That's a big, powerful team he's handling and a big wagon."

As time wore along, Mama noticed the hens in the box tied behind the Cooley wagon sticking their heads out and panting, and that reminded her that ours must need water. So Papa got out to go back and fill their water-dish—we carried a jug of water with us—and then, that was Papa all over, he went up to the Cooleys' hens and filled theirs.

The Cooleys' wagons went on ahead of us, onto the ferry, and we moved up to the edge of the bank to wait. That was a long time after Papa watered the hens. It was getting late, just at sunset, and Papa and Mama were afraid we'd have to camp there for the night, but they did so hope to get across that day, so we could make an early start in the morning. A storm was blowing up, so bad that some said the ferry wouldn't dare make another trip, till it was over, and goodness knows how long we'd have to camp there if it didn't. Papa wouldn't give up our place in line as long as there was any hope the ferry'd risk another trip.

So we moved up, right to the edge of the bank, and stood there. The bank went steep down from the horses' forefeet, far down and so steep it didn't seem a loaded wagon could get down it. It was frightening to see how steep and far down it was to the river's edge, and only to look at that river would scare anybody. There's something terrible about the Missouri River, sneaking and treacherous and terrible, like an enormous snake. That slow, sullen yellow water, just crawling along lazy and so powerful that nothing could stop it, it's poison and death to everything it touches—dead trunks of trees sticking up from it, and the dead land rots away under dead bushes.

We sat there and looked at it, at that awful river. It was so wide, too. The wagons on the ferry looked small, already, tiny and floating on no more than a chip, tipping a little and sliding the way a chip will on running water, and yet almost the whole width of that slimy river was beyond them. The far shore was just a low line of wild brushwood, flat, perfectly flat and thin and low, and nothing beyond it. Only great, wild, black storm clouds were rolling up the sky, rolling fast, and waves were curling up out of the river, pitching and tossing that little chip of a ferry.

I looked up at Mama, the way a child will, because somehow you always feel when you're little your mother is safe, and she wasn't looking at the river. She wouldn't look at the river or at the rolling, black boiling clouds. She kept her eyes fixed on the thin flat line of wild brushwood, and I remember how her voice sounded, faint and tight, saying, "So that's Nebraska."

Papa spoke up loud and hearty, like men do, making noise to fill the hollowness in them. "Yep! that's Nebraska!"

So I just sat there small between them, looking and not saying anything. And they didn't say anything more, either of them.

Then suddenly the wagon, the whole wagon that we were sitting in, rose up in the air and crashed down with a bang. The wind did it. The wind was rising behind us. Papa gave the lines to Mama right away quick, and got out rope to rope the wagon so we wouldn't be blown into the river.

It must have been longer than it was, the time that it took him to do it. Mama was having a hard time to hold the horses steady. But Papa would never hurry, he never got excited. Or maybe that was the way excitement took him, maybe it made him more steady and sure and precise. He had to hobble back to the rear end of the wagon, and hunt in it to get the picket pins that were packed under the bedding there, and the hatchet, and he had to drive the picket pins down into the hard ground, deep and firm enough to hold, and uncoil the ropes and snap them to the picket pins, and then rope down the wagon.

All the time the wagon was lifting, lifting and then crashing down and lifting again, as if there were no weight to it, no solid ground underneath it holding it down, and the next bounce might tip us right over, over the edge of that steep bank. Mama held on to the lines and kept talking to the horses, trying to stop their starting and jumping. Our hens were squawking like hens on a chopping block seeing the ax come down, and the wagons behind us were a hubbub of hens squawking and horses squealing and babies crying and children screaming.

We felt one hind wheel settle firm as Papa got a purchase on it, and then the wagon tipped and all Mama's dishes crashed one last big crash. It sounded as if every dish she owned was smashed to bits, except the ironstone platter. But in a minute, Papa roped down the other wheel, and then Mama got the horses calmed.

Papa didn't come right back, he was making a good job of it while he was at it, and both Mama and I looked around the edge of the wagon cover to see why he didn't come. And I will never forget that sight—the double line of wagons stretching far back in a strange, dead kind of light, men and women and children all a confusion along them, and behind them the whole earth rising up and curling in the sky overhead.

The sunset light turned that huge dust-cloud to gold, and Mama said to me, "That's your last sight of Dakota."

She said it in a queer way, hard and tight, and then she sat back on the seat and tears ran down her cheeks. She didn't make a sound, just sat there holding the horses and staring at them, with tears pouring out of her wide-open eyes. I was amazed. I had never seen anything like that before. Staring up at those tears startled me so, I just opened my mouth and bawled. Papa came as quick as he could get there, asking me what was the matter. Then he saw Mama.

"Why Laura, what is the matter?" Papa asked and he looked at her in wonderment.

Mama kept her face turned away. She reached across me and blindly gave the lines to Papa and then she put both hands over her face and said, "Let me be. I'll be all right in a minute. Please, just let me be."

"Well," Papa said. "You're tired. You'll feel better when we get across the river, if we're going to, and make a campfire and get a good hot cup of tea."

I remember all that so plain, and yet I hardly remember our crossing the river. I do remember getting down that bank, Papa holding on to our horses like iron, the horses braced back on their haunches and the braked wagon sliding. And I remember the storm-dark and the slashing rain and the lightning and the queer liquid unsteadiness under the ferry. Mama often said afterward how thankful we were to get across at all; the ferryman wished too late that they hadn't tried to make that one more trip ahead of the storm, and as soon as they landed us they tied up the ferry. We were the last load that got across that night.

Mama kept a journal of the whole trip.* People kept journals then; their lives were so interesting to them, they got all they could out of every minute and then wrote it down to remember. From the time we crossed the Missouri, it was all new country to Papa and Mama; they took the keenest interest in everything they saw, and at night by the campfire, with Papa prompting her, Mama wrote down every little thing. She had spent five cents to buy a small notebook for the purpose; it had blue-lined leaves, and she wrote small, three lines of writing to every blue line, to make the notebook last and get everything down. She prized that journal, she thought it would be highly valued someday in the future when everything was changed and people would like to measure their progress by what the country used to be.

It took us all summer to make the trip, and I wish I remembered more of it. I do remember a Sunday at the River Platte. Our wagon and the Cooleys' two wagons were camped together then, and in the afternoon we all walked to the river. Paul, George and I walked ahead, and our parents behind, to see that we behaved. I remember it, I suppose, because we were going swimming. Mama and Mrs. Cooley and I wore nothing under our long, modest dresses, and they were our oldest, patched and faded calico dresses. So we could go into the water just as we were, and let our dresses dry out afterwards while we walked back to the wagons. Papa and Mr. Cooley wore only overalls and shoes, and the boys only overalls,

---

*This journal was found among Laura's papers after her death in 1957. Rose edited it, annotated it, and had it published in 1962 as *On the Way Home*. Rose's description of crossing the Missouri corresponds to her mother's diary entry for July 23, 1894.

because of course in those days all children went barefoot in the summertime.

It was a long way to the River Platte, well over a mile, and all the way Paul and I insisted we were going in swimming, and George declared we wouldn't be let to do more than wade. I did not know the difference, to tell the truth, but I was determined to go swimming, whatever swimming was, and Paul sided with me against George.

We came at last to the river, and it was a straggling wide, long space of flat white stones, shimmering in the hot sun. There were some tangles of half-dead brushwood on it, here and there, and brush along its edges that gave no shade to speak of. Far out, across the drifts of stones, there were a few scattered small pools of glittering water.

The grown-ups had to think of their shoes. Walking on stones just cuts shoes to ribbons, and even if they walked very carefully, those stones were so hot that the heat alone would injure shoe-leather. We youngsters walked out a little way, we had been going barefoot long enough so that our feet were calloused and did not feel the burning unless we stood still, and we hoped to be allowed to go to the water. But the answer was "No." So we all walked back to the wagons again.

A good many days I was allowed as a treat to ride with Paul and George in the wagon that Paul drove, and I know how important they felt, taking care of me. They'd put me between them, and all day long we talked about everything under the sun. Paul would let me hold the end of the lines and pretend I was driving, and once, after I'd crossed my heart that I'd never, never tell, he let me really drive the big black horses. It was not as exciting as I thought it would be. The huge horses just plodded steadily along, and every instant Paul told me anxiously, "Just hold the lines, don't pull them." After a minute the road curved, and he took the lines away from me. I watched hard, to see how to drive horses around a curve, and I could not see that he did anything at all, but hold the lines, the horses seemed to follow the road themselves. But he would never risk letting me drive them again.

Kansas was wonderful. In Kansas, tall green trees full of thorns grew along both sides of the roads. They were Osage oranges. They bore a knobby green fruit that was the oranges, and we had heard of oranges but we hadn't expected to see them. Both Paul and George had heard that oranges were good to eat. We could hardly wait to taste them. But the knobby green rinds were so hard that we couldn't bite into them, and when Paul smashed one open between two rocks, it wasn't good to eat. The taste was horrid. Still, I never shall forget those beautiful roads in Kansas, the green trees as thick as a wall on both sides, and half the dusty road always shady.

In Kansas we were going through a great city, named Topeka. Papa and Mama kept me with them, the day we drove through it, for fear something might frighten the Cooley horses. We went slowly deeper and deeper into the confusion of tall brick buildings and crowds of wagons and buggies and carriages. In the very midst of the city, the ground was covered by some dark stuff that silences all the wheels and muffled the sounds of hoofs. It was like tar, but Papa was sure it was not tar, and it was something like rubber but it could not be rubber because rubber cost too much. The caulks of the horses' shoes sank into it, yet it was not dented everywhere, as it should be under the feet of so many horses.

At last Papa's curiosity got the better of him, and he stopped the wagon by the sidewalk and went to find out what that queer stuff was. While we sat waiting Mama and I saw ladies all in silks and carrying ruffled parasols, walking with their escorts across the street. Their heels dented the street, and while we watched, those dents slowly filled up and smoothed themselves out. It was as if that stuff were alive. It was like magic.

Papa came back amazed. He said all those streets were paved with a manufactured thing called asphaltum, and he told us how much it cost. Mama could not believe it. Well, Papa said, the merchants must save a loss from damage by dust, and a dustless city would draw trade, too, so in time it might be that asphaltum would be worth the cost.

"Not that much cost!" Mama said. At first she was sure Papa

had not heard the figures right, and then she said that the men he talked to must have been lying, bragging. And Papa decided that might explain it, they must have been bragging.

Somewhere on the trip, we camped among the Russians. Papa was stopping all along the way, of course, at almost every farm-house, trying to get a day's work to do for some eggs or milk or vegetables, anything to eat, and I think he got some work from the Russians. They lived all together in long, low houses, white-washed and very clean, and they spoke the Russian language. They were warm and friendly and golden; the men's long golden beards hung down the fronts of their blue blouses and the women's thick golden braids hung down their backs. The men wore their blouses outside their pants and the women wore short skirts, very full, standing out stiff and thick with petticoats underneath, and flow-ery aprons and flowery skirts and handkerchiefs on their heads, with the corners knotted under their chins. And one day a woman took out of the front of her blouse a whole tin of biscuits and gave them to Mama.

Mama could not manage to refuse them politely because she could not speak the Russian language, and while she was trying to, the woman hugged her and kissed both her cheeks and patted her on the back so heartily that Mama couldn't have said a word if she had known the language.

"They came right out of the front of her blouse, I saw it with my own eyes," she told Papa at suppertime. "I hate to throw food away, but I don't know as I can stomach them."

"They look all right to me," Papa said. "They look clean. These folks are clean people. They're good, light biscuits." He picked one up and broke it open, it was beautiful, so soft and white and clean. Then he fitted it back together and put it back and said, "Give 'em to the Cooleys and don't tell 'em. What they don't know won't hurt them."

For days and days Paul and George and I tried to cook wheat. We ate wheat whenever we could get any, it was good to eat, but hard to chew. It takes so long to chew a mouthful into a paste that you can swallow, that you can eat wheat all day and still be hun-gry. And we thought then that if we swallowed the whole grains they'd sprout inside us. I don't remember which one of us first thought of cooking wheat, but Paul was allowed to use one of his mother's cooking pots; she had two. Riding along in the wagon, George and I picked over about a quart of wheat, grain by grain, taking out every weed-seed and bit of chaff, and that night in camp, we washed it, and propped it over the fire to boil.

It seems reasonable that you could boil wheat soft, and maybe it can be done. But day after day we carried that pot of wheat in the wagon, and night after night we boiled it, and it never did soften. We drank the broth from it with spoons, and we filled the pot with water again the next night and boiled it again. And at last we ate it, hard, as hard as any unboiled wheat.

Of course we chewed elm bark, too, and wherever clover grew outside a field we gathered every blossom and sucked the sweet from the roots of the petals. We ate sheep-sorrel, leaves, blossoms, stems and roots, and dandelion leaves and bitter stems, and tender leaves of dock and soft ends of grass-stems pulled from the joints. The coarse stems and leaves of grass seem to have no nourishment in them, though you can chew and swallow them and fill your stomach, but there was plenty of grass so we usually ate only the juicy, faintly sweet stem-tips.

On Saturdays we camped early, to heat water and have all our baths before dark, and usually then Papa and Mr. Cooley went hunting. Sometimes Papa got a rabbit, and then we had rabbit stew for Sunday dinner, and once he shot a crow and prevailed on Mama to boil it, but it was very tough. Still, the broth was good. On Sundays, of course, we did not travel; the horses were picketed out all day to grass. They were getting thin; the trip was hard on them, pulling the wagons all day and picking their feed at night. But they had Mondays for eating too, while Mama and Mrs. Cooley did our washings and ironings and Paul and George and I watched the horses, changed their picket pins and carried them pails of water at noon. At sunset, those days, we watched eagerly for our fathers to come back, and quite often they had been working, and brought something—potatoes or young ears of field corn, cucumbers, even sometimes a few eggs and some milk in a little pail, though usually a farmer kept eggs to sell and milk to make butter to sell.

It was a happy summer. Papa and Mama, I know, looked on it as a kind of holiday, before they would have to come to grips with the hard, ordinary living again. This was a trip to enjoy and to take full advantage of. It meant a lot to them to be seeing Nebraska and Kansas, all the different places and people and cities, and besides they were looking forward to the Land of the Big Red Apple. Mama, I'm sure, never forgot for a minute that hundred dollars hidden in her writing case; we weren't going to start empty-handed as Grandpa always had to do. The Cooleys had something saved ahead, too, though not as much as a hundred dollars, but then they had two teams and wagons while we only had the one.

Only one thing happened on the whole trip to spoil it for me. I remember it yet with a kind of sickness of horror, though it was ordinary enough and probably I would have forgotten it if I hadn't been to blame. It was one night after supper, when the Cooleys had come over to discuss something with Papa and Mama. The four of them were sitting and talking in the firelight, Mama and Mrs. Cooley on boxes and the men standing up, and Paul and George and I were sitting on the wagon tongue. It was exciting to see them after supper, and the night was exciting and we were chattering together, for Mr. Cooley spoke to the boys and Mama said right away, "Rose, be quiet."

Of course we were as still as mice, after that. We sat without stirring for a long time, and then cautiously Paul lifted up his hands and twisted them together, and made them throw the shadow of a long-eared rabbit on the footboard of the wagon. He made the shadow move its ears, then he made it open its mouth and nibble, and I laughed aloud.

Mama said, "Rose." And childlike, without thinking, I gurgled out, giggling, "Paul tickled me!"

Mr. Cooley did not say a word. He stepped over, took Paul by the shoulder and lifted him off the wagon tongue. He was a big man, square and powerful, with the strongest arms and shoulders I ever saw, and something in the way he took hold of Paul struck terror in me. Paul tried to say something and gave up before he got a word out. Mr. Cooley led him away by the arm and Paul went stumbling as if he'd gone blind, and I choked out, "Mama, Mama, I—"

"Be quiet!" Mama said. I didn't dare to speak again. I guess I couldn't have, anyway. George and I sat there, just cold and stiff with horror, and we heard Mr. Cooley take Paul over to their wagon to get his blacksnake whip, and then we heard the whip. We heard it whine through the air and strike and curl, and hiss back and whine down, and strike. For a time, Paul didn't make a sound; then he began to, he couldn't help it. But they were only sounds he couldn't help.

He wouldn't cry. In those days many parents believed that a whipping did no good until it made a child cry. You had to keep it up until he cried.

Sweat broke out all over me, and then I shook as if I had the ague, and I felt as if I were going to vomit. Mama and Mrs. Cooley sat like statues, and once or twice Papa moved restlessly, but he could not do anything, it wasn't his business. And finally Mr. Cooley stopped. We heard him say, "Get on back there and behave yourself." We heard him put the blacksnake whip into his wagon, and then he came back and went on with the talk I had interrupted.

Paul came back and sat on the wagon tongue. He wiped his face on his sleeve and then put his elbows on his knees and rested his head on his hands. The wagon tongue quivered with his shivering. And there was nothing I could say or do. I hadn't meant that Paul had tickled my ribs, I meant that I was tickled by the rabbit-shadow he had made, but Mama had not let me explain. I could feel Mr. Cooley thinking that his children would be taught obedience whether Mama did her duty or not. I should not have spoken at all, I should not have laughed out loud, and now I could never change what I had done.

For a long time after that I did not ask to ride in the wagon with Paul and George. I did not ever want to see the Cooleys again. But of course I saw them every day, for now Mama and Mrs. Cooley were great friends. Only Paul looked the other way when he saw me, and I did not like George anymore. At last one day Paul said to me, "I wouldn't care about the whipping, but you told a lie. You said I tickled you. I wasn't even touching you."

He looked straight at me when he said it, and that was the first time I saw that his eyes were blue. They were blue-black, the color of a thunder-cloud, and his black eyebrows pinched down over them and his mouth pinched and curled, he despised me so. I cringed all over because I knew I deserved it, but not for lying. I hadn't told a lie.

"I didn't mean to tell a lie," I pleaded with him. "I didn't mean you *tickled* me. I only meant you tickled me. With the rabbit."

"Oh, was that what you meant?" he said. His whole face cleared up, but he wasn't going to be friends again so easily. He asked me, "Well, why didn't you say so?"

"I don't know why not," I told him. "Mama wouldn't let me. I couldn't, I was so scared." It made me feel sick again to think of it.

He said, "Huh, it wasn't anything to be scared of," and I knew that everything was all right between us, with a deep-down lasting kind of rightness that would be there without needing to be talked of.* But I was too young then not to go on pestering him. I had to make him admit that whipping did hurt dreadfully, and then I asked him why he didn't tell his father that he had not tickled me.

"Oh, shut up!" he said then. "Let's go look for hazelnuts."

"But why?" I kept on asking. "Wouldn't he listen if you—"

"Look here," he said. "I don't tattle-tale on anybody, even George, and you're a girl. I wouldn't tell on a girl to get her a licking, no matter how many lies she told. I wouldn't anyway, and if I did my father'd thrash the hide off me. So now you shut up, or I'll go get hazelnuts by myself and I won't give you any!"

---

*The "deep-down lasting kind of rightness" between Rose and Paul endured a lifetime. When the Wilders and the Cooleys settled in Mansfield, Missouri, the two continued to be close friends. They remained in touch until Rose died in 1968.

Laura Ingalls Wilder

# From Missouri

*As the Wilders traveled from De Smet, South Dakota, to Mansfield, Mis-*
*souri, in 1894, Laura faithfully recorded her impressions, writing in pen-*
*cil on a nickel note pad as the wagon jolted and swayed along the roads*
*south. Daily she recorded weather and crop conditions as well as descrip-*
*tions of the places and people they encountered. She also described the*
*landscape as it varied throughout the journey.*

*A sense of home seemed to pervade as the Wilders entered Missouri.*
*They had a destination and the security of the carefully protected one-*
*hundred-dollar bill. The Ozarks beckoned them; the hills, valleys, and shady*
*trees overhead were gentler and more comforting than the harsh, drought-*
*burned Dakota plains.*

*On August 23, a week before the Wilders reached their destination of*
*Mansfield, Laura condensed the trip into a travel letter for the friends and*
*folk back in De Smet. She mailed the account to Carter Sherwood, editor*
*of the* De Smet News, *who printed it in his weekly paper. Laura proudly*
*saved the clipping of her letter in her scrapbook; years later, by then the*
*famous author of the "Little House" books, she penciled a note in the mar-*
*gin of the yellowed newspaper: "First I ever had published."*

T HINKING OUR FRIENDS in De Smet might like to hear how
we are progressing on our journey, I will send you a short account of it so far.

We reached Yankton in just a week from the time we started,
crossed the Missouri river on the ferry and bade good-by to Dakota. The crops that far were about the same as they were around
De Smet.

The next town of importance we saw was Schuyler, Nebraska,
where we stayed a few hours for Mr. Cooley's people to visit
friends. We went through Lincoln and saw the capitol buildings,
the court house and a great deal of the city; then to Beatrice, which
is a nice city. The crops of wheat and oats through eastern Nebraska were good. Corn was damaged by the drouth.

We saw the capitol in Topeka, famous for the legislative war. It is a grand building. From Topeka we went to Ottowa and from there to Fort Scott, which is a lovely place. Coal crops out of the ground all through the country around Fort Scott, and at the mines it is only two feet below the surface. It is worth $1.00 per ton at the mines or $1.25 delivered. Crops through eastern Kansas are fair. It is a grand sight to see hundreds of acres of corn in one field.

We have had a very pleasant trip so far, no bad weather to delay us, having had only a few light showers, and those in the night. Our camping places have been delightful. We camped on the Jim river in Dakota, and on the Missouri and the Platte in Nebraska and the Blue in Kansas and nearly every night beside we have camped on creeks, among the trees. It is a continual picnic for the children to wade in the creeks and play in the woods, and sometimes we all think we are children and do likewise.

We have eaten apples, grapes, plums and melons until we actually do not care for any more, and to satisfy a Dakota appetite for such things is truly something wonderful.

There are hazelnuts, hickory nuts and walnuts along the road but they are green yet.

The country is full of emigrants traveling in every direction.

Our horses are in good condition and our wagons are whole yet, having had no accidents. We are near Lamar, Missouri, now and expect to be on the road a week longer before we reach the land of promise.

Rose Wilder Lane

# The Ozark Years

*Only the last stretch of the journey from De Smet to Mansfield remained when Laura drafted her travel account and sent it to De Smet. The Wilders and the Cooleys headed east as they passed through Ash Grove and Springfield; they crossed Pierson Creek and drove by Henderson and Sey-*

mour. The road wound around hills and ridges, and valleys dominated the landscape. "The Ozark streams have cut such deep valleys that the land between them is steep, high mountains," Laura explained. "But the Ozarks are not really mountains, they are valleys. So the skyline is always level and blue like the sea, and nearly always there is a lovely blue haze over the hillsides" (Stanley Kunitz and Howard Haycraft, eds., Junior Book of Authors, 2d ed. [Bronx, N.Y.: H. W. Wilson, 1951]).

The travelers had been on the road forty-five days when on August 30, 1894, the weary horses rounded a bend and, nestled in the hills, the village of Mansfield, Missouri, appeared. "This," said Laura in a voice filled with hope, "is where we stop."

Autumn was approaching, but the weather stayed warm long past the time of seasonal change the Wilders had expected in Dakota. With their hard-earned savings, Laura and Almanzo bought forty acres a mile east of Mansfield. It was not a promising piece of ground, covered with sassafras patches, rangy thickets, steep ledges, questionable slopes, and heavy woods. But there was already a log cabin at the top of a wooded knob, and below it, in a rocky, deep ravine, a clear spring fed a creek that wandered around the base of the hill.

Laura named the place Rocky Ridge Farm. Almanzo knew at once that there would be no smooth, wide fields of wheat on this place, but when he had cleared some land and planted some grass, cattle would thrive, and Laura's hens could scratch in the shady stands of tall oaks. The young couple automatically became fruit farmers when they purchased Rocky Ridge, for several hundred unplanted apple trees came with the farm.

When they were unpacked and settled in the cabin, Almanzo began to clear brush and to chop winter firewood. His sales of wood—at fifty cents a wagonload—bought groceries through the first winter. Laura often helped to "make an end" on the crosscut saw; selling that wood was essential.

The log cabin was primitive, but Laura made it cozy while they planned ahead to build a new farmhouse someday. The first year was a hard one; some days Almanzo was too weak to work, and money was scarce. Even so, the Wilders already loved their little farm, and they planned and hoped for a productive life in the Ozark hills.

Each morning Rose set out for the school in Mansfield and her parents went to work in the woods. Her memories of those school days and of the evenings at home overflowed into a lengthy diary entry in June 1920 when *she was traveling in Europe. Rose's nostalgia was bittersweet as she wrote of those earliest Ozark years.*

W HEN I WAS a little girl in the Ozarks I used to start every year to school. I had a donkey. He was a stubborn, fat little beast who liked to slump his ears and neck and shoulders suddenly when going down hill, and tumble me off over his head. I think he did it for the fun of looking at me in solemn sad forgivingness when I got up. I used to bridle him myself, and strap on the little home-made saddle. At such moments he drew in enormous breaths and held them, and I, who had been fed Black Beauty in my earlier impressionable youth, shrank at the idea of pulling the girths tight, so the saddle used to slide off sidewise as soon as I was on it. However, in spite of such mishaps, and though it cannot accurately be said that I *rode* to school, the donkey and I used to arrive there, usually together.

I carried a small tin lunch pail with an apple in it and several slices of brown bread spread with bacon fat, as we were too poor to have butter. We had not yet been able to afford a cow, or even a calf that would grow into one, as heifer calves cost seven or eight dollars. Besides, we had to sell the hay to pay the interest on the mortgage. However, I used to plan that when the apple orchard came into bearing—the trees were then six months old—we would have butter and Mama Bess [Laura] could have a new dress.*

Mama Bess often put surprises in the lunch pail. Sometimes the apple was cut in two without cutting the skin in any way—which is very surprising when you peel the apple and find it in halves already, but simple to do when you know how. Or sometimes there was a raw carrot—I loved raw carrots. Or sometimes—but not often, because sugar cost so much—there was a saucer pie. On such occasions she always told me there was a surprise and it was a point of honor not to open the pail till noon, in order to have all morning the delicious anticipation of the unknown.

---

*To distinguish herself from Almanzo's older sister Laura Wilder, Laura used the nickname Bess, derived from Elizabeth, her middle name. Rose called her Mama Bess.

Rose and Spookendyke, the balking donkey

So we went over the hills to school, the donkey, the lunch pail and I. First down the hill from the house, Fido following as far as the pasture gate, where he remained looking wistfully after us—and where with joyful barks he always met us on our return. Then we went across the "branch" on a wooden bridge built over the pool where the crawdads lived—and I was thirty before I knew that crawdads are fresh-water shrimp. Then up the lane between hedges of wild blackberry and past the path to Williams cave—where once I ventured alone nearly a mile underground, till I came to a great dark lake and waded it up to my armpits, when my torch went out, and the bottom of the lake shelved off abruptly to great depths, so I pondered, and decided to come out. Then over Patterson's Hill beneath which was the cave, and so into the hollow where the new log house stood in a clearing, and up and over another nameless hill, and down to the school-house, which stood at the end of the street, overlooking the town.

It was a square red-brick building in a grassless yard, one half for boys, one half for girls to play in at recess. Each side had a wall-less wooden shed to tie the horses under. The horses did not like

The Mansfield school

my dear donkey, whose name was Spookendyke. Spookendyke used to kick them; whenever I heard loud squealings from the yard I used to raise my hand and ask politely please might I be excused to speak to Spookendyke?

There were four rooms in the school-house, two downstairs and two upstairs. I was in the Third Reader, with the Fourth and Fifth Readers in the north room upstairs. All the desks were the same size and my feet ached from dangling. I was a poor girl from the country so I always had to sit with one of the horrid, snuffling, unwashed, barefooted mountain girls. I wanted to sit with one of the town girls—and they all turned up their noses at me. They wore wonderful dresses—red serge trimmed with satin and velvet, and big hats with ostrich feathers on them, and gold-plated bracelets, and they chewed gum and curled their hair and were always simply throwing nickles away on candy and new tablets.

The father of one of them owned a typewriter. He said it cost a hundred dollars; no one in town believed him, yet even at a reasonable price it was stunning to think that a man we actually knew owned a typewriter. Overpowering, really. Like owning a yacht. Only we wouldn't have known what a yacht was: it would have made no impression upon us. The typewriter did; he said he had bought it new, but we were sure he had got it second-hand just to impress people with his wealth.

He kept the Racket Store at the end of the muddy crossing, beside the Bank. He was a tall man with a drooping mustache always streaked with chewing-tobacco, and an Adams apple that moved when he talked and his stooping shoulders were always covered with dandruff. He came one day to "visit school." He was on the School Board. We were all very solemn and awed. The Professor asked him to speak to us. He stood up and made a long speech, telling us to improve the shining hours of our youth as he had done with his. "For," said he impressively, "I was once only a school boy like any of you and look at me now."

Sometimes when I went past his store I stopped to gaze at a box of spools of narrow baby-ribbon in the window among the heaps of second-hand clothing and misfit boots and bargain hats and hickory shirts. I liked to look at the colored ribbon. It was a penny a yard and I thought that when the apple orchard came into bearing I would buy a yard of it. I used to stand a long time deciding which color I would buy. But one day he saw me and asked me to come in, and after that I never stopped to look at the ribbon because I thought if I looked at it he would expect me to buy some then. I was conscious that my intention was honorable—I meant to buy as soon as I had the money, but I did not like to explain this to him.

The school-room was perfectly square, and all of the wall that was not blackboard or window was that shade of green that landlords paint the walls of cheap kitchens. It made a strange feeling in my insides. I told Mama Bess that the walls made me sick. She said I imagined it and must not be silly, besides, I would not be looking at the walls if I were studying like a good girl. I did not study much; the books were so silly. The grammar was all full of things like this:

"Exercise in verbs. Insert words in following sentences:

" 'The dog _____ at the cat.'
" 'The horse _____ the wagon.' "

Mama Bess said that school books now were not like those she used to study. In *her* school days children had to *work* to learn their lessons. So I got her old grammar out of the trunk behind the calico curtain in the corner and did all the lessons in it, and then I invented a whole language of my own, with verbs and nouns and prepositions and all, and used to talk it to Spookendyke. At that time I did not know there was any language in the world but English and my Fispooko.

In school I had all my lessons, so I used to sit and look at the Professor. He was much like the Racket Store man, except that he had long whiskers and was bald. He told us that the whiskers were useful because with them he did not have to wear a tie. I never knew whether this was serious, or a joke. He did not wear a tie, but when he was not teaching school he was auctioneer and made jokes professionally. When there was more than one "sale" a week we had a holiday in addition to Saturday. He got a dollar and his dinner wherever he auctioneered; for miles around, whenever a farmer sold out to move far west to Kansas, he called in Professor Kay to auctioneer. The Professor was still auctioneering when I was at home last summer, but his own son is teaching the school now.

In those days the Professor used to sit before us, tipped back in his chair, watching us study, ready to catch us if we whispered. He did not have any desk; he kept his chewing tobacco in his pants pocket. In one hand he held a long cane—it was intended to represent authority but he used in mostly to scratch his back. He could run it almost out of sight between his soiled white shirt and his skin, and scratch and scratch with it. Then he would straighten up and call a class.

We all lined up with our toes on a crack in front of his chair, he took one of our books and asked us questions out of it. For spelling there was "Head" and "Foot" to the line. When one of us missed a word it passed to the next, and if he could spell it he moved up one place. Because I was such a good speller I always had to start at the foot of the class. I could move up only when others missed a word, but usually I got to the head before the recitation was over.

This did not add to my popularity, but it was my one chance to feel superior to the town girls. They might laugh at my clothes but they couldn't laugh at my spelling. However, they didn't care about spelling.

In one corner of the school-room was the library. It was a book-case, a bottom part where the erasers and boxes of chalk were kept, and above it three shelves behind glass doors. Two of the shelves were almost full of books, "donated" to the school. At recess I used to get one out and read it and forget my clothes and the green walls and everything. At noon I took my lunch pail away from where the others were eating, so they would not become cruelly aware that there was no butter on my brown bread, and while I surrep-titiously ate it I read.

At night I took a book home, and after supper Papa would pop a big pan of popcorn and Mama Bess would read aloud while he and I ate it. She sat beside the table with the lamp on it. Her hair was combed back smoothly and braided in a heavy braid and the lamplight glistened on it. Her mouth was very sensitive and whenever she was amused it twitched at the corners. Her eyelids covered her eyes and her lashes were very long.

At one end of the table was the stove. I sat on the rag carpet be-side it and ate popcorn from my lap. Fido watched every kernel eagerly and I gave him every third one. At my back was the dark space under the bed.

Papa sat on the other side of the table, the pan of popcorn be-tween his knees, and ate slowly and methodically, kernel by ker-nel. He liked to look at the shape of each one; he often remarked that no two were alike and yet they were all pretty. He had taken off his shoes, because his leg was crippled and working the hilly, rocky fields hurt his feet cruelly. They ached so badly at night that he could not sleep. Usually he sat soaking them in a pan of hot water, and from time to time he poured in more hot water from the tea-kettle on the stove, and the lines in his face relaxed again. It was the cosy, comfortable hour for all of us. We had had supper, the room was warm, we were alone together, the horses fed and sleeping in the barn, nothing to worry or hurt us till tomorrow, and Mama Bess was reading. That was best of all.

I brought home one by one all the books in the library—all the books but one. Mama Bess read them aloud. *Conquest of Mexico* and *Conquest of Peru* by Prescott; *Orange Blossoms*, which was a series of little moral tales showing wives how to keep their husband's love by keeping their hair curled and always greeting him with a smile; *Afloat in the Forest* by Capt. Wayne Reid; the Leather-Stocking Tales; *Five Little Peppers and How They Grew* and *Five Little Peppers Grown Up; Sense and Sensibility; Pride and Prejudice; Dombey & Son; Nicholas Chuzzlewit,* until we came to the part about America, and then I had to finish it by myself in secret; *The House of the Seven Gables; Decline and Fall of the Holy Roman Empire; A Bow of Orange Ribbon; Maid, Wife or Widow?; Ben Hur;* and *The Hidden Hand, or Capitol the Madcap.* One book remained, I know not by whom. *Thaddeus of Warsaw* was its name.

And why we never read it, how the dog and the tin can intervened, how my education ended and that book was destined to be for twenty-five years a joy never tasted by me—all this must be told later, if at all. As usual, I have over-written my space.

# Laura's Land Congress Speech

*"In a few years we were not so poor,"* Rose said of her family's life in turn-of-the-century Mansfield (Cosmopolitan, June 1926). *Almanzo and Laura Wilder's goal was to develop Rocky Ridge, and they dreamed of building a farmhouse on the rounded knoll; for a time, however, they lived in a little house in Mansfield opposite the school building. Almanzo had entered the draying business and hauled goods regularly to Ava, twelve miles away. He also represented the Waters–Pierce Company, dealing in kerosene, coal, and fuel. Laura assisted by managing the customer billing and the account books.*

*Living in town, Laura could contribute to the family's income. She boarded the bachelor banker and cooked meals for the depot workers during the building of the Bluebird Railroad spur, which connected Mansfield and Ava.*

Whenever land adjoining their original farm purchase went for sale, the Wilders stretched their resources to add to Rocky Ridge. An "ideal home should be made by a man and a woman together," Laura stated in the Missouri Ruralist (February 18, 1911). Indeed, she was her husband's favored partner in all the work of the farm. Taking one end of the crosscut saw, Laura helped clear trees for smooth pasture land, and she helped pile brush to burn. She assisted Almanzo in the orchards, which were fruitful without the benefits of spraying. Eventually their fruit trees bore prime apples, peaches, and pears, and their produce was taken in carload shipments to Kansas City, St. Louis, and Memphis.

Almanzo's specialty was the herd of dairy cows, while Laura's domain was the henhouse. Her flock was carefully managed; her goal was to net a dollar in profit from each hen. Those chickens unwittingly provided a path for Laura from the henhouse to the publishing house.

Always willing to share her insights on successful poultry raising, Laura accepted invitations to speak at farmers' meetings and conventions on rural life. But she was still Almanzo's capable assistant on Rocky Ridge, and when he needed her she declined invitations, sending her paper to be read in absentia. John Case, editor of the Ruralist, happened to hear one of these speeches and was convinced that the absent Mrs. A. J. Wilder could submit copy to his farm weekly.

Although Laura had overcome her timidity in speaking before groups, she demurred at the notion of her words appearing in print. By 1910, however, she was recognized as an authority on country life and was active in upgrading the lives of rural Missouri families through club and organizational work. Particularly, Laura strived to enhance the lives of farm women. She abhorred the image of the lonely farm wife sitting uncomfortably in the farm wagon on a rare trip to town while her husband circulated and visited with the merchants and bankers. Laura personally organized farm women's clubs throughout southwestern Missouri, working to establish meeting rooms and restrooms for women. Though she scoffed at extreme feminism, she strongly protested any situation that demeaned women.

As a member of the Missouri Home Development Association, Laura was asked to address a group at a 1910 Land Congress meeting (the following typescript of her speech was taken from a clipping in her scrapbook). Laura made a pretty picture on the platform: plump, cheery, well dressed, sincere. And her speech drew more applause than any other.

M ADAME PRESIDENT—FRIENDS—I have been asked to say a few words about district organizations and I certainly appreciate the privilege.

The district vice-presidents have an important part in the work of our organization and I find that it is attended by a great many difficulties, the greatest of which is transportation. The work cannot be done by letters, for in most cases the personal touch is absolutely necessary.

The problem is first to reach and interest the women, then follow with the organization and leave with the new auxiliary association aglow with enthusiasm to help them over the hard places until they are well started.

I have had the pleasure to report the organization of an auxiliary association in each of the following places: Mansfield, Wright County; Ava, Douglas County; Hartville, Wright County; and Cabool, Texas County. The auxiliaries in Mansfield, Ava and Cabool have rest rooms in operation. At Cabool they have in connection a reading club and cooking class. At Ava and Mansfield the men have asked permission and were allowed to join as honorary members and at Mansfield the association this week will receive the first installment of a circulating library. The auxiliary at Hartville was the last organized and is not quite so far along. Of these four places I had to visit three in order to effect the organization. The district vice-president should be in close touch with all the auxiliary associations in her district, and be able to give advice when needed. Her fund of experience gained from the work of all the associations should be freely for the use of each one. She is then able to make intelligent reports to the secretary of the state associations and the president and her general officers can judge from these the situation over the state and be able to give their advice and help where it is most needed.

It is a great deal of work to reach and organize the women in every town in a district, but there is also great reward in the pleasure they show in the work when they are once interested, and in their satisfaction in the rest rooms, when they intend making a social center of the town as well as comfortable resting places.

That the rest rooms and auxiliary associations will help in the development of the state is shown by the fact that already several strangers have settled in these towns in preference to other places, so their women-folks might have these advantages. What a glorious thing it will be when the women of the entire state, in towns and country, feel themselves united in bonds of friendship & mutual helpfulness, all working together for the best interest of our dear home state—MISSOURI.

Mrs. A. J. Wilder

# Favors the Small Farm Home

*John Case persisted in persuading Laura Wilder to write for his* Missouri Ruralist, *and she finally agreed to try to express in writing what she had so often promoted in her speeches: that life was good in the country. "Plenty of woods for fuel and timber and rocks for building; with low lands for cultivation and upland bluegrass pastures for grazing; with game in the woods and fish in the rivers; and springs of pure cold water everywhere," Laura said as she listed the attractions of the Ozarks (*Ruralist*, December 1, 1923). "Here on the very peak of the Ozark watershed are to be found good health, good homes, good living, good times and good neighbors. What more could anyone want?"*

*In her first piece for the* Ruralist, *Laura wrote enthusiastically about small-scale farming in the Ozarks. This article, "Favors the Small-Farm Home," took the lead position in the February 18, 1911, issue. Laura Ingalls Wilder had just turned forty-four and was on the threshold of a long career as a country journalist and novelist.*

T HERE IS A movement in the United States today, widespread, and very far reaching in its consequences. People are seeking after a freer, healthier, happier life. They are tired of the noise and dirt, bad air and crowds of the cities and are turning longing eyes toward the green slopes, wooded hills, pure running water and health giving breezes of the country.

A great many of these people are discouraged by the amount of capital required to buy a farm and hesitate at the thought of undertaking a new business. But there is no need to buy a large farm. A small farm will bring in a good living with less work and worry and the business is not hard to learn.

In a settlement of small farms the social life can be much pleasanter than on large farms, where the distance to the nearest neighbor is so great. Fifteen or twenty families on five-acre farms will be near enough together to have pleasant social gatherings in the evenings. The women can have their embroidery clubs, their reading club, and even the children can have their little parties, without much trouble or loss of time. This could not be done if each family lived on a 100- or 200-acre farm. There is less hired help required on the small farm also, and this makes the work in the house lighter.

I am an advocate of the small farm and I want to tell you how an ideal home can be made on, and a good living made from, five acres of land.

Whenever a woman's home-making is spoken of, the man in the case is presupposed and the woman's home-making is expected to consist in keeping the house clean and serving good meals on time, etc. In short, that all of her home-making should be inside the house. It takes more than the inside of the house to make a pleasant home and women are capable of making the whole home, outside and in, if necessary. She can do so to perfection on a five-acre farm by hiring some of the outside work done.

However, our ideal home should be made by a man and a woman together. First, I want to say that a five-acre farm is large enough for the support of a family. From $75 to $150 a month, besides a great part of the living, can be made on that size farm from poultry or fruit or a combination of poultry, fruit and dairy.

This has been proved by actual experience, so that the financial part of this small home is provided for.

Conditions have changed so much in the country within the last few years that we country women have no need to envy our sisters in the city. We women on the farm no longer expect to work as our grandmothers did.

Rocky Ridge Farmhouse, built by Almanzo and Laura. The house is now preserved as the Laura Ingalls Wilder Home and Museum of Mansfield, Missouri.

With the high prices to be had for all kinds of timber and wood we now do not have to burn wood to save the expense of fuel, but can have our oil stove, which makes the work so much cooler in the summer, so much lighter and cleaner. There need be no carrying in of wood and carrying out of ashes, with the attendant dirt, dust and disorder.

Our cream separator saves us hours formerly spent in setting and skimming milk and washing pans, besides saving the large amount of cream that was lost in the old way.

Then there is the gasoline engine. Bless it! Besides doing the work of a hired man outside, it can be made to do the pumping of the water and the churning, turn the washing machine and even run the sewing machine.

On many farms running water can be supplied in the house from springs by means of rams or air pumps and I know of two places where water is piped into and through the house from springs farther up on the hills. This water is brought down by gravity alone and the only expense is the piping. There are many such places in the Ozark hills waiting to be taken advantage of.

This, you see, supplies water works for the kitchen and bath room simply for the initial cost of putting in the pipes. In one farm home I know, where there are no springs to pipe the water from, there is a deep well and a pump just outside the kitchen door. From this a pipe runs into a tank in the kitchen and from this tank there are two pipes. One runs into the cellar and the other underground to a tank in the barnyard, which is of course much lower than the one in the kitchen.

When water is wanted down cellar to keep the cream and butter cool a cork is pulled from the cellar pipe by means of a little chain and by simply pumping the pump out doors, cold water runs into the vat in the cellar. The water already there rises and runs out at the overflow pipe, through the cellar and out at the cellar drain.

When the stock at the barn need watering, the cork is pulled from the other pipe and the water flows from the tank in the kitchen into the tank in the yard. And always the tank in the kitchen is full of fresh, cold water, because this other water all runs through it. This is a simple, inexpensive contrivance for use on a place where there is no running water.

It used to be that the woman on a farm was isolated and behind the times. A weekly paper was what the farmer read and he had to go to town to get that. All this is changed. Now the rural delivery brings us our daily papers and we keep up on the news of the world as well or better than though we lived in the city. The telephone gives us connection with the outside world at all times and we know what is going on in our nearest town by many a pleasant chat with our friends there.

Circulating libraries, thanks to our state university, are scattered through the rural districts and we are eagerly taking advantage of them.

The interurban trolly lines being built through our country will make it increasingly easy for us to run into town for an afternoon's shopping or any other pleasure. These trolly lines are, and more will be, operated by electricity, furnished by our swift running streams, and in a few years our country homes will be lighted by this same electric power.

Yes indeed, things have changed in the country and we have the advantages of city life if we care to take them. Besides we have what it is impossible for the woman in the city to have. We have a whole five acres for our back yard and all out doors for our conservatory, filled not only with beautiful flowers, but with grand old trees as well, with running water and beautiful birds, with sunshine and fresh air and all wild, free, beautiful things.

The children, instead of playing with other children in some street or alley, can go make friends with the birds, on their nests in the bushes, as my little girl used to do, until the birds are so tame they will not fly at their approach. They can gather berries in the garden and nuts in the woods and grow strong and healthy, with rosy cheeks and bright eyes. This little farm home is a delightful place for friends to come for afternoon tea under the trees. There is room for a tennis court for the young people. There are skating parties in the winter and the sewing and reading clubs of the near-by towns, as well as the neighbor women, are always anxious for an invitation to hold their meetings there.

In conclusion I must say if there are any country women who are wasting their time envying their sisters in the city—don't do it. Such an attitude is out of date. Wake up to your opportunities. Look your place over and if you have not kept up with the modern improvements and conveniences in your home, bring yourself up to date. Then take the time saved from bringing water from the spring, setting the milk in the old way and churning by hand to build yourself a better social life. If you don't take a daily paper subscribe for one. They are not expensive and are well worth the price in the brightening they will give your mind and the pleasant evenings you can have reading and discussing the news of the world. Take advantage of the circulating library. Make your little farm home noted for its hospitality and the social times you have there. Keep up with the march of progress for the time is coming when the cities will be the workshops of the world and abandoned to the workers, while the real cultured, social and intellectual life will be in the country.

A. J. Wilder

# The Story of Rocky Ridge Farm

*A few months after Laura's first submission to the* Missouri Ruralist *appeared, John Case asked her to write the "success story" of Rocky Ridge Farm. The* Ruralist *was sponsoring a farm-home story contest, and though Laura was ineligible to participate because she was a paid contributor, Case printed "The Story of Rocky Ridge Farm" as the lead article in the July 22, 1911, issue. His editorial note remarked, "We certainly consider it worthy—and believe all contributors to this feature will approve of our giving it first position on this page since we cannot give it a prize."*

*"The Story of Rocky Ridge Farm" was not printed with Laura's byline. Instead, it was "written for the* Missouri Ruralist *by A. J. Wilder, Wright County, Missouri." The article was told from Almanzo's viewpoint and written by Laura, just as she wrote her husband's story in* Farmer Boy *twenty years later. The Wilders were partners in farm work, and now they were partners in Laura's new career as a writer.*

T o APPRECIATE FULLY the reason why we named our place Rocky Ridge Farm, it should have been seen at the time of the christening. To begin with it was not bottom land nor by any stretch of the imagination could it have been called second bottom. It was, and is, uncompromisingly ridge land, on the very tip top of the ridge at that, within a very few miles of the highest point in the Ozarks. And rocky—it certainly was rocky when it was named, although strangers coming to the place now say, "But why do you call it Rocky Ridge?"

The place looked unpromising enough when we first saw it, not only one but several ridges rolling in every direction and covered with rocks and brush and timber. Perhaps it looked worse to me because I had just left the prairies of South Dakota where the land is easily farmed. I had been ordered south because those prairies had robbed me of my health and I was glad to leave them for they had also robbed me of nearly everything I owned, by continual crop failures. Still, coming from such a smooth country, the place looked so rough to me that I hesitated to buy it. But wife had taken a violent fancy to this particular piece of land, saying if she could not have it she did not want any because it could be made into such a pretty place. It needed the eye of faith, however, to see that in time it could be made very beautiful.

So we bought Rocky Ridge Farm and went to work. We had to put a mortgage on it of $200, and had very little except our bare hands with which to pay it off, improve the farm and make our living while we did it. It speaks well for the farm, rough and rocky as it was, that my wife and myself with my broken health were able to do all this.

A flock of hens—by the way, there is no better place in the country for raising poultry than right here—a flock of hens and the wood we cleared from the land bought our groceries and clothing. The timber on the place also made rails to fence it and furnished the materials for a large log barn.

At the time I bought it there were on the place four acres cleared and a small log house with a fireplace and no windows. These were practically all the improvements and there was not grass enough growing on the whole forty acres to keep a cow. The four acres cleared had been set out to apple trees and enough trees to set twenty acres more were in nursery rows near the house. The land on which to set them was not even cleared of the timber. Luckily I had bought the place before any serious damage had been done to the fine timber around the building site, although the start had been made to cut it down.

It was hard work and sometimes short rations at first, but gradually the difficulties were overcome. Land was cleared and prepared, by heroic effort, in time to set out all the apple trees and in a few years the orchard came into bearing. Fields were cleared and brought to a good state of fertility. The timber around the buildings was thinned out enough so that grass would grow between the trees, and each tree would grow in good shape, which has made a beautiful park of the grounds. The rocks have been picked up and grass seed sown so that the pastures and meadows are in fine condition and support quite a herd of cows, for grass grows remarkably well on Rocky Ridge when the timber is cleared away to

"We cut and planed and fitted every stick of it ourselves," Laura said proudly of Rocky Ridge Farmhouse. This photograph, taken for the *Missouri Ruralist,* shows a corner of the parlor and part of the dining room.

give it a chance. This good grass and clear spring water make it an ideal dairy farm.

Sixty acres more have been bought and paid for, which added to the original forty makes a farm of one hundred acres. There is no waste land on the farm except a wood lot which we have decided to leave permanently for the timber. Perhaps we have not made so much money as farmers in a more level country but neither have we been obliged to spend so much for expenses and as the net profit is what counts at the end of the year, I am not afraid to compare the results for a term of years with farms of the same size in a more level country.

Our little Rocky Ridge Farm has supplied everything necessary for a good living and given us good interest on all the money invested every year since the first two. No year has it fallen below ten percent and one extra good year it paid 100 percent. Besides this it has doubled in value, and $3000 more since it was bought.

We are not by any means through with making improvements on Rocky Ridge Farm. There are on the place five springs of running water which never fail even in the driest season. Some of these springs are so situated that by building a dam below them, a lake of three acres, twenty feet deep in places, will be made near the house. Another small lake can be made in the same way in the duck pasture and these are planned for the near future. But the first thing on the improvement program is building a cement tank as a reservoir around a spring which is higher than the buildings. Water from this tank will be piped down and supply water in the house and barn and in the poultry yards.

When I look around the farm now and see the smooth, green, rolling meadows and pastures, the good fields of corn and wheat and oats; when I see the orchard and strawberry field like huge bouquets in the spring or full of fruit later in the season; when I see the grape vines hanging full of luscious grapes, I can hardly bring back to my mind the rough, rocky, brushy, ugly place that we first called Rocky Ridge Farm. The name given it then serves to remind us of the battles we have fought and won and gives a touch of sentiment and an added value to the place.

In conclusion I am going to quote from a little gift book which my wife sent out to a few friends last Christmas:

Just come and visit Rocky Ridge,
Please grant us our request,
We'll give you all a jolly time—
Welcome the coming; speed the parting guest.

Mrs. A. J. Wilder

# So We Moved the Spring

*Laura and Almanzo Wilder were enthusiastic innovators in modernizing Rocky Ridge Farm to make life easier. In fact, many of their improvements were copied and enjoyed by admiring neighbors. As the household editor for the* Missouri Ruralist, *Laura described many of the labor-saving devices and techniques that she and Almanzo had developed; relating their experiments on Rocky Ridge, she encouraged her readers likewise to improve and modernize their farms and homes.*

*The clear, ever-flowing spring on Rocky Ridge had been one of the attractions of the land when the Wilders had selected it in 1894. By 1912 they had completed the ten-room farmhouse and were considering arrangements for a permanent water source. Almanzo and Laura decided to "move the spring" to provide running water in the house, and Laura shared the story of the spring's rechanneling with her* Ruralist *reading family in the April 20, 1916, issue.*

*She neglected to say that her housekeeping duties were significantly reduced by the new water system. Almanzo had piped water into the kitchen, through the 1908 Montgomery Ward cookstove, and into the sink, so Laura "reveled" in both hot and cold running water in the house. Even the barns, gardens, and yard benefited from the improved water system on Rocky Ridge Farm.*

T HERE ONCE WAS a farmer, so the story goes, who hauled water in barrels from a distant creek. A neighbor remonstrated with him for not digging a well and having his water supply handier. The farmer contended that he did not have time.

"But," said the neighbor, "the time you would save by not having to haul water would be more than enough to do the work."

"Yes, I know," replied the farmer, "but you see I am so busy hauling water that I can't get time to dig the well."

There is a story of another man who also had trouble in supplying his place with water. This man hauled water for half a mile.

"Why don't you dig a well," asked a stranger, "and not haul water so far?"

"Well," said the farmer, "it's about as far to water one way as 'tis t'other."

I do not pretend to be the original discoverer of those stories, neither do I vouch for their truthfulness, but I do know that they correctly picture the fix we were in before we moved the spring.

We "packed water from the spring" for years at Rocky Ridge farm. Now and then, when we were tired or in a special hurry, we would declare that something must be done about it. We would dig a well or build a cistern or something, the something being rather vague. At last, the "something" was what we did. Like the men in the stories, we were too busy "packing water" to dig a well, and anyway it was "about as far to water one way as t'other," so we decided to make an extra effort and move a spring. There were several never-failing springs on the farm but none of them were right at the house. We did not wish to move the house and besides it is very easy to move a spring, if one knows how, much easier than to move a house.

Our trouble was to decide which spring. The one from which we carried water was nearest but it would require a ram to raise the water up to the house as the spring was in a gulch much lower than the buildings. Then, too, altho it never went dry, it did run a little low during a dry spell. There were the three springs in the "Little Pasture." They ran strong enough but they also would require a ram to lift the water. We wished our water supply to be permanent and as little trouble to us as possible when once arranged, so we looked farther. Up on a hill in the pasture about 1,400 feet from the buildings was a spring which we had been watching for a year. The flow of water was steady, not seeming to be much affected by dry weather.

We found by using a level that this spring at the head of a hollow in the hill was enough higher than the hill where the buildings were situated to give the water a fall of 60 feet. We decided to move this spring and the Man of the Place would do it with only common labor to help. The spring was dug out down to solid rock in the shape of a well, and a basin made in this a foot deep. In this well was built a cement reservoir 8 feet in diameter, the walls of which were 11 feet high extending 3 feet above the surface of the ground. It holds about 30 barrels of water. A heavy cement cover in the form of an arch was placed over the top. It takes two men to lift it so that no one will look in from curiosity and leave the cover displaced. The cement was reinforced with heavy woven wire fence to make it strong. The walls and cover are so thick and the shade of the oaks, elms and maples surrounding it is so dense that the water does not freeze in winter and is kept cool in summer. A waste pipe was laid in the cement six inches from the top of the reservoir to allow the surplus water to flow off if the reservoir should become overfull. It is in the nature of a water trap as the opening is beneath the surface of the water and both ends are covered with fine screen to prevent anything from entering the pipe.

The pipe that brings the water down to the buildings is in the lower side of the reservoir about a foot from the bottom. It was laid in the cement when the wall was built so that it is firmly embedded. The end which projects into the water was fitted with a drive well point, screened to keep out foreign substances and prevent sand and gravel from washing into the pipe. The pipe is laid 2 feet under ground all the way to the buildings and grass grows thickly over it for the whole distance. Because of this the water does not become heated while passing thru in warm weather and there is no danger of its freezing and bursting the pipe in winter. The screen in the drive well point is brass and the pipes are heavily galvanized inside and out. There is, therefore, no taste of iron or rust added to the water. We have moved the spring so that it flows into a corner of the kitchen as pure as at its source.

We have multiplied our spring as well as moved it. We revel in water! There is a hydrant in the hen house, one in the barn, one in the calf lot, one in the garden and one at the back of the house, besides the faucets in the house. The supply of water is ample, for we tried it thoroughly during a dry season. By attaching a hose to a hydrant, we can throw water over the top of the house or barn in a steady stream with the full force of a 60-foot fall and 30 barrels of water behind, so we feel we have protection in case of fire.

A man came out from town one day and after seeing the water works and drinking some of the water he exclaimed, "Why, this is better than living in town!"

We have saved more than time enough to dig a well but now we do not need to dig it so we find that time seems to run in doubles this way as well as the other.

We are told that "there is no great loss without some small gain." Even so I think that there is no great gain without a little loss. We do not carry water from the spring any more, which is a very great gain, but it was sometimes pleasant to loiter by the way and that we miss a little.

Mrs. A. J. Wilder

# It Depends on How You Look at It

*In 1919 the* Missouri Ruralist *created a section for Laura's columns, calling her niche "The Farm Home." After Laura had written eight years for the* Ruralist, Rocky Ridge Farm *near Mansfield was a familiar place to readers, as was the "Man of the Place," Mr. A. J. Wilder. People were also aware that the Wilders' daughter, Rose, was writing on the West Coast. Most of all, however, readers drew inspiration from the philosophies of living that Mrs. A. J. Wilder applied so well to country life. "It Depends on How You Look at It" typifies the simple, sensible style of Laura's thoughtful essays on the virtues of work and the satisfaction gained from having a positive attitude.*

T HE MAN OF THE PLACE and I were sitting cozily by the fire. The evening lamp was lighted and the day's papers and the late magazines were scattered over the table. But tho we each held in our hands our favorite publication, we were not reading. We were grumbling about the work we had to do and saying all the things usually said at such times.

"People used to have time to live and enjoy themselves, but there is no time any more for anything but work, work, work."

Oh, we threshed it all over as everyone does when they get that kind of a grouch and then we sat in silence. I was wishing I had lived altogether in those good old days when people had time for the things they wanted to do.

What the Man of the Place was thinking I do not know, but I was quite surprised at the point at which he had arrived when he remarked out of the silence, in rather a meek voice, "I never realized how much work my father did. Why, one winter he sorted 500 bushels of potatoes after supper by lantern light. He sold them for $1.50 a bushel in the spring, too, but he must have got blamed tired of sorting potatoes down cellar every night until he had handled more than 500 bushels of them."

"What did your mother do while your father was sorting potatoes?" I asked.

"Oh, she sewed and knit," said the Man of the Place. "She made all our clothes, coats and pants, undergarments for father and us boys as well as everything she and the girls wore, and she knit all our socks and mittens—shag mittens for the men folks, do you remember, all fuzzy on the outside? She didn't have time enough in the day to do all the work and so she sewed and knit at night."

I looked down at the magazine in my hand and remembered how my mother was always sewing or knitting by the evening lamp. I realized that I never had done so except now and then in cases of emergency.

But the Man of the Place was still talking. "Mother did all her sewing by hand then," he said, "and she spun her own yarn and wove her own cloth. Father harvested his grain by hand with a sickle and cut his hay with a scythe. I do wonder how he ever got it done."

Again we were silent, each busy with our own thoughts. I was counting up the time I give to club work and lodge work and—yes, I'll admit it—politics. My mother and my mother-in-law had none of these and they do use up a good many hours. Instead of all this, they took time once in a while from their day and night working to go visit a neighbor for the day.

"Time to enjoy life!" Well, they did enjoy it but it couldn't have been because they had more time.

Why should we need extra time in which to enjoy ourselves? If we expect to enjoy our life we will have to learn to be joyful in all of it, not just at stated intervals, when we can get time, or when we have nothing else to do.

It may well be that it is not our work that is so hard for us as the dread of it and our often expressed hatred of it. Perhaps it is our spirit and attitude toward life and its conditions that are giving us trouble, instead of a shortage of time. Surely the days and nights are as long as they ever were.

A feeling of pleasure in a task seems to shorten it wonderfully and it makes a great difference with the day's work if we get enjoyment from it instead of looking for all our pleasure altogether apart from it, as seems to be the habit of mind we are more and more growing into.

We find in the goods we buy, from farm implements to clothing, that the work of making them is carelessly and slightingly done. Many carpenters, blacksmiths, shoemakers, garment makers and farm hands do not care how their work is done just so quitting time and the pay check comes. Farmers are no different except that they must give more attention to how a thing is done because it is the result only that brings them any return.

It seems that many workmen take no pride or pleasure in their work. It is perhaps partly a result of machine-made goods, but it would be much better for us all if we could be more interested in the work of our hands, if we could get back more of the attitude of our mothers toward their handmade garments and of our fathers' pride in own workmanship. There is an old maxim which I have not heard for years nor thought of in a long, long time. "To sweep a room as to God's laws makes that, and the action, fine." We need more of that spirit toward our work.

As I thought of my neighbors and myself it seemed to me that we were all slighting our work to get time for a joy ride of one kind or another.

Not that I object to joy riding! The more the merrier, but I'm

Laura and Almanzo spent long winter evenings by the hearth in their living room at Rocky Ridge. This photograph was taken for the *Missouri Ruralist*.

hoping for a change of mind that will carry the joy into the work as well as the play.

"All work and no play makes Jack a dull boy," surely, and it makes Jill also very dull indeed, but all play and no work would make hoboes of us. So let's enjoy the work we must do to be respectable.

The Man of the Place had evidently kept right on thinking of the work his father used to do. "Oh, well," he said as he rose and lighted the lantern preparatory to making his late round to see that everything was all right at the barns, "I guess we're not having such a hard time after all. It depends a good deal on how you look at it."

"Yes," said I. "Oh yes, indeed! It depends a good deal on how you look at it."

Rose Wilder Lane

# Faces at the Window

*Ironically, Rose Wilder grew dissatisfied with the very life her parents promoted. "No one can tell me anything," she wrote in 1925 in the* Country Gentleman, *"about the reasons why young people leave farms. I know them all—the drudgery of farm tasks; the slavery to cows and pigs and hens; . . . the restlessness of ambition, with its sense of missing, on a farm, all the adventures and rewards that one dimly feels are elsewhere. Stronger than these, there is the lure of material things, and of satisfied vanities."*

*In 1903 Rose spent her last year of school in Crowley, Louisiana, where she lived with her father's sister, Eliza Jane Thayer. Rose was a brilliant scholar at the high school, which ambitiously offered two more grades than the Mansfield school. She had to learn four years of Latin to graduate from Crowley, and this she accomplished in a single year: "from Grammar to Caesar to Cicero, inclusive," she said (quoted in William Anderson, ed.,* A Wilder in the West *[De Smet, S.Dak.: Laura Ingalls Wilder Memorial Society, 1985]). She graduated from high school at the top of her class, writing and reciting a poem in Latin for the graduating exercises.*

*Back home in Mansfield, Rose learned telegraphy at the local railroad station, and she dreamed of life beyond the Ozark hills. At seventeen she left home, proficient as a telegrapher. Her first post was in Kansas City, where she was proudly self-supporting at $2.50 a week as a Western Union operator. A bachelor girl, Rose Wilder quickly established her innate independent spirit.*

*Rose often liked to tell her famous ghost story of those early telegraphy days. Again and again she spellbound friends and family with what she called "Faces at the Window." She never published her story, but fortunately for her readers she left a typed draft of the strange but true tale. (The* Laura Ingalls Wilder Home and Museum in Mansfield issued "Faces at the Window" as a booklet in 1972.)

I HAVE NEVER SEEN Mayfield, Kentucky. It happens that, so far as I know, I have met only three persons who came from that probably charming small city; they were unknown to each other, I met them at widely separated times and places, and in combination they gave me the strangest report of the supernatural that I have ever heard. It seems worth setting down. There must be persons living in Mayfield who know the facts or have investigated the reports. I can tell only what I heard; and this is not fiction; it happened exactly as I shall tell it. I cannot explain it. Whatever the explanation may be, here are the facts:

In 1904 I was a young Western Union telegraph operator, working the night shift at the branch office in the Midland Hotel in Kansas City, Missouri. The Midland Hotel has vanished now; it was then the pride of a newly opulent era of magnificence. I remember its lobby as a dazzle of white marble and red plush under a glitter of crystal chandeliers pendant from a ceiling of gold. Revolving glass doors guarded it from the streets. When I first reached the city after daring the railroad journey from Sedalia, and the Western Union manager told me to report at the Midland Hotel, these doors baffled me. My every attempt to enter the vast place ejected me, and I circled it in growing desperation, renewing my attack until by some accident in utterly blind panic I found myself inside the overpowering lobby. Thereafter I never passed competently through that revolving door without feeling the superiority of my sophistication.

I came through it every afternoon at six o'clock, breathless after running at top speed up the block-long hill from KC Main Office. For my boundless ambition, unsatisfied by an 8-hour day, had got me a Main Office job, too; I was working 16 hours a day seven days a week, earning $60 a month, and riding on top of the world. I accepted formal transfer of MD branch office from Miss Hamilton, the day operator, who waited gloved and hatted and left at once. Behind the marble counter I peeled off my gloves, pulled out hatpins and removed my hat, fluffed up my front hair, with firm hands on hips pushed down my corsets, smoothed my skirt-placket; then I took from my purse a paper-wrapped bottle of alcohol, and with it signaled across the lobby to Gladys, the Postal operator.

Rose Wilder at the time of her high school graduation in 1904

Gladys was a thin and pale but lively blonde, with freckles. Her hands were peculiar, having six fingers each and extremely long, flexible thumbs, and her life was even more oddly fascinating. I anticipated the evenings during which she told me bits of her experiences. It was Gladys who had walked nonchalantly up the lordly curve of wide marble stairs mounting from the lobby to the

Rose, the "bachelor girl," as a Kansas City telegrapher in the early 1900s

mezzanine, discovered the public dressing room, and led me to it.

Western Union and Postal Telegraph companies were competitors; I would not have dreamed of leaving my Western Union post if Gladys had stayed at hers beneath the rival Postal sign. In faithful loyalty to our employers, we left both offices empty and while the Midland's guests wandered about the lobby carrying unsent telegrams and bellboys soothed them, Gladys and I whiled away the hours happily in the dressing room on the mezzanine.

It was a place of incredible magnificence. The floor and the walls were made of some substance then unknown to us, apparently china, for it was smooth, hard, and white as a plate. All along one wall was a thick, astonishingly clear mirror, and beneath it a row of white china basins, into which water, either hot or cold, could be made to pour, simply by turning the (apparently silver) handles of faucets. At that time I had once seen a porcelain bathtub, but never before such a place as this.

Gladys brought an alcohol stove. It was a flat tin can, filled with some substance that did not burn, covered with a fine wire mesh. I brought the alcohol and matches. Each had a curling iron. We took out of our hair the rhinestone-studded shell hairpins and little combs and barrettes, and the wire hairpins; we unbraided the braids and combed out our hair; we set the alcohol stove on the edge of a washbasin, poured alcohol into it, and lighted it, safely. We heated the curling irons in the smoky flame, testing them with licked fingertips. When the irons barely sizzled, each deftly rolled up a long lock of hair on the hot iron, and stood holding it tightly close to her scalp. Meanwhile, of course, we talked. In the white glare of light and the faint oily odor of hot hair, Gladys told me the enthralling story of her life.

She was next to the youngest of thirteen children, and all alone in the world. Where her twelve brothers and sisters were, she had no idea at all; she had not seen nor heard of any of them since she was eight years old, because then her mother died and her father just went away. They did not know what to do, and sort of scattered. I had the impression of a nestful of little quails, scattered and cowering in the grass without a mother. Gladys stayed with a neighbor for a while but they made her work too hard, so she left there. She walked into Memphis, where a policeman took her to a police station and some people wanted to put her in an orphan asylum, but she got away from them. She went to back doors asking for work, and she had worked a year for a nice woman who had three little children and gave her some clothes. But then there was yellow fever in Memphis and so many people died that everyone left Memphis that could. That nice family left, and Gladys was scared of yellow fever, so she left Memphis, too.

When she was fourteen years old, but she said she was fifteen, she was clerking in a bookstore in Colorado Springs. It was easy, clean work and she liked it; $3 a week and they let her read the magazines. There she met a girl named Amy, who came in to buy books. Amy was fourteen and she was an only child. She was in Colorado for her health; she had consumption and she was living in a hotel with her parents until she got well. Gladys and Amy became great friends; they were together all the time and Amy's parents were pleased because Amy was so much happier, she was always laughing when she was with Gladys; they had such good times! Gladys was almost one of the family. Then Amy got well, and they were taking her back home to Mayfield, Kentucky, so she and Gladys had to part.

Gladys felt bad about it, but not as bad as Amy. Amy cried and cried, she said she'd die without Gladys; they couldn't get her to stop crying and sure enough, she cried herself so sick that they had to call the doctor again. The doctor advised them not to take her away from Gladys. So her father and mother talked to Gladys and said she was all alone in the world, there was nothing to keep her in Colorado Springs, and if she would come with them they would sort of adopt her as a sister to Amy and she could live with them like one of the family as long as she wanted to, or for always if she wanted to. And she did want to. This was the most wonderful thing that ever happened to her in her whole life.

I remember Gladys' face when she said that; she meant it. Nothing else so wonderful had happened to her in her life, and it had not happened. For here she was in the Midland Hotel in Kansas City, a Postal branch-office operator earning $30 a month and living, as I knew, in a $2-a-week hall bedroom in a rooming house. What happened? I wanted eagerly to know.

Well, Gladys said, it was queer; it was very queer and she did not understand it at all, and maybe I wouldn't believe it, but it was so; cross her heart and hope to die, it was the honest truth. They went to Mayfield, Kentucky. They traveled in the sleeping cars;

Gladys slept in a Pullman berth, and ate in a dining car. Maybe they weren't exactly rich, not as rich as Rockefeller and people like that, but they did have a lot of money and Gladys' keep was no burden to them. When they got to Mayfield, at first they had a hard time finding a place to live. Amy's father owned a business there, but they had sold their house when they went to Colorado for Amy's health, not knowing how long they would be gone. Now Mayfield was growing fast; the hotel was full, all the nice places were rented, and they had to buy or build a new house. That would take some time. So meanwhile they rented what they could get, and it was an old house, not even painted, right on the bank of the river. They rented it by the month, till they could get into their new home.

It was a big house, bare and sort of echoing inside. They didn't really furnish it; their furniture was in storage and they only took out a few things like beds and some chairs and lamps, and a stove and table in the kitchen, because they were only camping there till the new house was ready. The first thing that happened was, in the middle of the first night, every one of them had the most frightful nightmare. They were all so scared that they got up and lighted lamps, and at midnight they were all together in the kitchen. They made some coffee and drank it and stayed there till daylight.

The next night, exactly the same thing happened. They were all in the kitchen again, all scared by nightmares. In the daytime, it seemed so silly to act that way for nothing but a bad dream, probably from something you'd eaten or maybe because you were sleeping in a strange place, and you were so tired you were sure you'd sleep tonight. They'd all be laughing at each other for yawning, and right after supper, as soon as Amy and Gladys did the supper dishes, they all went to bed and sound asleep. Then in the middle of the night it happened again; they'd wake up screaming, and light lamps, and all get together in the kitchen. The queer thing was, not one of them could remember what they'd dreamed. At first Amy's father wouldn't let them talk about it; but now, when they did, they could not remember what they had dreamed that scared them so.

Amy's mother said probably it came from drinking so much

coffee, in the middle of the night too, so she made cocoa. They all agreed that they'd have a nice cup of cocoa and then go back to bed, but they didn't; they just sat there in the lamplight till morning. Every morning the whole thing seemed so silly and everything was all right all day, and then at night the same thing happened again.

Gladys said she supposed you got used to almost anything in time, and after a couple of weeks they were sort of used to having those awful nightmares and anyway she was too sleepy to care much, but then they saw the faces. They were not real faces, they couldn't be, but whether I believed it or not, she saw them. They all saw those faces. At least, Amy said she did, her father and mother said they did, and Gladys knew she did. She would swear it on the Bible.

When they went in the kitchen, in the night, with the lamp lighted and it was black night outside, they saw those faces looking in through the kitchen window. You know how sometimes you see your face reflected in a window pane? These faces were like that, but they were not reflections of anyone inside the kitchen. They were faces of old men, and young men, and women and boys and girls. Different faces, sometimes a crowd of them, and then only one.

Amy's father said they were all worn out and imagining things; he said there was nobody outside that window. They all knew there was nobody there; there couldn't be because the kitchen wall was at the very edge of the river bank. The bank went straight down to the river below, and outside that window there wasn't ground enough for anyone to stand on.

Next day Amy's father put a window-shade on that window. He said that nothing was hurting them; they were only imagining things that weren't so, and he had bought another house; they would move into it six weeks later, when the owner had agreed to move out. Gladys had looked out of the upstairs window and made sure that nobody could possibly stand outside the kitchen window looking in. That afternoon, before sunset, Amy's mother pulled down the shade. Nothing happened that night but the nightmares. The shade at the window was down, and stayed down till broad daylight.

Gladys said she should have been able to stand it for six weeks. They pulled down the shade every day before sunset. She saw the faces only that one time, and she never could remember a single one of those horrible dreams. But she always knew that the faces were outside that shade trying to look in, and she couldn't stand it. One day she just left. She went to the depot and bought a ticket with almost all of her money and left on the next train, with a few things wrapped in a bundle. She did not take any of the things that Amy's folks had given her, and afterward she wrote to them and tried to explain but she never mailed the letters.

What happened to Gladys after that doesn't belong to this account. I do not remember when or why she left the Postal's Midland Hotel branch office, and I have heard nothing of her since then. Her inexplicable experience in Mayfield, Kentucky, was only a chapter in the short but adventurous autobiography that she told me in vivid bits while we curled and combed our hair in the sophisticated luxury of the Midland's public dressing room on the mezzanine. I do not remember that we discussed it all; I would certainly have forgotten it but for subsequent events.

In 1908 I was manager of the Western Union's office in Mount Vernon, Indiana. I was also telegraph operator, clerk cashier, janitress, and stern though frequently baffled chief of the staff, one messenger boy aged 13. Mine was a position of dignity, leisure, and affluence; I worked only ten hours a day, only six days a week, and my salary was $50 a month. I lived well, dressed fashionably, and every payday gaily added $25 to my savings bank account. The memory lingers with me still of those huge, delicious 5-cent sandwiches, buttered buns enfolding a major portion of a sizzling fried fish fresh-caught from the Ohio.

One day a briskly important young man breezed (as he would have said) into the office, dashed off (as he would have said) exactly ten words on a telegraph blank, and swirled it around on the counter to me. It was the routine message from husband to wife, announcing his arrival and ending, "Meet me," as such messages always did. I was surprised to hear myself exclaiming the address aloud, "Mayfield, Kentucky!"

"Oh, you know Mayfield?" the customer said. In some confusion, I said that I didn't. He guessed, then, that I'd been reading about the excitement there, in the newspapers. I hadn't; then as now I was unperturbed in placid ignorance of the newspapers.

Unquestionably my first surmise had been correct; this customer was what I would have called "a traveling man"; in 1908 only a hayseed still said "drummer." He pushed his hat back, lounged jauntily against the counter, and told me all about the excitement in Mayfield.

There had been an old house there, he said, in the edge of the town on the bank of the river. It was a ramshackle old place, nobody had lived in it for years; there were stories that it was haunted, but nobody pays any attention to such notions any more, do they kiddo? Well, here last week the railroad was putting in a new side-track, and they had to widen the flats along the river, where the railroad yards are, so they wrecked the old place and brought in steam-shovels and dug into the bank underneath where it was, and what do you suppose they dug up? Bones, girlie, human bones. It's in all the newspapers. They got reporters there, taking pictures, from St. Louis and Chicago and everywhere. It's a big sensation, a BIG one.

Yes siree sir, those steam-shovels have brought to light any amount of skeletons. Skeletons of old men and women and middle-aged, and young ones, children, they say even babies. They haven't sorted them all out yet, but there's dozens of skulls and skeletons, some say hundreds. Buried all these years under that old house. And it turns out, the papers say, that that old place was an inn, once, in the early days before Mayfield was built, when the early settlers were coming west. They say there was a good many such places, along the trails, that took in travelers and their families for the night and then murdered them in their beds and buried their bodies, for whatever goods they had with them. They had horses or oxen and wagons, and their supplies, of course, and guns and clothes, and these inn-keepers murdered them in cold blood, for things like that. Whole families. And now those steam-shovels are digging up their bones. Though they've stopped them now; there's men there digging now with picks and shovels, it seems more respectful to the dead. But nobody even knows their names today. There's probably no way to trace them. Nobody'll ever know who they were. Nothing but bones. Lying there all these years under that old house. It gives you something to think about, don't it?"

I said yes, it did.

He said that it was a big excitement in Mayfield, the biggest sensation maybe that Mayfield ever had yet, and I certainly ought to read the papers, a big sensation like that even in St. Louis and Chicago and probably New York by this time.

I said I certainly ought to read about it; I said, "This will be twenty-five cents," and he paid for the telegram and left. I didn't remember his name and I did not read the papers. I thought of Gladys, but I had not thought of her for years and didn't know where she was.

As everyone knows, a mention of the supernatural in any group of persons will produce strange anecdotes. Someone or several in the group will relate an absolutely trustworthy friend's inexplicable experience. The narrator does not believe in ghosts, of course; no one present does; but can you explain this actual occurrence? The traveling man's sequel to Gladys' tale was a coincidence that served me well in such anecdotal groups, for many years. I thought the story ended, but it was not.

In 1928 I completed the typical American circle by returning from Baghdad via Tirana, to the farm from which I had set out. This farm is near Mansfield, Missouri, The Gem City of the Ozarks, pop. 811. I like it; I like Mansfield and Mansfield people and the Ozarks, their sea-level blue skyline, their clear limestone streams, their early blossoming springtimes, their incredible massed expanses of summer's wild flowers, their winters brown with oak leaves, their fox chases and frolics and speeding motor cars filled with singers playing guitars.

Mr. N. J. Craig was President of the Farmers and Merchants Bank in Mansfield. The Craigs and my family were old friends, and often I listened entranced to an eveningful of Mr. Craig's stories and modestly tried to repay him with some of my own. So one day when Mr. Craig telephoned to ask if he might bring an acquaintance out to tea, I was pleased, and I thought nothing of it when, over the teacups, he asked me to tell the anecdote about the haunted house in Mayfield, Kentucky.

I told it unusually well, I thought, for no one had ever listened more attentively or appreciatively than Mr. Craig's acquaintance. He was a quiet young man, intelligent, somewhat reserved but observant and quick-witted; the perfect listener who doesn't miss or fumble the most subtle nuance. I finished the tale; there was a brief pause. Then he thanked me.

"It is an extraordinary story," he said. "I think I have never heard a stranger one, and I am greatly obliged to you for telling it to me. I cannot explain it at all. Because, you see, I was born and brought up in Mayfield, Kentucky; I have lived there all my life and live there now. And there is no river in or near Mayfield, Kentucky."

Rose Wilder Lane

# A Place in the Country

*Rose's job as a Western Union telegrapher took her to cities across the United States. By 1909 she had settled in San Francisco, where she married Gillette Lane and where the couple sold real estate—with great success—until the onset of World War I caused a decline in land sales. At that point Rose turned to newspaper writing, gaining quick renown as a top reporter for the* San Francisco Call-Bulletin; *for four years she wrote feature stories and serial fiction.*

*After the Lanes' divorce in 1918 Rose traveled abroad for three years, and in 1920 she accepted a post as publicist for the American Red Cross in Paris; while there, she translated the book* Dancer of Shamahka *from French to English and sent foreign correspondence to the American press. As she journeyed through Europe, Rose dispatched travel articles to the magazines back home. Later, her affiliation with the Near East Relief took her through central Asia and into the Middle East as she investigated post– World War I conditions.*

*On some of Rose's reporting excursions, her addresses were the finest European hotels, and she was lionized as a celebrated American author. Other trips included trekking across deserts, picking her way through dangerous mountain passes, and dodging gunfire in minor revolutions.*

*In a chance visit, Rose became fascinated with the Balkans area and the primitive, proud, independent people of Albania. On one daring trip through the mountains of northern Albania, Rose was the first foreign woman the highlanders had ever seen. Her Albanian adventures inspired the book* Peaks of Shala, *published in 1923.*

*Through all her adventures, Rose faithfully wrote home to the "dear folks of Rocky Ridge Farm," keeping her parents and their Mansfield friends abreast of her experiences, wanderings, and whereabouts. "We're being treated as visiting princesses," Rose wrote from war-torn Armenia when she anticipated anxiety at home over her safety and that of her traveling companion and photographer, Peggy* (De Smet News, *September 16, 1922). Rose's frequent letters—some of them typed on her reliable Underwood, held steady on her lap in moving, jolting boxcars—and her strange postcards with foreign postmarks kept her parents assured of her safety.*

*In one letter Rose spoke wistfully of Rocky Ridge Farm and Mama Bess's good meals: "Peggy says . . . could you fry a chicken and send it to us, please? These have been long, lank dry years, with no fried chicken. Some day we'll come home to fried chicken and on that day we get home for fried chicken it'll be a happy day" (March 11, 1923).*

*That day finally came. In time for Christmas, 1923, Rose's train from New York City, via St. Louis, chugged into the Mansfield station. Mama Bess was there to meet her with a taxi, and Almanzo had brought the lumber wagon to collect the trunks and luggage, travel worn and covered with hotel stickers. At home on Rocky Ridge, there was a fire in the fireplace and chicken pie for dinner. Rose settled back into her old quarters in the sleeping porch upstairs. She set up her Underwood on the desk in front of the bank of windows that overlooked the wooded ravine.*

*Rose had two goals in returning to the farm: to spend a year with her parents after her long separation from them and to sell enough magazine*

Rose in 1924, when she returned to live on Rocky Ridge Farm

*articles to buy comforts for the old farmhouse and establish security for her parents.*

*Wherever she was, Rose Wilder Lane had an uncanny sense for finding writing material in her surroundings. The Ozark Mountains breathed dozens of story ideas for her to spin out as magazine fiction for the* Country Gentleman. *The hills and hollows of the Mansfield vicinity suggested the settings for two of Rose's full-length novels,* Hill Billy *and* Cindy. *Both stories were purchased by the* Country Gentleman *as serial features,* Cindy *yielding Rose a check for ten thousand dollars.*

*Not long after Rose had rejoined Almanzo and Laura on Rocky Ridge, she wrote this portrait of her home place and the two people who had created it. "A Place in the Country" appeared in the March 14, 1925, issue of the* Country Gentleman.

T HIS MORNING WAS not yet light when I woke and stretched an arm out of coziness into the chill of my room. A glow of lamplight came up the back stairs into the hall outside my open door, and from the kitchen I heard my mother's steps going back and forth, the rattle of wood going into the cookstove, a clanking of milk pails, then the slam of the kitchen door. Nero, the Airedale pup, barked in circles around the milk pails as they went toward the barn, and my father's voice replied to him indulgently.

The chimney from the dining-room heater comes up through my bedroom, and I dressed close to its warmth. The bathroom water heater is out of order, has been out of order for months, while we send the leaky fittings back and forth between the farm and the plumber's shop in the city. Seems like you can't get an honest job done anywhere, these days.

My mother had a basin of soft water warmed on the stove for me when I went downstairs. It had been a cold night; an edging of frost on the windowpanes was melting in the warmth.

### Hen Tending

It doesn't do to let laying hens awaken to cold feed and icy water. For thirty years my mother has been a servant to hens, and many times I have raged against any woman spending her life in that way. Now that I'm on the farm again, it has often surprised me that we must have so many affectionate rows about which of us shall do the work.

This morning I left her to watch the breakfast while I trudged to the henhouse with the pails. There is a warm, feathery feeling in a henhouse. The feed steamed as I spooned it into the troughs, and the hens came fluttering from their perches. Their sleek bodies and red combs clustered around my feet, and already they be-

The kitchen wing of Rocky Ridge Farmhouse, with Rose's upstairs writing study–sleeping porch. Rose took this photograph on a visit to Mansfield in the 1950s.

gan their crrr-ing of contentment while I moved among them like a benevolent goddess.

"This is sheer egotism," I said to my own feeling of happiness in dispensing such complete happiness to those hundreds of hens.

I came back through the barn alley. Overhead the hay is crammed to the ridge pole—sweet, well-cured hay, with hardly a weed in it. There is a feeling of opulence in all that hay. My father handled it so well, too, getting it all safely under cover in a season of uncertain showers which caught some of our cleverest neighbors' new-mown harvest.

The Best Cow

On one side of the alley are the box stalls, where Fanny and Kate and gentle Governor, the Morgan stallion, had finished their bran and were turning floury noses to their mangers. They whickered greetings as I passed. On the other side are the cows. My father, in his milking apron, was lifting a pail of milk to the hanging scales; at his feet Nero sat, intent upon him, and the barn cats washed their faces by half-emptied saucers of milk.

"That Jersey's the best little cow I ever raised," my father said, transferring the scale's figures to the Jersey's record with a carpenter's pencil. "If she don't give pretty nearly her weight of milk in another thirty days I miss my guess."

There was deep satisfaction in his voice and eyes. It was the indescribable feeling I have when I have written a story that is the very best I can do; there was the sense of creation in it, and the workman's joy in a good job done.

It was more than these; it was also the owner's pride in a fine possession, the triumph of outdistancing rivals, and even something of the delight in a friend's achievement.

For the Jersey is, in a way, a friend—one of the personalities on the farm, known in all its developments since calfhood. It was she who nearly strangled to death on an apple one frantic morning in her adventurous youth; and mild as she looks, she is the most ornery cow on the place when it comes to driving her from pasture at night. Yes, she is a character, and though she cannot conceivably feel pride in her milking record, she does in a way share the honor.

"Yessir, a darn good cow!" my father said, slapping her flank, while she turned large eyes upon us in the lantern light, and licked her nose. Nero whined for attention, and we looked down at his eagerness of uplifted paw. That exuberant pup is constrained by affection to obey our laws, but sometimes it's very hard for him.

He besought special dispensation from us, his Providence; his own milk was licked clean, and there was still milk in the cats' abandoned saucers. His eyes directed question marks toward them. My father decreed rapture for Nero with a nod, and waited an instant to watch the waggle of thanks and the red tongue lapping, before he picked up the milk stool and turned to the spotted cow.


A Fresh New Day Is Born

Outside the barn the morning was gray, and as I came up the path I was surprised to see my mother, wrapped in a shawl, standing outside the kitchen door. "Hurry!" she called to me. "It's changing every second!"

The barn behind me was black against a rosiness in the east, but it was not the sky she wished me to see. It was the evanescent colors, the lights and shadows subtly changing down all the length of the valley at the coming of the dawn. We stood and watched them silently till the rosy sky faded to the color of water, and sunshine came yellow across the fields. A new day was there, a day as miraculous and fresh as though it were the first that ever dawned, and a chill little wind that ran before it went westward, followed by a promise of warmth.

It looked like a good day for setting fence posts, and my mother said so while taking the biscuits from the oven. "Some morning early, when I can get away, I want you to come with me along the edge of the hill in the wood-lot," she continued. "When the shadows of the trees begin to come down the slope, as the sun rises you feel the turning of the earth. You feel the whole globe under your feet rolling into the sunlight. . . . That's something I found one morning when I was driving the calves to pasture. I've been saving it up for you. I wonder if you've seen a more beautiful dawn in any of the places you've been."

On my fingers I count the dawns I have seen—memorable, just in being dawns. Sleepy-eyed dawn from the Paris markets after a night of dancing; misty dawn against which I was just too late to see the minarets of Constantinople—all the fault of the stupid stewardess who didn't wake me in time; one startling moment of color on the hills around the Dead Sea before they went colorless in merciless heat; sudden dawn like a clap of light over the freezing-cold Syrian desert. Four dawns in twenty years. No, I do not know dawns as my mother does.

Twenty years ago I left this farm. No one can tell me anything about the reasons why young people leave farms. I know them all—the drudgery of farm tasks; the slavery to cows and pigs and hens; the helplessness under whims of weather that can destroy in a day the payment for a year's toil; the restlessness of ambition, with its sense of missing, on a farm, all the adventures and rewards that one dimly feels are elsewhere. Stronger than these, there is the lure of material things, and of satisfied vanities. I know all these reasons, for they took me to the cities.

For twenty years I have lived in the cities: San Francisco, still pioneer on her hills above the Golden Gate; New Orleans, soft and southern under her alertness; Kansas City, St. Louis, Cincinnati, so different, yet alike in that strong, building spirit of the Middle West; New York, labyrinth of stone and steel from subterranean depths to the skies; and farther abroad, London, the center of Empire; Paris, strait-laced and shrewd and incomparably lovely; Prague, the medieval; Vienna, the gay and tasteful; Rome, Athens, Constantinople, Cairo, Tiflis, Damascus, Bagdad—the cities of all the Western world and of Western Asia.

Now I have come back to the farm.

And this is a joke on me. For it was fifteen years ago, when I was still intoxicated with all that the city offers, that my parents were offered an opportunity for city life. The offer was a good one, meaning at once as much money as the farm was giving them, and opening vistas that were positively glittering.

I was enthusiastic for the change. I was a newly grown-up daughter, and if that alone had not made me feel infinitely wiser than my parents, my city experience would have done so. They were dears, but they couldn't know as much as I did. I took their life in hand and splendidly made it over in every detail; I knew exactly what they should do and exactly how they should do it. The only difficulty with my plan was my parents. They wouldn't move.


Mother Stands Her Ground

Driven by my fierce arguments to her last defense, my mother said: "I don't see why we should. Why should we move to a city and work fifteen or twenty years to get money enough to retire to a farm? Because I notice that that's what city people are always planning to do and working for. We already have the farm."

"That's different," I said impatiently. "City people don't mean ever to live on a farm. What they want is a country place."

"Well," my mother said mildly, "this farm is a country place. We can move to St. Louis and work hard fifteen years or so, save our money and then have a country place. Or we can stay here and keep on working hard enjoying the country place as we go along, and then have it. It comes to the same thing in the end."

My mother was, of course, an exceptional woman. I was not. It must be said in my defense that the farm then was not what it is now. It was forty acres of partly cleared poor land, with a barn and a three-roomed house on it—four rooms, counting the attic bedroom.

There is a great deal of talk about the cultural advantages of the cities. I talked largely about them at the time. But it isn't the desire for education and culture that takes us from the farm. No, the lure of the cities is in the material things they offer.

We felt inferior, we country people, when I was a girl on this farm. That was largely due to the cheap superiority felt by the merchants of our little town, who wore city clothes and thought of us as hicks and hayseeds.

A great deal has changed in America since then, but at that time this sense of the countryman's inferiority was a strong part of the driving force which sent the multitudes of us into the city. There, without realizing it, we truly became inferior. We lost two things we might have had on the farm—independence and leisure. Yes, leisure.

There are very few jobs in cities that will give an honest living, with independence, self-direction and some freedom as to hours.

I was lucky enough to fit into one of them. I became a writer.

But last week I received a letter from one of the girls I knew nineteen years ago. She writes joyfully that she and her husband have at last been able to buy — with a mortgage — a suburban house.

"You remember Mrs. Evans?" she adds. "She is still working in the same office."

For twenty-two years now, Mrs. Evans has been every day at that same desk. It is only by rare and fortunate accident that I have not been there too.

Twenty-two years! A lifetime of being a living human attachment to a machine, of doing the work of a machine.

There is no machine in the world that can raise a calf or direct the destinies of an Airedale pup.

It has taken me twenty years to realize that the things I have

The Wilders on a visit to the Wilson farm near Mansfield in 1929. From left to right: Laura, Almanzo, Jim Wilson, Wilson's hired man.

fought for in the cities all my life have been all that time here on the farm.

I sit here at my desk by the big window that looks out through tree tops down to the brook and up the wooded hillside where squirrels are scampering, and I add up the values of my life spent in cities and values of my mother's life spent here.

There are the pictures I know—my hours in the Louvre, in the Paris salons, in the galleries of the Vatican in Rome. Beauty! But my mother has had beauty too.

The big living room downstairs has four great windows, framing landscapes of forest and meadow and hills curving against the sky. Their curtains hang straight on either side, leaving the glass uncovered. "I don't want curtains over my pictures," my mother says. "They're never the same for two hours together, and I like to watch them changing."

She has windows everywhere, not only in her house, but in her mind. One window in the kitchen—the one in her built-in kitchen cabinet—was put there for a special purpose, because she hates kneading bread. All her life she has hated it, and baked twice a week. So the window is there. She forgets the kneading in looking at the sheep pasture.

Success. The joys of creative work, the joys of its recognition. I have written my books. But my father and mother have made their farm; two hundred acres of good land, well fenced, productive.

They made it, with their hands and brains, from poor acres of thin hillside land, from washed gullies and sassafras patches. They built this house, with its sleeping porches and verandas, its big stone fireplace, its filled bookshelves, its white-enameled kitchen, its modern bathroom. This was a dream of theirs, realized through creative labor, as my books are made. The reward of it to them is the same as mine to me.

So, as my mother said, it comes to the same thing in the end. Here I am, back on the farm, and finding here all the variety, the beauty and the human satisfactions that can be packed into my days.

Laura Ingalls Wilder

# My Ozark Kitchen and The Farm Dining Room

*When Rose returned to Rocky Ridge in 1923 after traveling in Europe and Asia for three years, she resumed her role as Laura's writing coach. Three years earlier she had arranged for the publication of her mother's story "Whom Will You Marry?" in* McCall's *(June 1919), but since then Laura had seldom stirred from her regular and comfortable niche in the* Missouri Ruralist. *Rose's continual production of top-paid magazine fiction and articles on her typewriter in her upstairs room in the farmhouse was infectious; Laura was again encouraged to submit her work to better-paying, widely circulated magazines.*

*Rose saw her mother's progressing from the* Ruralist *to magazines of* Country Gentleman *stature as a possibility needing only intelligent manipulation. She was confident that Mama Bess could forge a reputation as an expert on country living for the publications that paid so handsomely. Not only would it transfer her mother's talents from regional to national exposure, it would also generate the income for the family that Rose considered herself responsible for providing.*

*Late in 1924 Rose visited New York City, and through her agent, Carl Brandt, she obtained two assignments for Laura from the* Country Gentleman. *Laura could handle the topics easily; one assignment was to deal with the farm kitchen, the other with the farm dining room. Furiously Rose wrote her mother copious instructions on how to proceed with the articles, how to structure the writing, and how to obtain photographs suitable for publication. She also explained how she was marketing the material between her agent and Loring Shuler, editor of the* Country Gentleman: *"What I am trying to do is give you the benefit of these ten years of work and study [in her own writing career]. I'm trying to train you as a writer for the big market" (November [?] 1924).*

*"Here is your chance, Mama Bess, to make a real income," Rose exhorted her mother with a tinge of desperation. "For God's sake," she wrote, "get yourself free to go after this. There is no reason under heaven why you should not be making four or five thousand dollars a year" (November 12, 1924).*

*"My Ozark Kitchen," by Laura Ingalls Wilder—a new byline after years of appearing as Mrs. A. J. Wilder—was published in the January 17, 1925, issue of the* Country Gentleman. *In the same issue was Rose's Ozark story "The Hill Billy Comes to Town," later incorporated into her book* Hill Billy.

*The Wilder dining room was next to be featured in the pages of the* Country Gentleman. *It had been renovated, as Rose reported to Guy Moyston, her New York friend who had visited the farm for several months in 1924:*

You wouldn't recognize the dining room. The floor has a linoleum rug on it; brown and cream and tan. The old table and chairs are gone, and in place of them is a drop-leaf table, painted cream, with a dark blue edge, also simple plain wooden chairs—kitchen chairs, with rungs up the rounded backs—painted cream, with dark blue seats and dark blue on the rounded tops. This I had decreed before leaving for New York, and it was done when I returned. It's the smartest, cutest little dining-room you ever saw. And looks about twice as large as it did. (January 20, 1925.)

*Laura's article "The Farm Dining Room" was published on June 13, 1925. Each of her* Country Gentleman *submissions brought a check for $150, and Rose remarked, "Mama Bess is very much pleased" (Letter to Moyston, January 17, 1925).*

W E MADE A false start with the kitchen when we remodeled an old building into our Rocky Ridge Farmhouse. And I should have known better.

But my ideal kitchen had been made of ideas taken from women's magazines. It was almost the perfect room in which to cook, but when it was done it was not what I wanted. I had not realized that a farm kitchen must be more than merely a kitchen; it is the place where house and barn meet—often in pitched battle. My "city" kitchen was too small for the conflict and so placed that the sights and sounds and smells of the struggle penetrated the rest of the house.

I wanted a little, white, convenient, modern kitchen. I wanted it as badly as my neighbor, Mrs. Parsons, who made her husband get a job in the city machine shops because she wouldn't put up any longer with her farm-kitchen work. In a way I couldn't blame her, for the average farm kitchen is enough to break the strength and spirit of any woman.

But I meant, somehow, to bring my ideal kitchen to the farm. It had to be done by sheer brain power, for in the first place I could find no kitchen plans that provided for chickens' feed buckets, swill buckets, taking care of oil lamps, storage of foodstuffs and all my other problems. And in the second place we had very little money. But we country people are accustomed to using our brains; we must use them in our work. That is one of the great advantages of living on a farm.

Behind my unsatisfactory kitchen was a woodshed, separator room and junkshop combined. Here I had been meeting the barn, and trying to keep it from coming farther into the house. But in cold weather the skimmed milk and the swill buckets would freeze and have to be brought in to thaw at the kitchen stove. I studied this room for some time before I proposed that we finish it up for a kitchen.

The Man-of-the-Place is a very good jackknife carpenter, and was an expert painter before that kitchen was done. We thought we could lessen expense by doing the work ourselves, and we did. The kitchen has cost just $49.84. But it took us a year to finish it, working at odd times.


Here's the Secret

We began by putting wall board on the walls and ceiling; we cased the windows already there and put in others. Then we began to build cupboards. The secret of my kitchen is there—windows and cupboards.

"Why, this isn't a kitchen; it's a kitchen cabinet!" exclaimed the first friend who saw the completed triumph. The only wall space left of the original 12 × 14 room is the bit behind the range. All the rest is windows and cupboards.

The windows are large, with one clear pane of glass in each sash, and no curtains. They let in light and sunshine—and beauty.

The cupboards have several things in common. They are all built straight to the ceiling and to the floor, leaving no spaces beneath to be swept or above to be dusted. They are all closed with light doors, made of wall board framed in wood.

Every floor cupboard has a floor of its own, made of one broad three-quarter-inch board laid on the kitchen floor and sloped to it at the cupboard threshold, and as the whole front of every cupboard is a door one whisk of the broom sweeps out the cupboard. There are no corners to clutch dust and no maddening obstacles over which it must be lifted with a whisk-broom.

Beginning with such windows and such cupboards, the only problem that remained was to arrange them to meet the needs of a farm kitchen.

The east wall looks toward the barn, with a glimpse of wooded hill beyond it, and the orchard and pastures to the north. All of this wall not occupied by the half-glass back door is filled by a large double window and the barn cupboards. These cupboards are under the sixteen-inch-wide window sill.

## Places for Everything

The swill buckets for the pigs, the skimmed milk for the hens, the lanterns and the kerosene can all have their places in these cupboards. There is a shelf for the shoe-blacking outfit. The cupboard doors shut them all out of sight.

On the top of these low cupboards is a hand basin and a jar of soft water. A towel rack is fastened to the window casing and a small mirror hangs against the double window.

Here I wash my hands and tidy my hair after excursions to the henhouse or hasty dashes to settle the affairs of colts or dogs. Here, too, the men wash up when they come in to meals on cold days. In the mornings I wash the lamps on this shelf and fill them from the oil can beneath it before I set them up in their own cupboard.

I chose the north side of the kitchen for my mixing and bread making because it has the best view. The two wide north windows give me hills and woods and the slopes of the sheep pasture to occupy my eyes and mind while I am kneading.

Between these two windows is my mixing cabinet. The lower part of it is a cupboard eighteen inches deep, holding baking pans and tins and cake board. The top of this is a wider shelf, 24 × 34 inches, and nineteen inches above this is the bottom of the shallow upper cupboard, which holds spices, baking powder, soda, and so forth.

Against the wall, under this upper cupboard, my egg beater, skimmer, wire strainer, spoons, paring knives and butcher knives hang all in a row. Not all the spoons, and none of the knives, had anything to hang by, but the Man-of-the-Place put screw eyes in knife handles and with a small drill bored holes in the handles of the spoons.

Nor is this the whole of my mixing cabinet. Under the windows

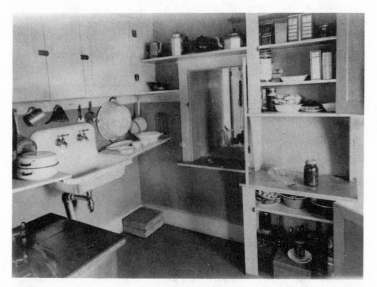

Taken especially for her kitchen article in the *Country Gentleman*, this photograph shows Laura's Ozark kitchen as she was using it in 1924.

are built-in chests, 32 × 15 inches, their tops making the window sills. These tops are hinged and the fronts of the chests are doors, to allow easy cleaning. In the chests are white flour, graham flour, corn meal, brown and white sugar, all in tin containers. Weevils and all bugs that delight in flour bins are baffled, for when a container is empty I lift it out, scald and scrub and sun it. And before I put it back a whisk of broom and mop scrubs out the chest.

There was still wall space between the windows and the corners of the room, so we filled it with two shallow cupboards. The one near the back door holds my preserving outfit. The one near the dining room door is the broom closet.

When all these were against the north wall it still seemed to lack something. So across the tops of the windows we put two narrow shelves, and on one I set a fantastic row of china animals. On the other shelf I put a Chinese teapot and cups.

There are two doors in the west wall, one full-sized door into the dining room and one little door, set high, opening onto the dining room sideboard.

After a meal I put the dishes and food from the dining room onto the sideboard. Then going into the kitchen I open the little door, and without taking another step I put the food into the food cupboard and the dishes into the sink.

Over the little door is a broad shelf on which I keep my several teapots, the percolator and the coffee pots.

The sink, the range, the wood box and the woodshed door occupy the fourth wall of the kitchen. Above the sink are cupboards, one for cooking dishes, the other for the lamps, laundry soap, scouring powders, and so forth. Under one cupboard, against the chimney, is a shelf for my flat-irons, and the towel rack is fastened to a corner of this shelf.

One step takes me from sink to range, which is set close to the wall with its pipe going directly into the chimney.

On the other side of the range is another duplicate of the central cupboards in my mixing cabinet, and this I think is my greatest triumph. With one stroke it abolishes the two greatest nuisances of a farm kitchen. It has always seemed to me that if there is anything more untidily exasperating than the wood box, it is the mess of barn coats, old sweaters, hats and overshoes that invade the kitchen on the farm.

That innocent-looking double cupboard beside the range wipes out both my exasperations. The upper cupboard hides all the barn wraps on their hooks. The wider lower cupboard is really a wood box, 15 × 24 × 22 inches, hung in the wall, its bottom eight inches from the floor, balanced so that it can be tipped outward into the woodshed and filled, then tipped back into place. Beneath it is a place for rubbers and overshoes, with its own door.

We painted the whole room white—two coats of flat white and a finishing coat of white enamel. I would hardly have attempted this in an ordinary farm kitchen but mine has no places to catch dust; no baseboards, no window sills, no beveling on doors. Wherever there is a corner it is rounded with a piece of molding, and white paint is really much easier to keep clean than dark paint.

It is a kitchen to be happy in. The convenience and the neatness of it and the whiteness are a continual joy.

# The Farm Dining Room

I SEE THAT THE general trend in American home architecture is toward eliminating the dining room. There was a time when the cozy breakfast nooks in kitchens and the dining alcoves in living rooms had quite a charm for me. They seemed to fit into my plan of combining, here on Rocky Ridge, the comforts and graces of city life with the greater advantages of life and work on a practical farm.

But I have since tried eliminating the dining room, and I have come to the conclusion that architects are even less concerned with farming than I am with architecture.

Eating in the kitchen is nothing new. Farmers did it long before architects existed. When there were only two rooms in Rocky Ridge Farmhouse, we ate in the kitchen.

At mealtime I tried to make it appear that we only incidentally cooked in the dining room. But a farm kitchen is difficult to disguise. Too much, in addition to cooking, is being done there; it refuses to be ignored.

Besides, in summer the whole room was an oven. One of the advantages of the farm is that it supplies our fuel, but a wood-burning range throws out too much heat to be a good neighbor for a dining table on a hot day.

Long before we were able to remodel the house, I had thought a great deal about the dining room problem.

## The Apartment Idea Failed

My kitchen was not merely a kitchen; it was my workshop and office, the place where I conducted my business of canning and preserving and pickling, of counting and packing eggs, of preparing fruits and vegetables for market, of handling meat, and milk and cheese and butter. Like any other woman, I wanted to get away from my workshop and my job while I was eating. So when we remodeled the house I borrowed an idea from the city apartment, and moved the dining table into the living room. Eating in the living room was not a success. The table was never a pleasing sight after a meal was eaten, and when company came I had a choice of leaving the table in disorder and in plain view while I entertained the guests, or of leaving the guests more or less in disorder while I attended to the table.

Also, there was another problem peculiar to the farm—the hired men. I have no snobbish attitude toward a hired man. Indeed, he is becoming so rare as to be more precious than fine gold.

But when a threshing crew of husky, dusty, sweat-stained harvest hands invaded either my crowded kitchen or my immaculate living room, there was little left of the grace of living in my house. And if they did not invade, but were set to eat outdoors, with the cool large house empty before their eyes—well, next time they worked for "more neighborly folks."

I perceived that a dining room is absolutely necessary to a farmhouse. Still I admitted to myself that it might prove to be a luxury, very expensive in time and strength, for unless it were carefully planned it would mean a large additional burden of work and innumerable extra steps. Every step counts when so many must be taken in house and garden and poultry yard, especially in summer when fresh vegetables require so much time and hired help must be cooked for.

Nevertheless, I must find some way of combining my work with the niceties of living or confess myself a failure. Being a farm woman, I could not separate my business career and my home life. I had to take them both together and keep the best values of each.

I needed a dining room that would mean no more work than eating in the kitchen; that would be cool in summer and warm in winter; that would be beautiful, completely simple, easy to keep clean. When we moved the kitchen into the woodshed, my opportunity came to meet all these necessities of the farm dining room. The only materials I had were the abandoned kitchen, with its built-in kitchen cabinet, and the old back porch, which fortunately faced north and was shaded by oak trees.

And of course we had very little money for the house, since the farm offered dozens of business opportunities that begged for every spare penny.

Helpful Difficulties

Now I have found many times that if I treat "the lion in the way" as a friend, it becomes a good house dog. These very difficulties led eventually to the making of a dining room so satisfactory that if I were building a new farmhouse, with unlimited space and money at my disposal, I would duplicate it exactly.

The first thing we did was to throw the room and porch practically into one, by putting a large window and a glass-paned door in the wall between them. The Man-of-the-Place extended the porch past one kitchen window, then screened it and painted the interior white, like the house, with a blue ceiling and a brown floor.

These changes gave light and air and a sense of space to the room, but it was so small and the kitchen cabinet was so large that there was no place for the furniture.

The cabinet reached from floor to ceiling and across the entire east end of the room, except for the door into the kitchen at the corner. A ladder-sized little stair began by this door and ran upward, behind the cabinet. Under this stair, and in the center of the cabinet, was my work shelf, with cupboards at either side and above it.

The whole thing seemed a white elephant. But I hit upon a happy idea.

We cut an opening through the wall, above the shelf, as large as the space between the cupboards, with a door made of wall board framed in light lumber.

When this little door is open, besides increasing light and ventilation, it seems to add to the size of the dining room, and the view of the white kitchen seen through it is not unpleasing. Through this opening food is served and dishes passed between dining room and kitchen. And when the door is closed the kitchen is shut out.

I gave the whole cabinet, inside and out, two coats of white paint and then enameled it. And when I had put my china and silver into the dish cupboard, my glassware on the shelves, my table linen into the drawers, and canned fruit into the closet under the shelf, I had a sideboard, china cabinet and linen closet combined.

Combining the porch and the small room gave us a half summer, half winter dining room. There was light and air and enough space, for we now needed room only for table and chairs. All the other dining room furniture was combined in the cabinet. So I turned my attention to decoration.

The screen walls of the dining porch were pictures of field and meadow, woods and sky, and I knew they would be all the colors from the exuberant canvas of spring to the etchings of winter. The walls of the dining room were paneled in wall board, and I must color them myself. I painted them a silvery gray—the lightest shade of a white oak's bark—which would not be discordant with any of Nature's colors, and I made the woodwork snow white to match the cabinet. Around the outer edge of the floor I painted a border of rich brown, like the floor of the porch, and covered the center with a linoleum rug in tones of brown and tan and ivory.

I did not like the oak dining table and chairs in their new setting. They were heavy and cumbersome, and their color brought too much darkness into the room. But I had them, and it seemed an extravagance to buy others. This made me quite unhappy, until one day a large department store in the nearest city, trying to get the farmers' patronage, sent me advertisements of a furniture sale, and I read that for only $10.95 I could buy an unfinished dropleaf kitchen table and six chairs to match. Delivery charges were included.

Two days later one of my neighbors was delighted with her bargain—my good oak table and chairs for only eleven dollars—and a truck delivered my new ones. Their lines were simple and charming. I gave them two coats of paint and one of ivory enamel, with a line of blue. It is surprising what a pretty dining room set they make.

The last question was curtains. Nothing that I could see or plan seemed to fit the character of the room and to add the exact touch

Almanzo's cabinetry in the Rocky Ridge dining room

that my imagination demanded. But at last, rummaging among my stores in the attic, I found some pieces of white scrim and a remnant of fine blue-and-white gingham plaided with brown and tan. I made the curtains of the scrim, to hang in straight folds at each side of the window, and edged them with narrow strips of the gingham.

When they were hung our dining room was complete. The blue in their trimming picks up the blue on chairs and table, the blue of my willow-ware dishes, the blue apple plate on the sideboard and the blue match jar on the clock shelf; the brown and tan plaid brings up to the walls the colors of the rug.

In summer this combination dining room and porch is as airy and cool as a tent with the sides raised. The doors into kitchen and living room are opposite each other; a door opens into the bedroom with its large double windows, and the whole dining room is open to the north porch.

There is air from every direction, and the little open stairs concealed by the sideboard act as a chimney. When upstairs windows are open this stairway draws air in and down, or pulls it up and out, according to the direction of breezes outdoors.

The porch end of the room is open to north and east, with a window to the west into the living room, and near the other end a window into the kitchen. In summer this porch is the dining room. The porch table is painted to match the chairs of the dining room set. There is no other furniture except a little sewing rocker, and decoration is unnecessary, for the porch is outdoors.

# An Actual Noon Dinner in the Ozarks

*Laura Wilder had been fascinated by Ozark folkways ever since she and Almanzo had settled in Missouri in 1894. Though she never wrote about her life in Missouri for her "Little House" reading audience, Laura continually jotted down country folklore, tall tales, and music of the mountains. When asked to share an anecdote, Laura usually chose an Ozark story.*

*In a letter to Rose, who was doing historical research at the University of Missouri, Laura included several pages of notes on Ozark life. She wrote, "I have just discovered some notes I made years ago. . . . Perhaps you can use them as anecdotes or in some way. . . . They were written when Wilson was president and are true" (August 19, 1937). This menu was one of the items.*

A dinner of 93 different dishes:

Fried ham, boiled ham, sausage,
beef boiled, beef roasted,
chicken, fried, stewed and
baked with dressing.

Sweet potatoes baked and fried.

Irish potatoes creamed, baked and
boiled with beef.

Three different gravies with meats.

Light bread, biscuit and cornbread.

Onions, beets, cabbage boiled,
cabbage slaw and kraut.

Beet pickles, cucumber pickles,
piccalilli, pickled green tomatoes,
peaches, pears and onions.

Tomato preserves,
crab apple preserves.

Stuffed mangos.

Citron and melon preserves.

Gooseberry, current, blackberry,
plum, grape, peach, apple, jellies and
marmalades.

Tomato catsup, horseradish and
mustard.

Six kinds of pie.
Six kinds of cake.

"Well set up!" said Uncle Jim.
"We haint got much to eat now,
but I aim to kill a sheep next week."

And the friends he had brought
with him from church for Sunday
dinner "set up."

Rose Wilder Lane

# Autumn

*Having returned to Mansfield in 1923 after her years abroad, Rose Wilder Lane enthusiastically invited her many literary friends to visit in her country surroundings. "The farm is grand, really," she wrote to Marian Fiery at Knopf, "quite cool and remote and covered by big trees. We have a good Middle-Western German cook and Simmons beds and saddle horses and dogs, and we'll take you on an Ozark fox hunt. . . . And by the fireplace of evenings I can tell you such true stories of the people here as never can be printed. We'd love to have you drop in, anytime. New Yorkers often do" (May 27, 1931).*

*And the friends came: the Stellmans from San Francisco; Dorothy Thompson, when she was married to Sinclair Lewis; Mary Margaret McBride, radio commentator; Guy Moyston, New York journalist; and groups of staff writers from the nearby* Springfield News and Leader. *Two more permanent houseguests were Catharine Brody, New York novelist, and Helen Boylston, nurse, writer, and Rose's traveling companion throughout Europe and in Albania. Helen, nicknamed "Troub," lived on Rocky Ridge for four years.*

*In Mansfield Rose became reacquainted with old friends. Some of her girlhood memories of Mansfield were bittersweet; it had not made her popular to be the smartest girl in school or to dreamily write stories. But Rose's writings became eagerly read in Mansfield, and some of her fiction used her hometown as a setting, as did the* Harper's *story "Autumn," published in June 1924.*

THE WEATHER WAS milder than she remembered it. She had remembered October days crisp with frost and bright colored with autumn leaves. The voices of farmers had sounded strong and round, the horses' harness had merrily jingled, and the wagons had rattled over frozen ruts in the street. A smell of apples had jolted from them. Every detail had remained in her memory through all the years. The road coming under the oaks from the high-shouldered brick schoolhouse, the wooden bridge where

Rose in Paris in the 1920s

horses' hoofs had sounded hollowly, the long upward slope past little houses painted white or yellow, and the jog in the street at the top of the hill—these were like beloved objects worn by much handling. They had been part of her thought of Harry, and somehow, under all the other occupations of her mind, she had always been remembering him.

The weather made the difference. The little town that had been purposeful and energetic was limp in lukewarm dampness. Brown leaves fell heavily, and did not rustle underfoot. A stain of moisture spread on her glovelike kid shoes. How strange to be walking here! Her shoes, and her frock, and the coat with its collar and clever cuffs of *kolinsky*, were strange. *"Mais, il vous va à merveille, mademoiselle!"* Who was this stranger walking here in clothes from the Place Vendome? Would no sharp edge of reality pierce through this dream and with its pain wake her to knowing who she was?

Rose slipped a hand into the crook of her elbow and gave her arm a little squeeze. "It's good to have you home again, Evie," Rose said. "I was scared at first you'd be so changed I shouldn't know you, but you aren't changed a bit. You're just the same old Evie you were when—" Rose's voice stumbled, and went on quickly. Rose had thought of Harry.

But there was no longer any pain in that. She had put the thought of him away from her, desperately, for so long, because she could not bear the pain of it. During those years, in some mysterious way, its power to make her suffer had gone. Remembering him had become a part of her so deeply rooted that to tear it out would make her bleed to death. She had wanted to tear it out. Loyalty had not restrained her, nor sentimentality about love. Quite simply, no other man could be to her what Harry was.

They came to the top of the hill, she and Rose. The new cement sidewalk began here, and there before them was the Square, its wooden hitching-rails replaced by iron ones. Farmers' wagons were thick around it, their wheels in mud. Under pale sunshine the street was pathetic. A country road, at home in woods and hazel thickets, it was miserable before false second-stories and harsh brick fronts. The farmers, who had once seemed bold and hearty men, wore now the sad aspect of those whose lives are eaten away by the land. Peasants. In every country the same bowed shoulders, crippled hands, and wintry smiles in cheeks of leather. Oh, piteous strugglers that we are, upon the indifferent earth! Something in her put its arms round them all, to weep with them. But a little smile came out to run along her lips and hesitate in their corners.

Yes, after all the years and beneath all the differences they had made, she was still the girl who had strolled past this Square on moonlit nights, coming home with Harry—the serious girl whose cheeks had shone with scrubbing and whose serge dress, trimmed with pink baby ribbon, had cost so many anxious days of sewing.

Rose still wore a "best dress." She was wearing it now, for this was a great occasion. Rose was taking her famous sister to a reception given by the wife of the banker. The farmers stepped stiffly aside to let them pass, and followed them with oblique glances. Rose was proud and excited. She was wearing a new hat from Paris, France, brought by her famous sister, and beneath it two spots as red as rouge burned in her cheeks. Rose, too, was a stranger. One saw only the outside. One saw, with aching fond amusement, this climax to her long social striving.

"I hope you'll be awfully nice to Mrs. Mason, Evie. She'll be hurt if you don't. She's read every one of your books, and she was so nice to me last summer when Mrs. Hornbrook was so mean. Just because she comes from Kansas City, that Mrs. Hornbrook thought she could just run this place and she'd have taken the Embroidery Club right out of my hands if Mrs. Mason and I hadn't got together. I know it doesn't seem important to you, Evie, after all the places you've been, but to me—"

"Rose dear, if you only knew how unimportant I am in all the places I've been!"

"You aren't, Evelyn! Knowing Cabinet Ministers, and Princes, and everything! You're the most important person that ever went out of this town. I want you to remember that, I want you to remember it every minute!" Rose's voice was shrill with earnestness.

But who knew what Rose really was, deep, deep underneath? Rose, who had not been jilted; Rose, who had married Bob and borne her children and been—happy? One saw only the outside of Rose—the new house with a bathroom, the little car, the trip to Los Angeles, where, for a dollar, she had seen everything from a sight-seeing bus. That was the successful Rose whom others saw.

There was another Rose whom only Rose saw, when she had shut all the doors of herself and sat peaceful in loneliness. It was this Rose who did not speak of Harry.

This was the corner by Latimer's store, where he had stood with other boys on summer evenings while she went laughing past with other bareheaded girls on imagined errands. Here unchanged was the gravel walk that went by the old unchanged white church.

"Latimer's sold out," said Rose. "It's a wholesale feed-and-grain store now. The town isn't what it used to be; it gets deader every year. I guess it's the mail-order houses; they've killed everything. Mail-order houses and automobiles."

"Our old-fashioned little towns seem doomed," she answered. "The small stores can't outlive their economic usefulness."

All the time, silently, she was talking to the other Rose. "You need not be tender with me now. Truly, truly, all the old hurt is gone. So much of it was vanity—seeing pity in all the eyes, and I so young and naked to them. Oh, a great deal of my pain was vanity. How amusing we are, in the tragic solemnities of our little lives! Yes, but—I do love him. I've never been able to get over that. But I am not ashamed or hurt or struggling about it anymore. It is just something one accepts, even with gratitude for the little that it is. And I have built myself a good life. There is one thing you could tell me, perhaps, if we spoke aloud. Why did he do it? I have never understood that. Because he loved me, too."

The giant oak was gone, the oak whose shadow in the moonlight had sheltered the awkwardness of their first kiss. She smiled at that memory now, as a mother smiles at the funniness of a child. But the oak, now only a ghost, wakened two other ghosts who lingered in its vanished shade.

They had sat pressed together by the crowd on the benches of the church. The smell of oil lamps and of sweat was in her nostrils. Light and color and white faces blurred before her eyes. For hours they had risen and sung, sat and prayed, controlled by the exhorter's passionate voice. "Come to Jesus, come to Jesus! Come and be washed in the blood of the Lamb!" Sobs and cries rose round them. Weeping, on their knees, calling to God for help, the girls she knew struggled with their sins. "Come to Jesus, come to Jesus!" She trembled, tears ran down her cheeks. All of her melted into one ache of longing. Somewhere, waiting for her—"Jesus is calling, Jesus is calling you!"—unimaginable power and glory and joy! A thinning resistance held her still until one intolerable shriek broke it. Shaking and blinded, she stumbled to her feet—and felt his hand firm on her arm. "Let's get out of this," said his unshaken voice.

He had taken her from that orgy into the sanity of darkness and stars. Breathing the clean air, she was grateful and ashamed, like one rescued from degradation. She trembled, clinging to him, more entirely his than she knew. But he must have known. He said, "Religion is all right, but that back there—it isn't healthy." Always, with a word, he could show her what she had known. For a long time they had walked up and down past the oak, talking: "I feel I want to do what I can to make the world better," he said. She was reproved. Her ambition to escape and to accomplish great things was selfish. His was noble. At that moment she had first loved him.

Yes, there had been in him a fineness, a strength, that she had never found again. His steadiness had never failed her in the crude years of their growing up together. Never until that last inexplicable month that had ended with his marriage.

"But how cleverly you managed it!" she said, to the end of Rose's long story of Mrs. Hornbrook's defeat. An automobile passed, flinging mud from its sucking wheels. Far in the depths of her were echoes of that crude and terrible battle: the intolerable pain of jealousy that tore her like claws; the night of wind and freezing rain when she lay and beat her hands to bleeding on the icy ground, waiting to hear them pass together; the question, never answered, "What did she give him that was finer and deeper than I could have learned to give?"

Automobiles stood in a row before the banker's many-gabled house. Rose's breath came fluttering. "If only our car hadn't been laid up for repairs!" The picket-fences were gone, too; there was no gate to click behind them. But there on the lawn was the old cast-iron dog, holding as always an empty flowerpot on his rusty head.

She and Rose were going up the walk to the scrolled porch of the banker's house. The house was conscious of its importance on this afternoon; it wore an air of festivity as farmers wear Sunday coats, and figures moved as if embarrassed behind its staring windows. Strange. When there had been a picket gate it had never clicked behind them. She and Rose had never been invited to the banker's parties; their father was the drayman. Now the house was agitated because of her coming. The drayman's daughter was stiff with self-consciousness, and some one else within her smiled, and some one else was bored, and everything was strange. Her finger pressed the bell.

There was desperation in Rose's clutch on her arm. "Oh, Evie, I just can't let you—without telling—please don't be mad at me— Harry," Rose gasped, "he's going to be here."

She stared at Rose's rounded blue eyes. This must be what writers meant who wrote, "The blood drained from her cheeks." There was a tingle in her fingertips. Because of the dampness the door was sticking in its frame, and through the glass scrolled with frosted flowers she saw the banker's wife in undignified struggle with it. She heard the laughter of the gods. The door opened with a jerk.

She had been told that he was in Washington. She should have remembered that Congress was not in session.

The banker's wife was nervous, and her face was red. Perhaps tight corseting, perhaps the struggle with the door. "I am pleased to meet—to welcome our noted authoress," said the banker's wife. The others said, while looking at her with shy keenness, "I am pleased to—pleased you're home again." Some added, "Are you going to stay here now?" He was not in the parlor, where women who had been girls she knew sat on rigid chairs. What atrocious wallpaper! "Are you glad to be home again, Evelyn?" "You look just the same, you haven't changed the least bit." "Well, now you're here we hope you'll stay a long time." No, he was none of the men who stood together as if for self-defense in the doorway to the back parlor. But surely, surely, she would have recognized him instantly. Rose was garrulous. "Well, as I tell Evie—"

What was she doing here, in this *petit bourgeois* atmosphere? Her chair pressed gilt scrolls against her knees, held her upright as in a vise. Inside the constraint of her self-conscious muscles something ran about wildly, trying to escape. The smile on her face was hardening like a mask. Her polite voice repeated, "Yes, I am glad to be here again." A phonograph ground derisively in her mind, setting the words to a tune. "Yes, we have no bananas"—That was what they did to Handel's Messiah. How piteous they were, the eager young girls she had known! They looked at her helplessly through eyes dulled by commonplace. They, who had been so sure and happy, were wistful now as she had been.

At any moment he would come.

Was there no end to meaningless phrases? The young and eager girls were still there, behind softening cheeks and thickened bodies. They were like animals born in captivity, wistful behind inevitable bars. They wished to ask her the news of the far places, but they did not know how. "Give us the scent of wind on mountain tops, and the taste of the fears and the kills you have known in the jungle," that was what they wanted to say, while they spoke phrases without meaning: "Paris is awfully wicked, isn't it?"

His step was on the porch; she would have known it anywhere. Her blood answered it with a leap, as it had always done. The mask of her face broke. The banker's wife was struggling with the door. A little smile scampered over her lips and quivered in their corners.

He was unchanged. The same Harry, he stood in the doorway of the parlor, and his smile expressed the same confidence and good humor. "Well, folks—!" The old, remembered heartiness in his greeting! Their voices answered him in chorus.

Her chair was no longer uncompromising in its rigidity, it seemed soft to her relaxing body. A fountain of laughter flung a jet from her throat. Love him? Love that man? She did not love him. She had never loved him. The laughter of the gods swelled to a roar at this climax of comedy. So all our tragedies become comedies in the end? Farce, broad farce. Here were the girls who had risen, fearing they had not done the proper thing, and sat down again in imitation of her!

His clasp, the warm one of the successful politician, enfolded her fingers. How could he know that the sparkle in her was not for him? Indeed, there was something of the moving-picture actor in all American politicians. This was delightful. Her gesture settled him in the chair beside her.

He had still the habit of running his fingers through his thick hair. Then they sought a watch-chain no longer looped across his front. His talk sounded well to the ears for which it was intended. He had ideals, purely emotional. Words like Mother, Home, and England struck in him a chord of noble feeling. He was inconsistent, illogical, and usually right. One must admit that minds made by newspapers were more normal than those of independent thinkers; human beings were created to feel in crowds. His kind was the preservative of nations, institutions, customs, morals. Every Sunday morning he would eat the same thing for breakfast. No doubt he was an admirable husband and father. No doubt. If one were to ask him, "What do you think of women in politics?" he would clear his throat and answer seriously, "Well, of course, I believe that woman's place—" All the time, a wilder sense of freedom was intoxicating her.

The banker's daughters gave them each a plate on which was set a cup of coffee beside a slice of brick ice-cream and a slice of layer cake. Oh, of course! "Refreshments." The talk became animated, as the end of the reception was perceived. She had forgotten to be nice to Mrs. Mason. It was not difficult; Mrs. Mason stammered in her pleasure. "I've always thought I c-could write, myself," Mrs. Mason confided. "Things come into my mind, sometimes—Do you ever run out of ideas for stories? I—I'd be glad to give you some, if—"

She thanked Mrs. Mason. Now all at once everyone rose, with an outbreak of farewells like a chattering of sparrows. Everyone was shaking hands with everyone else. They crowded the hall where the banker's wife stood by the open door, smiling in relief. They overflowed upon the porch and their voices sounded shrill on the quiet air as they had sounded long ago at the end of a schoolday.

She went down the walk with Rose. Beside his car Harry hesitated. He thought of taking them home in his car. Then he thought, better not; it might make talk. He held his hat in his left hand and took her gloved fingers in his right. "Good-by, Miss Evelyn, it's been a pleasure to meet you again." A timid look came for an instant to the surface of his eyes—his vanity looking out to see if it were hurt. But no, it could see nothing, and whisked into hiding again. Better let sleeping dogs lie, he thought.

"And I'm very glad to have seen you, Harry. Good-by."

In the moist air there was now a promise of frost. Behind them automobile engines complained of the prodding of self-starters, then one by one rushed down the street. The last team of horses at the hitching-rails tossed their heads with jingling of bits. The buildings round the Square seemed to huddle together for warmth. In the yards of little houses women with knitted scarfs over their heads were bringing in wood. Rose hurried. "I'm afraid I'll be late getting supper," Rose said in a strained voice.

"Never mind, Rose, I'll help you," she said, giving Rose's arm a little squeeze. Better than joy or happiness was this sense of wholeness, of oneness with herself. With pleasure she felt her muscles moving as she walked. There was exhilaration in the chilling air. Her feet marched to the rhythm of a tag of verse: "I will run and stand in the wind on the hill, now that I am lone and free."

Late that night she was still too much alive to sleep. Supper had been mirthful, Rose and Bob answering her laughter until the children grew hysterical in their milk cups. Evening had been prolonged round the lamp after the children had been forced to bed. Now she was alone, and sitting by her window, wrapped in a dressing gown, she looked at the moon in the cold sky. A branch of cherry tree made a Japanese print across it. She knew that her door was opening softly before she heard the whispered, "Evelyn?"

"Yes? Come in, Rose."

"Where—? Oh, I thought you'd be in bed." Rose stood hesitating. Then in the darkness, that Rose whom only Rose knew spoke shyly, "Evie—you aren't mad at me, are you?"

Softly, softly, not to frighten her away. "No, I'm not mad at you. Come and look at the moon."

Moonlight fell on Rose's thick body, huddled in a shawl over her nightgown. The night was still, and bare twigs were delicate against the sky. "It's pretty, isn't it? I like to look at it. . . . Evie, I didn't mean to be mean to you. You're the only sister I have."

"Yes. I know."

"It—didn't make you feel bad?"

"No."

"You see, Evie, all that was a long time ago. I've thought about it so much. I thought it must be the reason—Evie, I hate for you to be an old maid. You miss so much. I thought if you could only see him again—and I knew talking to you wouldn't do any good." She was trembling. "Don't you think, maybe now—?"

"Rose dear, how did you know?"

"I'm awfully glad." Their hands clasped in the shadows that veiled their faces. "It doesn't much matter who, Evie—who you marry, I mean. Just so he is a good man." The secret Rose came shyly again into her voice. "Men are only what we make them, you know. In our minds, I mean. What they *really* are—But you find they are just as—lost and—fumbling, as we are. And they cling, like children. So you have to be brave for them. It doesn't last, the— feeling you have at first. They say that at the last, when your children grow up and go away and have their own lives, that then— I don't know." Rose leaned her forehead against the cool pane of the window, her voice spoke quietly to herself. "Maybe we are always alone, really."

There was companionship in that knowledge shared.

Rose shivered, drawing the shawl closer. "I declare, the nights are getting chilly. You'll catch cold, sitting in that thin thing." Her fingers felt it expertly. "What is it?"

"It's an *abba*—the Bedouins wear it. The silk? Handwoven; I got it in Damascus."

"Oh, Damascus." Rose's mind slid absently over that jeweled word. "Sure you have enough covers on your bed?"

Alone, Evelyn lay with hands clasped above her head. She felt the weakness and the surging energy of convalescence. Her life had been wasted? She smiled. Dear Rose, poor Rose. Wise, illogical Rose, urging marriage now. To each human being one thing is solid, stable, an anchor to which to tie. That is the thing not yet examined. How merry and busy Rose would be, too, when the children were grown and she was free! So all the ecstasies and the heartbreaks come to one end, and the end is freedom from them all. Freedom. And the good years still to be lived!

Rose Wilder Lane

# Thirty-Mile Neighbors

*Laura told Rose this humorous yarn about the first automobile seen in the Ozarks:*

A family heard it coming through the woods. They knew it was some kind of varmint but had never heard one like it. Mom hid behind the brush pile; the young'uns scattered in the brush like rabbits but Pop gathered him some big rocks and when it came in sight he began rocking it. He hit it good and it left the road and tried to climb a tree, but it could get only part way up when it fell back and ran away down the road.

Mom stuck her head up over the brush pile and hollered, "Did you kill it, Pop? Did you kill it?"

"No," Pop answered, "but I made it turn that man loose. Thar he is in the road!"

*The coming of the automobile was inevitable in the Missouri country-side, just as it was in the rest of rural America. Rose had owned and driven a car since 1912 and missed its convenience when she returned to live on Rocky Ridge. The Wilders still admired horseflesh and resented what Laura called "tin can tourists" whizzing along peaceful country lanes. But eventually a handsome 1923 blue Buick replaced Buck and Billy as trans-portation for the Wilder family.*

*"The car is a most tremendous sensation," Rose wrote enthusiastically*

to Guy Moyston. "I think it will work a complete revolution in their [her parents'] lives. There is so much liberation in a car; it extends horizons so."

It was also inevitable that the winding lane through the woods in front of the Wilder farmhouse would change; it became a modern highway, Route 60. Almanzo and Laura mourned the loss of their narrow roadway; even though the new highway increased the value of their land, they knew that the quiet back roads were doomed.

The Wilders' Buick suited Rose well. As she related, "I got behind the wheel, started the engine, put it in the various gears and drove off sweet and smooth as cream." Of Mama Bess she boasted, "She's learning to drive like anything." And Rose extolled the Ozark roads, which had proven quite adaptable to the automobile:

These roads are really quite excellent for cars. I now go to town and back, using gasoline less than half the way. Shut off the engine and coast. In gear, the car makes 22 miles, which is fast enough; throw it out of clutch, and it picks up to 36 and climbs the next hill on the momentum. I'm going to try to make it all the way and back without starting the engine someday. I bet it can be done. Well, no; would have to start the engine to get out of the garage. But from our doorstep to the post office the car will go by itself. And from Hoover's livery stable back to our doorstep. That would mean running the engine about 200 feet in all. For a mile and a half trip. How's that for Ozark roads? (Letter to Guy Moyston, July 11, 1925.)

Almanzo's transition from a lifelong horseman to an automobile driver was not without mishap. One April morning he and Rose were driving aimlessly down a road near Rocky Ridge, with Almanzo at the wheel. Rose wrote Moyston about the prized Buick's collision:

I was nearly killed today. . . . My father and I were out in the car, I was teaching him to drive, he was at the wheel and there was a mix-up on the road—two cars caught us between them and Papa from experience driving with horses braced his foot hard down on the gas and pulled on the wheel! Made it hard for me to turn the wheel. I missed both cars, grazing one's front fender and the other's hub cap and then the car went into the ditch and charged up the bank, took down six fence posts with barbed wire between, hit a tree fair and square—a bright, young living oak tree about 8 inches through, uprooted it neatly. We would apparently have been going yet, only the butt of the tree rose up under the rear axle and lifted it off the ground. Somehow I never thought of flopping the little lever and cutting off ignition. It all happened quite quickly. So I went head-first into the wind shield and was cut a bit. My nose feels like a bushel basket full of groans.

The poor, sweet car—its engine began to purr as soon as I tried the starter. I shut off its roaring just while I was pitching into the wind shield. As soon as I got out and ran to see that nobody was killed, because I knew we had hit the other cars, I came back and the engine sang—purred—so nicely. I could have cried, the way we'd treated it. Bumper and radiator are smashed. And of course the wind shield. . . .

In no time at all there were fifty cars there at least. Everyone came hurrying out from town. I said I thought it showed great intelligence in us, when the road got so dangerous with cars, to quietly leave it and climb a tree. Everyone crowded around congratulating me—it was like being the bride at the wedding reception. I got so tired of shaking hands. . . . We did not hurt the other cars in the least bit. (April [?] 1925.)

*The damaged Buick—which the Wilders had given a name, Isabelle, just as they had named their horses in the past—was quickly repaired and repainted. Almanzo became a capable driver, but he stayed at home when Rose, Laura, and their rather permanent houseguest, Troub (Helen Boylston, whom Rose had first met in Europe), left for a trip to California. In the fall of 1925, it was uncommon for three women to venture out on an extensive automobile trip alone, without the protection of a man, but the trip was made without difficulty. "Isabelle has behaved well all the time," Laura wrote to Almanzo from a hotel in Wichita, Kansas (September 18, 1925).*

*Within a year, both Laura and Almanzo were driving with ease and enthusiastically jaunting through the Ozark hills in their own car. Rose*

Rose in the 1923 blue Buick. She purchased the car in the East as a gift for her parents and shipped it by train to Rocky Ridge.

*knew that her family was typical in its transition from the trusty old team to the newfangled automobile. Using the Wilders' experiences, Rose wrote "Thirty-Mile Neighbors," which appeared in the* Country Gentleman *on May 6, 1925.*

T HIS MORNING AT breakfast I said to my father, "Well, what are you going to do today?"

There is a lavishness, an exuberant abundance in farm life. It begins to be evident at breakfast, which is so different from the restraint of breakfasts in the cities, where food is precious. Here on the farm is no meager arrangement of slices of bacon, no single piece of toast delicately browned on an electric toaster.

No. Here are bowls of oatmeal, with whole pints of cream, large dishes of baked apples, the big blue platter full of sizzling ham, with many eggs disposed upon it; here are hot cakes piled by tens and dozens, with melting butter and brown sugar between them, and hashed brown potatoes, Graham bread and white bread, fresh butter, honey, jam, milk and the steaming pot of coffee.

Here are doughnuts or gingerbread to accompany the coffee cups' second filling, and then—for he was a boy in New England—my father likes just one medium-size wedge of apple pie, to top off the meal and finish the foundation for a good day's work.

This sense of abundance extends forward into the unrestrained day. It is the medium in which, unconscious of it as a fish of water, the farmer's life moves.


The One Independent Man

After the morning chores are done there is nothing inevitable in what the day will bring him. There is no certain street car or subway train to catch, no door that must be reached at a definite time, no routine waiting to seize upon him like the cogs of a machine.

The only rhythm in his life is the rhythm of the seasons, which is varied by the weather's moods. From day to day he chooses, out of a large variety, the task he will do.

Among all the working men and all the employers of America, it is only the farmer who is asked, "What are you going to do today?"

"Well," my father said, while with leisurely enjoyment he ate the apple pie, "I don't know's I know. There's that tool-shed door I'm working at. Then I did think some of mending and greasing harness. Yet on the other hand, there's that spring-tooth harrow; it ought to be put in shape for early spring work. Well, and then there's some corn out in the granary that isn't shucked yet. Oh, I've got plenty to do! Seems like a farmer always has."

It was left at that, and the floors had been swept, dishes washed, beds made, lamps filled and set away, before he came from the barns, letting into the house a sudden current of crisp air and prancing of Nero's muddy paws.

"I clean forgot what day it is," said my father. "It's Jeff Morgan's sale today. He's got a couple of pretty good young heifers, grade Jerseys; I'd like to see what they bring. Want to go along? Well, I'll have old Buck hitched up in two jerks of a lamb's tail."

Thus swiftly the day became a holiday. Old Buck tossed his head, jingled the harness and set off at a smart trot. Twenty-four years old. We are proud of old Buck.

"Knows as much about the farm work as I do," my father

bragged. "Take him into any field, he knows which way to run the furrows; he knows how to turn hayrake or harrow at the end of the rows. And as for the hayfork, he draws up the hay, dumps it, whoas and turns round for another load, without a word said to him."

The clean woodsy air blew cold against our faces. The light buggy made little sounds of creaking as its wheels rattled over the pebbles of the creek road. There were patches of snow here and there, dappling the hillsides brown with fallen leaves. Gray squirrels and red squirrels frisked, with flickering tails, on the gray tree trunks.

"We'd get there quicker on the highway," my father said, "but I take the creek road when I can. Not that it's as pretty now as it will be later, when dogwood and redbud are out. You wouldn't ask a prettier sight than this stretch of road, along in March and April. Violet time, you'll see these creek banks blue with 'em, hazel and sassafras in bloom and the oak leaves red as flowers themselves. There aren't many roads like this one left," he said, grieving.

"It's all highways nowadays. Good roads, they call 'em, and they're good enough underfoot. But what people get out of the country, racing through it in a cloud of dust at forty miles an hour, I don't know. Give me a horse and a winding kind of wild road like this when I want to enjoy the sights."

## Jeff Morgan's Sad Mistake

My father admitted to being old-fashioned on the subject of automobiles. They've just about ruined country life, he said. Folks no longer hitch up, pile into the farm wagon with the wife and the children and go to spend a long neighborly day with friends a few miles away.

No; they jump into the flivver, go tearing fifty miles to the city, see a movie, do some shopping, come racing back again.

Why go anywhere in such furious haste? Life is speeding up too much. Nobody has time for good old-fashioned neighborliness, for leisurely enjoyment of talk, for careful handwork any more.

"That was Jeff Morgan's mistake—buying that second-hand car

of his. That young man's a fool to give up that good farm. But his wife will have it so. Ever since they got that car nothing will suit her but moving up to the city. Her cousin's up there and he writes he's getting six dollars a day, at day's wages.

"Yes, but I notice he isn't laying by anything. Now it's just two years ago that Jeff started out on this forty of his father's, with one team and a cow. Maybe he didn't make six dollars cash a day, but he's lived well, he's fixed up the house and barns and he's bought that car.

"If he'd keep on working and saving, in a couple of years he could buy the farm, with our Farm Loan Association to help out. And if he sells out today for less than twelve hundred dollars, I miss my guess. That's fifty dollars a month laid by during the time he's been working, and I doubt if he saves as much at any kind of city wages.

"But his wife won't be satisfied till he tries it. It's this automobile idea of getting there quick, that's what's the matter with her."

So, slowly and surely, enjoying along the way the busy affairs of woodpecker and squirrel, we came at last into view of the Morgan house and barns.

The pasture that sloped to them was black with parked automobiles. Small and large, cheap and medium priced, they all wore the practical, hard-driven aspect of farmers' cars.

The crowd of men in khaki trousers, puttees and short wool-lined coats, with a few shawl-wrapped women, was congregated in the barnyard, where already the horses were being led out and the auctioneer was mounting his box.

My father hurriedly tied and blanketed old Buck, while I went into the house. Its bare rooms were mournful with that look of the dismantled home, which so quickly takes on an air of abandonment and desolation. Most of the women who were there, waiting for their husbands to return from the barns, were walking about on the carpetless, mud-trampled floors.

The numbers of automobiles outside had surprised me, for it seems only yesterday that only the banker owned an automobile, and certainly these are hard times for farmers. But this crowd of women gave me two profound shocks.

Almanzo with Governor of Orleans, the prized Morgan stallion of Rocky Ridge Farm

One was in the fact that here, within a mile of my home, were dozens of women who were strangers to me. The other shock was in my discovery that I had been snobbish.

Now in all my years of city life I had never "looked down" on farm women. Why should I? Born—like most city people—of a long line of farmers, bred on a farm, knowing the sturdy characters and good hard-headed intelligence of farm people, of course I hadn't felt superior to them.

But I had not seen farm people in a group for twenty years. In those twenty years something had happened. I was out of date in my thoughts of farmers, and this, I realized, had made me snobbish.

The fact is that I had almost "dressed down" to these women. To spare their feelings, I had thought, it might be better to wear something—well, rather cheap and worn, so that I wouldn't be conspicuous among them.

But I had had a second thought—no, I wouldn't be condescending to my own people. I'd dress just as I would to go anywhere in the city in the morning. They would enjoy seeing how city people dress. Didn't I remember how we used to talk for days about what a city woman wore when by chance we saw one?

Standing among these women, I had just one thing to be thankful for, and that was my second thought. Thanks to it, I was dressed in as good taste as any of them. My mind staggered. What has become of the toil-worn farmer's wife, with her bad teeth and thin hair, her awkwardness and confusion with strangers, her piteous homemade dress that sagged in back and wabbled on the armhole seams.

## A New Spirit Abroad

She did exist. I didn't dream her. I was once a young edition of her myself. Apparently she has disappeared. Where? Why? How?

"Yes, it took us fifty-eight minutes to make the twenty miles over here," one was saying. "But the roads are bad south of Norwood; we had to put on the chains. Last year, on our trip to Kansas, we—"

"My, what a pretty hat!" one said to me.

And I remember how we used to look and look, in silence, and would not for worlds have admitted such frank admiration and envy into our voices.

It is certain that I have been cheated of something. If I had gone to the city forty years ago I might have come back twenty years ago and been a sensation. But I was born too late. Now I am no sensation at all. I am taken quite calmly. There is a new spirit abroad among farmers.

We used to feel inferior to city folks. We used to be considered so. City people spoke contemptuously of the "country hick," the "country jake." And wasn't there resentment, though, in our spat-out phrase "city dude"!

Now both the hick and the dude seem to have vanished.

Poor pretty little Mrs. Jeff Morgan seemed a bit overwhelmed at what she had done, now that she saw the ruins of her home. She sat with her baby on her knee, talking to the woman who had bought her hens.

"I started out with just that old biddy and a setting of eggs," she was saying, "and if I do say it, there isn't a better little flock of Rhode Island Reds anywhere. I certainly hate to let old biddy go; she's an awfully good mother. I hope you'll keep her, even if you do use an incubator. She's never lost a single chick for me; she's got awfully good sense."

## Mrs. Jeff's Misgivings

Now and then the door was opened by a man coming to get his womenfolks, and every time Mrs. Jeff looked up eagerly. "Has old Star-Face gone yet?"

"Well," she sighed, "I certainly do hope we're going to like it in the city. I don't know—it seems awful good money, the wages they're paying—"

"If you don't like it you can come back," we reassured her.

"My brother Jim's folks, out in San Francisco, write they're coming back as soon as they get money ahead for the fares," said a thin and mournful woman. "Seems they sold their car, and Jim's been sick and all."

We murmured sympathetically.

The door opened again and a stout woman entered in tall boots and well-worn black coat, a knitted muffler wrapped around her head.

"My goodness, Mrs. French, aren't you almost frozen!" somebody exclaimed.

"Is Star-Face sold yet?" Mrs. Jeff wanted to know.

"Yes, we bought her. Thirty-seven fifty," said Mrs. French. "She looks like a good breeder to me, and I'm the one that has the say-so about cows at our house. Our cream check was forty-nine dollars last month; I guess John's got no complaint."

"Oh," said Mrs. Jeff faintly.

"I never mind how cold it is," Mrs. French continued heartily. "My land, hot or cold, rain or shine, I'd rather be outdoors than cooped up in any house. Whenever I've got to stay inside walls a week or so—sewing up for the children or the like—well, I just say to John, 'Either I'm coming out in the woods with you or I'm going to be took to a hospital up in Springfield; you just make your choice right now.'

"You know that cold spell two weeks ago? Right around zero, a couple of days. Well, those two days John and I cut four loads of stove wood, me on one end of the crosscut saw, and we took 'em up to town and sold and delivered 'em."

"Mrs. French, you didn't!"

"I did so. I said to John, 'My land, when I think of those poor folks up in town, pretty near freezing to death, and us with more wood than we can use—'

"They paid us two dollars a cord for it; I guess nobody asks better wages. Enjoyed every minute of it too. I was that warm with sawing I took off muffler and coat and rolled up my sleeves. And it was right pretty in the woods. I always did admire woods in winter, all white and black, with the red-headed woodpeckers.

"I guess you're going to miss 'em, Mrs. Morgan, up in that slushy, muddy city. My land, I guess I've seen it! Snow gets dirty just falling through the air, it's that thick with smoke and soot. Last time we went up to the city I just said to John, 'I wouldn't live here, not if they gave me the city hall! I like to be in a place where the snow's clean,' I said."

## Familiarity Breeds Respect

The door opened on the crowd of men, scattering in groups through the yard; automobile horns honked. The women collected purses and gloves and bundles. The sale was over.

My father was taking the blanket off old Buck, folding it under the buggy seat, untying the halter. Automobile after automobile swooped past us scattering mud. My father climbed into the seat beside me, shouted a last word to Jeff Morgan and the auctioneer and gathered up the lines. The yard behind us was a criss-cross of wheel tracks; that neighborly gathering, from thirty miles around, had vanished like an Arab enchantment.

Old Buck jogged more soberly now. Slowly the creek road unwound behind us. It seemed a long way home, and rather a lonely way. Once it would have echoed to many buggy wheels and to the sound of voices. Times change. Neighborliness goes now on rubber tires and takes in, more swiftly, a wider radius.

My father was recounting a fund of farm news gathered from far and wide. I was thinking of automobiles. It used to be said that farmers would never "get together." Now our Farm Loan Association has more money out on farm mortgages than the local bank; our Farmers' Exchange is the biggest building in town—and what have become of the old hitching posts along the sidewalks? We used to be "country hicks"—unless we became "city dudes."

Now, after all, it's only fifty miles to the city, and this seems to be a case where familiarity breeds understanding, mutual respect and self-respect.


## Father Falls in Line

My father was telling about the day Gord Parsons passed him on the way to town in his new car, my father driving old Buck; how the car had a flat tire and after all my father beat it into town.

"Horses don't have flat tires anyhow," he said.

"What kind of a car was it?" I asked.

"It was this new type C, six cylinder, chummy roadster Maxmobile, $1162.50 f.o.b. Detroit," replied my unsuspecting father. "Some say it'll do more miles to the gallon than the Studeford, but it looks to me like—"

So that's why he's been widening the tool-shed doorway!

"While we're about it," I said, "why not get a sedan? It'd be more comfortable in bad weather."

My father grinned sheepishly. "Well now I don't know," he replied. "Of course, if we should get a car, I'd figure on taking cream and eggs to town in it. We could always get a winter top."


Laura Ingalls Wilder

# The Sunflower

*When Laura was sixty she stopped submitting articles to the* Missouri Ruralist. *She also completed her work as secretary-treasurer of the Mansfield Farm Loan Association, proud that she had dispersed a million dol-*

lars in federal loans to her Ozark neighbors. Under her management there had never been a bad loan or a delay in repayment.

What could be next? She and Almanzo now rented out parts of Rocky Ridge, and Almanzo had a hired man to help him with the small load of farm work that was left. Almanzo's crippled feet had grown worse, and he thought of retiring from farming. Rose encouraged her parents to sell the farm; they could move to a warmer climate where Manly might move around more easily. She suggested that they move to California or to England. She was in Albania, and if they lived in England she could travel by steamer and train to visit them.

But Laura could not leave Rocky Ridge. Most of her life had been devoted to building up the place, and she loved her quiet walkways through the woods, the birds and animals, and the running creek under the tall trees. On one of her solitary walks on the farm, nostalgia flooded Laura; she longed for the old faces and familiar voices of home. Lovingly she thought of her girlhood days and all she had learned from them. How she longed to write about Pa and Ma and their little houses in the Big Woods and on the prairies! In one of her final *Missouri Ruralist* columns (published on August 1, 1923), she expressed gratitude for the home of her childhood and its love, which still nurtured her as an adult.

Gather ye rosebuds while ye may,
Old time is still a-flying
And this same flower that smiles today,
Tomorrow will be dying.
(Herrick)

O UT IN THE meadow, I picked a wild sunflower and as I looked into its golden heart such a wave of homesickness came over me that I almost wept. I wanted mother, with her gentle voice and quiet firmness; I longed to hear father's jolly songs and to see his twinkling blue eyes; I was lonesome for the sister with whom I used to play in the meadow picking daisies and wild sunflowers.

Across the years, the old home and its love called to me and memories of sweet words of counsel came flooding back. I realized that all my life the teachings of those early days have influenced me and the example set by father and mother has been something I have tried to follow, with failures here and there, with rebellion at times, but always coming back to it as the compass needle to the star.

So much depends upon the homemakers. I sometimes wonder if they are so busy now, with other things, that they are forgetting the importance of this special work. Especially did I wonder when reading recently that there were a great many child suicides in the United States during the last year. Not long ago we never had heard of such a thing in our own country and I am sure that there must be something wrong with the home of a child who commits suicide.

Because of their importance, we must not neglect our homes in the rapid changes of the present day. For when tests of character come in later years, strength to the good will not come from the modern improvements or amusements few may have enjoyed, but from the quiet moments and the "still small voices" of the old home.

Nothing ever can take the place of this early home influence and, as it does not depend upon externals, it may be the possession of the poor as well as the rich, a heritage from all fathers and mothers to their children.

The real things of life that are the common possession of us all are of the greatest value; worth far more than motor cars or radio outfits; more than lands or money; and our whole store of these wonderful riches may be revealed to us by such a common, beautiful thing as a wild sunflower.


Laura Ingalls Wilder

# My Work

*In 1928, after returning from two years of travel in Albania, Rose offered to build a retirement home on Rocky Ridge Farm for her parents. She enthusiastically planned an English-style cottage built of Ozark rock for a* site across the ridge from the old home place. It was completed in time to be a Christmas gift from Rose to her parents in 1928. Laura and Almanzo gratefully settled into the modern house, which was an Ozarks showplace for miles around.

For herself Rose modernized the family farmhouse. Busy in her second-floor combination sleeping porch and writing studio, she turned out fiction for the Country Gentleman, the Saturday Evening Post, the Ladies' Home Journal, and Harper's. Laura observed her daughter's brilliancy and skill in her work. Could she do the same? Years before, Rose had advised her to write about what she knew and to use her own life as the basis for a book. Laura finally decided to try.

In verse Laura expressed to Rose the significance of her girlhood memories—the very stories Rose had urged her to set down in prose—and her wishes for her daughter.

My pictures hang in memory's hall,
Both pictures grave and pictures gay,
And some are great and some are small,
And some, alas, are sad and gray.

But as you go from day to day,
Painting your pictures one by one,
May brightness touch your brush alway
And shadows flee before the sun.
May steady hand be yours, that you
May blend their tints in harmony,
And pictures bright and brave and true
Hang on the walls of memory.

In 1930 Laura decided that her cherished pictures in "memory's hall" were "stories that had to be told." She wrote her autobiography and called it "Pioneer Girl." Rose took time from her own schedule of deadlines to edit her mother's manuscript, type it, and encourage her New York agent to sell it. But the story failed to excite an editor during the Depression. Nothing happened until Rose's friend Berta Hader, who with her husband, Elmer, wrote and illustrated children's books, introduced Laura's work to an editor they knew.

Laura had reworked her autobiography into a collection of stories about her Wisconsin childhood—stories sparked by the tales Pa had told around the fireplace on long winter evenings in the Big Woods. *The stories immediately roused an editor at Harper and Brothers. On Thanksgiving Day, 1931, a telegram arrived at Rocky Ridge from* Harper's: *they would like to publish Laura's book the following April.*

*When published, Laura's* Little House in the Big Woods *was an instant success. It was the runner-up for the prestigious Newbery Award (presented annually to the outstanding children's book published during the previous year), and* Harper's *wanted a second book from Laura Ingalls Wilder.*

*While Rose worked on her* Saturday Evening Post *serial "Let the Hurricane Roar," she advised her mother on the second book. The story was not Laura's; this time she wrote about Almanzo's boyhood in Malone, New York, and titled the book* Farmer Boy. *Laura and Almanzo were again working as partners as she wrote the descriptions, details, and narratives that he supplied.*

*In the Ozarks, the news was surprising that Mrs. Wilder of Rocky Ridge Farm was now Laura Ingalls Wilder, the authoress. People knew her as the lady who wrote for the* Ruralist, *the farm woman who walked into Mansfield with a basket of eggs over her arm to trade, the mother of the famous Rose Wilder Lane.*

*While Laura was working on her fourth book,* On the Banks of Plum Creek, *she was invited to address members of the Mountain Grove Sorosis Club to tell about her new career as a children's writer. "My Work" was the title of the talk Laura gave. (The manuscript for this speech is at the Laura Ingalls Wilder Home and Museum in Mansfield.)*

I HOPE YOU WILL pardon me for making my work the subject of this talk for I had no choice. The children's story I am writing completely filled my mind.

And again I must ask your indulgence for reading it. Since ten years have passed without my speaking to a crowd, I am some like one of the boys in the recent speaking contest. He said to me, "I was scared plum to death and it was actually pitiful how my knees shook."

When I began writing children's stories I had in mind only one book.

For years I had thought that the stories my father once told me should be passed on to other children. I felt they were much too good to be lost.

And so I wrote *Little House in the Big Woods*.

That book was a labor of love and is really a memorial to my father. A line drawing of an old tin type of father and mother is the first illustration.

I did not expect much from the book but hoped that a few children might enjoy the stories I had loved.

To my surprise it was the choice of the Junior Literary Guild for the year 1932. In addition to this it ran into its seventh edition in its third year and is still going strong.

Immediately after its publication I began getting letters from children, individually and in school classes, asking for another book. They wanted to hear more stories. It was the same plea multiplied many times that I used to hear from Rose: "Oh tell me another, Mama Bess! Please tell me another story!"

So then I wrote *Farmer Boy*, a true story of Mr. Wilder's childhood. This was a few years farther back than my own in a greatly different setting. Little House in the Big Woods was on the frontier of Wisconsin, while the Farmer Boy worked and played in Northern New York state.

Again my mail was full of letters begging for still another book. The children still were crying, "Please tell me another story!"

My answer was *Little House on the Prairie*, being some more adventures of Pa and Ma, Mary, Laura and Baby Carrie who had lived in the Little House in the Big Woods.

Again the story was all true but it happened in a vastly different setting than either of the others. The Little House on the Prairie was on the plains of Indian Territory when Kansas was just that.

Here instead of woods and bears and deer as in the Big Woods, or horses and cows and pigs and school, so many years ago, as in *Farmer Boy*, were wild Indians and wolves, prairie fire, rivers in flood and U.S. soldiers.

And again I am hearing the old refrain, "Please tell another!" "Where did they go from there?"

After being crowded on from one book into another I have gotten the idea that children like old fashioned stories. And so I have

Laura in 1937, as she looked while writing the "Little House" books

been working in my spare time this winter writing another for them, which will likely be published within the year. It will tell of pioneer times in western Minnesota, of blizzards, of the 1873 plague of grasshoppers, of Laura's first school days, of hardships and work and play. With the consent of publishers, I shall call the story *On the Banks of Plum Creek*.

The writing of these books has been a pleasant experience and they have made me many friends scattered far and wide.

Teachers write me that their classes read *Little House in the Big Woods* and went on to the next grade but came back into their old room to listen to the reading of *Farmer Boy* and that the next class was as interested as the first had been.

A teacher in Minneapolis writes me that *Little House in the Big Woods* and *Farmer Boy* are in every third grade in the state.

There is a fascination in writing. The use of words is of itself an interesting study. You will hardly believe the difference the use of one word rather than another will make until you begin to hunt for a word with just the right shade of meaning, just the right color for the picture you are painting with words. Had you thought that words have color?

The only stupid thing about words is the spelling of them.

There is so much one learns in the course of writing, for instance in writing of the grasshopper plague. My childish memory was of very hot weather. In making sure of my facts, I learned that the temperature must be at 68 degrees to 70 degrees for grasshoppers to eat well and it must be above 78 degrees before the swarms will take to the air. If the temperature is below 70 degrees the female grasshopper doesn't lay well, but above that she may lay 20 or more "settings of eggs."

In writing *Little House on the Prairie* I could not remember the name of the Indian chief who saved the whites from massacre. It took weeks of research before I found it. In writing books that will be used in schools such things must be right and the manuscript is submitted to experts before publication.

I have learned in this work that when I went as far back in my memory as I could and left my mind there awhile it would go farther back and still farther, bringing out of the dimness of the past things that were beyond my ordinary remembrance.

I have learned that if the mind is allowed to dwell on a circumstance more and more details will present themselves and the memory becomes much more distinct.

Perhaps you already know all this, but I will venture to say that unless you have worked at it, you do not realize what a storehouse your memory is, nor how your mind can dig among its stores if it is given the job. We should be careful, don't you think, about the things we give ourselves to remember.

Also, to my surprise, I have discovered that I have led a very interesting life. Perhaps none of us realize how interesting life is until we begin to look at it from that point of view. Try it! I am sure you will be delighted.

There is still one thing more the writing of these books has shown me.

Running through all the stories, like a golden thread, is the same thought of the values of life. They were courage, self reliance, independence, integrity and helpfulness. Cheerfulness and humor were handmaids to courage.

In the depression following the Civil War my parents, as so many others, lost all their savings in a bank failure. They farmed the rough land on the edge of the Big Woods in Wisconsin. They struggled with the climate and fear of Indians in the Indian Territory. For two years in succession they lost their crops to the grasshoppers on the Banks of Plum Creek. They suffered cold and heat, hard work and privation as did others of their time. When possible they turned the bad into good. If not possible, they endured it. Neither they nor their neighbors begged for help. No other person, nor the government, owed them a living. They owed that to themselves and in some way they paid the debt. And they found their own way.

Their old fashioned character values are worth as much today as they ever were to help us over the rough places. We need today courage, self reliance and integrity.

When we remember that our hardest times would have been easy times for our forefathers it should help us to be of good courage, as they were, even if things are not all as we would like them to be.

And now I will say just this: If ever you are becoming a little bored with life, as it is, try a new line of work as a hobby. You will be surprised what it will do for you.

Rose Wilder Lane

# Object, Matrimony

*The two writers on Rocky Ridge Farm exchanged what each knew best. Laura's memory was laden with tales from the pioneer days, and Rose's keen professionalism enabled them both to transform memories into published works.*

*"What this country needs is more Rose Wilder Lane stories," declared George Bye in an encouraging letter to Rose (November 27, 1931). Bye was the agent for both Rose and Laura; he followed the progress of each "Little House" book closely, and he urged Rose, "his distracted Ophelia," to keep a steady stream of her short stories directed to his New York offices.*

*During the summer of 1934, Laura was toiling on her "High Prairie" manuscript, which finally became* Little House on the Prairie. *Over tea one day, she shared a tale that she thought Rose might develop as a short story for her eager agent.*

*When Charles Ingalls was justice of the peace in Walnut Grove, Minnesota, he held court in the front room of the family's home. Pa was often busy at carpentry jobs in town, but as Laura explained in her "Pioneer Girl" manuscript, "when he was wanted as Justice of the Peace he just laid down his tools, took off his carpenter's apron, and stepped into this office." Thus, while official business was being conducted in the front room, Ma and the girls retreated to the kitchen.*

*When the Welch and the Roy families appeared before Pa to negotiate some papers, Laura was interested. She knew Mrs. Welch to be an outlandish woman, prone to violent outbursts, quarrels, and odd behavior. She listened carefully through the door as Pa performed the legal work for the coarse-looking woman, her meek husband, and her visiting married sister. That Mrs. Welch had been a mail-order bride gave her an even more unusual aura. She had answered a newspaper advertisement, and on the day she arrived in Walnut Grove she and Mr. Welch were married beside a haystack.*

*The treachery that the embittered Mrs. Welch wrought upon her unsuspecting sister, Mrs. Roy, marked one of Pa's most sensational cases.*

*Rose developed the incident into the short story "Object, Matrimony,"
which appeared in the lead position of the September 1, 1934, issue of the*
Saturday Evening Post.

F OR TWENTY YEARS Jed Masters' wedding was a mystery.
No one asked him to explain it. Good-natured and obliging as
he was, Jed was a man whose toes were not to be stepped on. No
one suspected that he could not explain his wife's astounding behavior, even to himself. It is not known by what resources of patience or philosophy he supported that unanswered question during so many years of their life together.

There were few strangers among the Western pioneers. Homesteaders on the prairies had known each other in Missouri, in Iowa,
in Minnesota or the Big Woods east of the Mississippi. No one had
seen Jed Masters' wife until the day she stepped from the train at
the end of the line. And twenty years did not make other women
forget that incredible wedding day.

Steel rails had reached the town-site two weeks earlier. Now a
train came every day. Men nailing rafters on new buildings saw it
crawl from the cut away off in the east. They watched it grow larger, its smoke stretching and fading above the prairie. When the
puffing locomotive whistled by Lone Tree, they came down. Saloon and store emptied and every man hurried to the depot.

The iron horse came snorting, clanging, and with a clashing jerk
it halted express car, immigrant cars, box cars, flat cars and passenger coach. Men shouted greetings to engineer, brakeman, fire-
man, they hailed acquaintances looking out of immigrant cars; the
bell clanged, the whistle tooted, boys yelled. But silence spread
around the girl who stepped down from the passenger coach.

She was traveling alone. No one met her, no one knew her. She
was graceful, slender, and hardly yet an old maid. Dark braids were
heavily massed above the white nape of her neck, a fashionable
small bonnet tied with ribbons under her chin. Her mouth was
compressed and pale. Shadows lay under her eyes, and the eyes
were startling. They were the blue of lake ice in zero weather.

The conductor set two carpetbags at the edge of her hoop skirts.
She thanked him and said she would require a porter, please.

Someone guffawed and was abruptly silenced. Eastern dudes were fair prey, but a lady was a lady. Several men stepped forward, taking off their hats.

She looked past them at the town. There were already half a dozen buildings. The depot, the saloon and the store had weathered a little, the others were raw boards. A number of shanties were being built, and there were tents, and families camping by covered wagons.

"Isn't there any Town Hall?" she asked, as if frightened.

They told her that the county had been organized that spring.

"Where can I get a marriage license?" she said clearly. No color came into her pale cheeks.

Some of the listening men later contended that she couldn't exactly be called hard. They said she was going on her nerve. Ever watch a gambler betting his last chip, and his gun, and his horse, on maybe two pair? She was like that.

At the time, they were flabbergasted. In their silence, Gid Donovan said she'd better see the county clerk. "Come on, Slim," he said, daring Slim Jeffries to pick up her other satchel. Married men stood back to let them pass. Her slim, tightly buttoned bodice seemed to sail on those wide hoop skirts. Her hands, incased in black lace mitts, clasped a small reticule. The men felt baffled; she seemed not to know they were there.

Harvey Denning was then the county clerk. Embarrassed and doubtful, he said he guessed it could be done to oblige a lady. Her hoop skirts gathered dust as they crossed the street to his shanty. Mrs. Denning shooed the children out of the front room and moved the lamp from the center table, while Harvey pulled the box of county papers from beneath one of the beds.

In due form he made out a marriage license for Clarinda Jane Lewis, age nineteen, of South Duxbury, Massachusetts, and Jedediah Masters, over twenty-one, of Sioux County, Dakota Territory.

"Has something happened to Jed, is he hurt?" Mrs. Denning asked.

"How much is it, please?" Miss Lewis said.

Mrs. Denning noticed that she broke the last bill in the reticule.

She also noticed that the back of the hoop skirts was draped in a way never before seen in the Territory.

"Well!" she said to her husband. "Why for goodness sakes if he ain't crippled don't he get his own marriage license, I'd like to know. I never heard of a woman so bold and brash!"

Slim followed Miss Lewis sheepishly, but Gid was enjoying the sensation in the street. Miss Lewis wanted to find a minister. Gid told her that the preacher had gone on west, through the construction camps.

"The Reverend's a missionary preacher," he said. "But how about a justice of the peace? Won't he do?"

Miss Lewis said he would do.

"He's on his claim now, four mile west," said Gid.

"Mr. Masters' claim is west, too, isn't it?" she asked.

"Yes, ma'am, nine mile."

"I can engage a carriage?"

"You can hire a rig at the livery stable," Gid told her.

At the livery stable she hired the buckboard and the roans, to drive first to the Peter Allen claim and then to Jed Masters'. "And back?" Old Bill Higgins asked her.

"I don't know," she said.

Bill Higgins always drove a sharp bargain with Easterners. "Four dollars to take you out," he told her. "Five, round trip."

Miss Lewis opened the reticule. "I will pay you four, now."

Gid Donovan wanted to go along to see what happened. He offered to drive her for nothing, and Old Bill Higgins snorted.

"I know you young scalawags," he said. "All you think about is speed, these days. Forty miles a day, and durn a horse's wind— that's you. No sir-ree bob, you don't drive them roans. What am I paying Al's wages for?"

Al drove out the roans. They came eagerly, prancing, and Old Bill had difficulty lifting Miss Lewis into the back seat. It was not her fault that he caught a glimpse of a slim ankle in a white stocking. She tucked the bulging skirts inside the buckboard and he gave her a lap robe to spread over them. Gid and Slim found room for the carpetbags ahead of the front seat.

"Thank you," she said. But she had never given them an impression that she saw them.

The roans swiftly left the town-site. Al handled them with skill and wished he could smoke. He could light a cigar in the forty-mile wind, but he was driving a lady.

"It's a great country," he said. She did not answer; perhaps she did not hear him, in the wind. He shouted, "Great country, out here!"

For a few minutes he despised these Easterners, too high-and-mighty to behave like ordinary decent folks. Then he turned slightly and glanced at his passenger. She was sitting upright, her hands folded, and her wide-open eyes stared through him. They gave him a shock. She seemed to be scared almost to death.

"There's nothing to be afraid of, lady," he said, sawing on the bits and pulling the roans to a trot. "They're gentle as kittens, but I won't let 'em out if you don't say so. We got all the time there is."

"No," she said. "Go on, please. As fast as you can."

"You looked like you're scared," said Al.

"Oh, please go on! Go on and don't talk!"

Al let the roans go and did not say another word to her. At the Allen claim they stopped only long enough to pick up Peter Allen. He was breaking sod, but he unhitched his horses and put them on picket lines to graze. He was glad enough at prospect of a wedding fee. The Allens had foolishly spent money for a frame shanty, and they must live on game until they could raise a crop. Peter Allen took his gun along, to shoot a jack rabbit on the way back. Mrs. Allen and the four scrawny little Allens watched them drive on.

Jack rabbits were plentiful. They bounded from the tall wild grass beside the wagon track and leaped away. Now and then a prairie hen scuttled in front of the roans. Masses of wild pink roses mottled the enormous prairie, which stretched on all sides to the edge of the sky. Dust from the railroad grade was blowing along the horizon.

It took a practiced eye to find Jed Masters' sod shanty amid the wavering shadows on miles of blowing grass. But the sharp green oblong of his wheat field shouted that a homestead was there.

Two miles away, the shanty began to stand up. There was also a sod barn, and a haystack. A crawling insect could be perceived to be a wagon and horses.

Jed Masters was putting up slough hay. He had picked out a fine quarter-section, with a slough across its corner. Cut when young, the slough grass made good hay. The tougher autumn grass, when expertly twisted into solid sticks, made fuel in a land without a tree.

On the loaded hayrack, Jed looked at the approaching buckboard. He pushed back his hat and with a finger wiped the sweat from his forehead. Then he pitched hay to the stack until the buckboard was near enough to hail. He waved his hat to it, jumped to the ground, and stopped short when he saw a woman in the back seat.

Jed Masters was then twenty-one, though he had already lived two years alone on this homestead claim. When he took it he had solemnly affirmed that he was twenty-one, though in reality he had been nineteen. No one else knew this. Since he was supposed to be two years older than he was, women spoke of him as an old bachelor. Little girls frankly told him they would marry him when they grew up.

Al pulled up the roans and backed them, cramping the wheels so that the girl could get out. For some reason, no one spoke.

Jed took off his hat and his eyes narrowed a little. They appeared bluer than they were because his face was burned red by sun and wind. The sun had bleached his eyebrows and mustache, but his hair and the stubble on his unshaved cheeks were brown.

Peter Allen jumped over the front wheel and took the girl's hand, and Jed politely looked the other way while she got her swaying skirts safely to the ground.

"Well, here we are!" Peter Allen said.

The girl looked steadily at Jed. Her rapid breathing shook her voice.

"Are you Mr. Masters?" she asked. Peter Allen was thunderstruck.

"That's right. Jed Masters' my name," said Jed.

"I got your letter. I'm Miss Clarinda Lewis."

Jed pulled himself together. "Please to meet you, Miss Lewis. I—well, I figured maybe I'd hear from you. I was going to the townsite next Saturday to see if a letter'd got here."

She opened the reticule. "Here's the license. I brought it."

"You did?"

"You asked me to marry you. In that letter."

"Yes," Jed said.

"I will. Here I am."

Jed's sweat-stained face could not turn redder than it was. He pulled out his handkerchief and mopped the back of his neck.

"I don't go back on what I wrote you," he said. "But I figured we'd have a little time to—"

"No," she said. "Now. Right away."

Peter Allen was behind her, Al was in the buckboard. They could not see her face. The whole thing astounded them. Jed looked at her for a long moment, then taking a deep breath he said, "All right. Go ahead and marry us, Pete."

The girl was trembling all over. Peter Allen did not know what to do. He read the license slowly, twice, and cleared his throat and asked, "You don't mean right now, do you, Jed? Maybe you better take a little time to—kind of think it over, or maybe fix up a little?"

"Now's as good a time as any," Jed said. "Go ahead, Pete."

They stood there by the haystack and Peter Allen married them. As soon as he pronounced them man and wife according to the ordinance of God and the law of Dakota Territory, Jed dropped the bride's hand.

"Much obliged, Pete," he said. "How much do I owe you?"

There was a slight difficulty about the certificate. Jed's Bible was a small one which his mother had given him when he left Wisconsin. It was not a family Bible with a decorated marriage-certificate page. Peter Allen said he would write their certificate when they got a family Bible. But Jed, glancing at the girl, said he'd better write it now. So Peter Allen wrote it on the flyleaf of the little Bible.

It did not seem quite regular, but it was legal enough. Al witnessed it, and Peter Allen wrote Mrs. Allen's name, too. "Don't worry, you're married sound and solid, Mrs. Masters," he said.

She was fumbling for the pocket in the folds of her skirts. She took out two letters, sealed and stamped, and asked Al to mail them for her in town. She thanked him and thanked Peter Allen and said good afternoon.

"Well, I'll be durned!" Al said as they drove away. They did not look at the letters till they were well out of sight. The thin one was addressed to a Boston newspaper, the other to Miss Abigail Lewis, South Duxbury, Massachusetts. Before night almost everyone at the town-site was wondering what was in those letters.

Jed and his wife stood by the haystack and watched the buckboard going away. Then she looked at the sod shanty and said, "Do you live in that?"

It was a good sod shanty, thatched with slough hay. Grass had covered the walls, and grass and flowering weeds grew thick on the roof. Jed pulled the latchstring and swung the door open. His wife looked in.

There was a board floor, and one window was glass. The bunk was neat against the wall, and the breakfast dishes were washed. Frying pan and bread pan hung on the rough studding by the rusty stove. Clothes, quirts, wash rags and towels, a buffalo-hide lap robe and a saddle, spurs, and pieces of harness which Jed was greasing in the evenings, hung from nails. Jed had made the stout table and benches.

Not many men, baching, kept a place as tidy as he did. She made no comment, and he said, "I guess you're tired. Come all the way from Duxberry without stopping?"

"From Duxb'ry, yes," she said.

"Well, make yourself at home and rest. I'll bring in your satchels."

When he came in with the carpetbags, she was examining the door. The narrow space squeezed her hoop skirts into a grotesque shape. He laughed a little.

"'Fraid I didn't plan for hoops," he said. "Better take 'em off."

She gasped. Her eyes were the eyes of an animal in a trap. Jed stepped outdoors and put on his hat. "I'll finish getting in the hay."

"Isn't there any lock?" she asked him.

"Sure. Pull in the latchstring and drop the bar. Like this, see?"

"Thank you, yes," she said faintly.

"Aren't going to lock me out tonight, are you?"

She shook her head, mute.

Jed hauled the rest of the hay. He built the stack into a firm, weatherproof pile. The placid horses started nervously at the feel of his hand on the reins. Now and then he glanced sidewise at the shanty. The door remained shut, the latchstring pulled in.

At sunset he unhitched and watered the horses. In the barn he fed them, gave them fresh bedding and hay. He padlocked the barn door as usual, and went to the house.

The door was ajar. He pushed it open. Coffee boiled on the stove and his wife was turning slices of fat pork in the frying pan. Her light calico dress, without hoops, made her appear impossibly thin. The yards of skirts were pinned up at the bottom so that they barely touched the floor. On the wall the hoops hung collapsed in concentric circles of wire held together by white tape.

"You do burn this twisted grass?" she asked.

"Yes. We call it sticks of hay. Takes quite a knack to twist it like that."

"I thought you must burn it, it was in the wood box," she said. The table was set with two tin plates.

He took the water pail and brought fresh water from the well by the slough. At the bench outdoors, he washed thoroughly and combed his wet hair. Color had gone from the sky and night was coming over the prairie. In the shanty his wife lighted the lamp.

When he went in, her shaking hand poured a wabbling stream of coffee into his cup. The pork was on the table. They sat down.

He noticed that she ate with her fork. He had heard that Easterners did that. It was a newfangled way of eating, not practiced in the West. But she was only pretending to eat. He looked at her haggard face in the lamplight. There was a beautiful line from temple to chin, and the dark hair grew softly from her white forehead. Suddenly and roughly he shoved away his plate and folded his arms on the table.

She started, and was tense and quivering, looking straight at him.

"Look here," he said. "Tell me what it's all about?"

"I don't know what you mean," she answered.

"What's your reason for acting this way? What's all the hurry about? I figured you'd come out and stay with some nice woman at the town-site till we got kind of acquainted."

Her whole face became painfully red, her lashes fell. He waited, hearing the tiny hum of the lamp drinking oil and the lonely sound of the wind in the dark.

Brutally he said, "Are you in trouble?"

She blazed at him, "No!"

"Well, I didn't think so, I thought that wasn't it," he muttered hurriedly. The color left her face and he was savage. "You're going to tell me, you hear?"

Her teeth left small marks on her lower lip. She said, as if she had rehearsed the words, "It's a fair bargain. You advertised for a wife because you wanted a woman, any woman. I married you because I wanted a husband."

"Today?"

"Yes," she said harshly. "Today."

"But why, why today? That's what I intend to know."

"I'll never tell you," she said.

She was on her feet, facing him as he came around the table. "You can kill me, but I'll never tell you."

"Kill you?" he laughed at her. Her mouth was cold, passive to his ferocious kisses. Her whole body was unresisting, uncaring. Under the hard corsets and folds of cloth there was the lifelessness of a doll. In rage he shook her, and let go of her so suddenly that she staggered against the wall.

"My God," he said. "What are you? What is it? What—"

Her knees were sagging. Her body slid and toppled, and on the floor her face was like that of a dead woman.

He felt for the pulse in her wrist. He dashed water on her face. Her clothes baffled him, he ripped off layers of cloth and with his hunting knife cut the corset strings and tore the whale-boned thing off her. He splashed more water on her and slapped the cold cheeks. Her eyelids twitched. She gasped, shuddered, and while he rubbed her hands the gray-blue eyes opened.

"Lie still," he said. "You're all right."

She huddled instinctively and he pulled some fold of cloth over her.

"I tried not to," she murmured. "I'm very strong, like I wrote you. I never swoon."

"That's all right," he said. "Lie still and don't talk."

He went to the door and stood looking out. The dark prairie spread endless under the paler dark of the sky. Large quivering stars hung so low that it seemed an outstretched hand might touch them. Their liquid brilliance was mocking. Far away a wolf howled. Then another, nearer.

"What's that!" she exclaimed. He heard the rustle of her sitting up.

"Wolves," he said absently. Slowly he turned. An arm in a torn sleeve supported her. Her hair was dripping wet, a few wisps plastered to cheek and neck. Her left hand held the hem of her skirt to her throat.

"I'll send off an order for a wedding ring next time I go to the town-site," he said. She did not speak. "You feel able to get to bed?"

"Yes," she said.

"Look here. We're man and wife."

"It's a fair bargain," she repeated.

"Damn it, shut up if you can't talk sense!" he said roughly. "What bargain? I didn't make any bargain. Here we are, married. We've got to live together the rest of our lives. We've got to figure out some way to get along, somehow. Can't you see we've got to— we can't— The two of us, alone out here— What is this thing you're hiding? What is it you're using me, my name, for?"

Her mouth hardened.

"Well," he said at last, "tomorrow's another day. Go to bed and get some rest. I'm sleeping outside tonight."

The hoops jangled startlingly when he blundered against them, taking down the buffalo robe. Her faint voice stopped him on the threshold.

"The—wolves—"

"Wolves?" he said. "Oh, that's right. Maybe I better take the gun." He took it from the wall.

She did not speak. He went out by the haystack and lay down on the ground, rolling himself in the buffalo robe.

Jed Masters and his wife seemed to get along together as well as any married couple, perhaps better than most. That fall they attended singing school at the town-site. Both had good voices and they sang together while they drove home across the prairie. When the church was organized, both joined it. The second winter of their marriage he bought a sleigh, and in warm spells when the mercury rose to zero they came out of the sod shanty and went speeding over the snow with a jingling of sleigh bells. Everyone agreed that Jed was a good husband and that Mrs. Masters was a helpmeet to him.

Mrs. Allen was with her when their baby was born. Mrs. Masters had a hard time, and during the second night Jed drove like a madman, thirty miles east, to get the doctor. The doctor was out on a call. It was the fourth day before Jed could get back with him, and the baby was dead then. But Mrs. Masters pulled through. Jed couldn't do enough for her. He paid a hired girl for several weeks, and after that he waited on his wife hand and foot till she was strong again.

They were among the first homesteaders to build a frame house. In time, with additions, it became a substantial two-story building, painted white. The cottonwoods they had planted and watered shaded it in summer, and in winter Mrs. Masters kept its sunny windows full of blossoming geraniums. The wagon track had become a road then. Jed owned a half-section, all wire-fenced, and a big red barn.

Not an acre of his land was mortgaged and he had money in the bank. His wife's garden stuff and butter, chickens and lambs, had helped him make it. She was thrifty and hardworking, but she held her age well and was considered handsome for an old married woman. She made her clothes from Eastern fashion plates and was always stylish. It was rumored that she had business interests in the East. She wrote and received an increasing number of Eastern letters, but she had never again written to Miss Abigail Lewis in Duxbury.

Trains were commonplace now. Young folks, born in the town, knew nothing of covered wagons or claim shanties, wolves, Indians, horse thieves. Even more than the milder weather, these young folks made the old-timers feel old. When the morning passenger train whistled at the wheat elevator, it was odd to meet young fellows carelessly going the other way.

"We're not as young as we was, Slim," Gid Donovan said, and the fat station agent, coming from the clicking telegraph office with a bunch of orders in his hand, answered, "No, Gid. And we're not getting any younger, fast."

He hurried on, but Gid, lounging against a loaded truck, saw Jed Masters' black team swiftly coming down West Commercial Street. The mares' necks were arched, shining manes and tails fluttering, oiled hoofs spurning little plops of dust. There wasn't a better driving team in the country. Jed pulled them up and jumped out to tie them.

"Hello, Jed," said Gid, lifting his hat to Mrs. Masters in the buckboard.

"Lo, Gid. It's a fine, large morning."

"Sure is. You folks expecting somebody on Number Four?"

"Yep. Wife's cousin and her husband coming out from the East to pay us a visit."

Mrs. Masters was a fine figure of a woman. Her back was as straight and her waist as slim as a girl's. This was a week-day morning, but she was elegant in brown-and-white striped lawn, with intricately puffed bosoms and sleeves, and yards of flounces. Curled bangs fluffed above her eyes, and the color in her cheeks was as bright as paint.

Gid turned to watch her crossing the platform beside Jed. One gloved hand deftly bunched her skirts at one side, and she held above her sailor hat one of the newfangled tiny parasols with a long, jointed handle.

The locomotive rushed by, steaming and clanging, drawing a long line of coaches with strangers' faces looking out. Roustabouts raced trucks toward express and mail cars. Startled sheep baaed in the stock pens, and with a rattle and rush the wheat elevator began to fill freight cars on the spur track. Strangers came down the steps of several coaches, and in the crowd Gid could not be sure which were the Eastern cousins.

He saw them coming toward the buckboard—a thin, tall, stooping old gentleman and a birdlike little woman in rusty black. Brown and stocky, Jed stowed satchels under the seats.

"My, is this your carriage?" the little woman said, darting quick glances everywhere. Her eyes were bright brown, her withering face and frizzled hair were the color of oatmeal.

"I have a phaeton," Mrs. Masters replied. Her cheeks were white as chalk. "We brought the buckboard so we wouldn't be crowded. Mr. Lansing, if you will ride in front with my husband, Abby and I will gossip on the back seat."

"I shall be most happy to do so," the elderly gentleman replied, stroking his white goatee. "But surely, ah, since we are cousins, my dear Clara, we may address each other by our Christian names?"

The little woman gushed. "My goodness gracious, why, yes, of course! I won't be jealous!"

"Certainly, if you wish it, Perley," said Mrs. Masters, flushing.

Indian summer was on the prairie. Wheat stubble stretched golden in the mellow sunshine, dusty goldenrod and wild sunflowers bordered the road. The rolling land was dotted with farmsteads in groups of trees. The town became a mass of green from which rose white church steeples and the elevator's towers.

"My! I had no idea the West was like this!" Abby Lansing exclaimed. "For all you wrote you liked it so much from the first— What pretty horses!"

"My husband's horses," Mrs. Masters said, watching the flight of colts across the pasture. "I am glad you like the West, Abby. I hope you will make us a long visit."

"Oh, we can't, we couldn't," Abby Lansing began, and her chatter about the farm in Duxbury, her son in college, her married daughter, was interrupted only by exclamations about the windmills, the barns, the wind and the immensity of the sky.

Jed set the satchels on the side porch and drove on to the barns. He unhitched and rubbed down the black mares. He never let hired men handle those blacks. He noted that the windmill needed oiling again, but he went on to the house.

His wife was inspecting the roast in the oven. He stepped into the shed and refilled the coal hod. Setting it by the range, he asked, "Where are they?"

"Upstairs, in the front bedroom."

"Look here," said Jed. "How long they going to stay?"

"I want them to stay all winter."

Jed slowly whistled. "Well you're the doctor. Needs a change of climate for his health, uh? He'll get it out here, all right."

His wife turned to him suddenly and said with intensity, "Jed, what do you think of her?"

"What's the matter?" he asked, putting an arm around her. Her hands gripped the front of his blouse.

"Tell me! What do you think of her?"

"Her? Oh, faded little blond nitwit. Clara, what is the matter?" His arm shook her gently. "What are you all wrought up about?"

Wildly laughing, she jerked out, "So that's what you think of her!" She stopped that laughter. "I must put the potatoes on."

Still holding her, he asked, "What about a kiss?"

She kissed him. He said, "You do like me."

"You know it's more than liking."

"Not much more."

"Don't say that," she pleaded. He let her go then, and taking the oil can from the shed he went out and stopped the windmill.

Everyone for miles around soon knew Mrs. Perley Lansing. Every fine afternoon Mrs. Masters took her somewhere in the phaeton. She furbished up her old dresses with bits of lace and ribbons, dangling chains and tinkling bracelets, and her light voice chattered at church sociables, at ladies' meetings and dances and harvest parties. Everyone heard about her son in college, her married daughter, her beautiful old home in Duxbury. Twice she made a round of farewell calls, but Mrs. Masters persuaded her to stay a little longer. Then the bitter weather came.

An early November blizzard buried the prairie in snow and piled drifts against barns and houses. Storm doors and storm windows were on, the big coal burners would not be cool till spring, and only reckless young folks and men on business ventured far from home. Trains fought through storms and were delayed by snow-packed cuts. It would have been folly for the Lansings to leave before spring.

Jed's hired man left him in February. It was no time for a man to throw away a good job, but the hired man said he did not like that house. He did not like the evenings by the heater, with Jed and the missus and them Easterners. They talked like butter wouldn't melt in their mouths, but all the same he didn't like it. Something funny was going on, underneath.

"Jed knows it, too," he said. "Sets there looking at the almanac and not turning a page. Like he was listening to something he can't hear."

"What's he suspicious of?" Gid Donovan asked.

"I don't know," the hired man said. "'Tain't the old gentleman. She don't favor him any. Polite, but that's all."

Late one March afternoon, Jed drove from town against a northwest wind. He stamped into the warm house, red and stiff with cold, his arms full of packages. Taking off his icy buffalo coat and cap, he threw some letters and newspapers on the dining-room table and warmed his hands by the heater. "Brrrh!" he shivered. "We'll have a cold snap tonight."

"I'll get you some hot coffee, Jed," his wife said, going to the kitchen. The old gentleman courteously handed the letters to Mrs. Lansing, and opened a newspaper.

"Ah," he said, clearing his throat. "I see there are no limits to Mr. Cleveland's rascality. An autocratic President, sir, and a cringing Congress—"

In the rocking-chair by the geraniums, Abby Lansing screamed. Her shriveled face contorted like a child's, tears gushed under the steel-rimmed spectacles. She clutched a letter and sobbed, "No! No! Oh, Jed! Perley, our home—"

Mrs. Masters set down the cup of coffee. "Why, Abby!" she said.

Jed glanced at her under his eyebrows. He took the letter, read it slowly, then read it aloud.

By the terms of their contract, copy inclosed, Mr. and Mrs. Lansing had forfeited possession of their farm in Duxbury. Merely as a matter of form, the present owner would pay twenty-five dollars for a quitclaim deed. This letter was signed, with assurances of esteem, U. S. Stebbins.

"But Lawyer Stebbins told me we could live there all our lives!" Abby Lansing wept.

"Let me get this straight," said Jed. He asked questions patiently. It appeared that the Lansings were desperately poor. The old Lansing place was all that was left, and they had sold a deed to it, but they held a contract allowing them possession of the house as long as they lived. Now the contract was void, because they had left the place long enough to lose their legal residence.

"I guess all you can save is that twenty-five dollars," Jed decided heavily. He looked with pity at the old gentleman, who walked up and down, agitating his coat tails with nervous hands. Mrs. Lansing collapsed, and Mrs. Masters supported her upstairs to bed.

"This is preposterous, sir! Preposterous!" Mr. Lansing insisted. "I—I find it difficult to conjecture what we shall do. Twenty-five dollars— Why, it is mere chicanery! It is dishonorable, sir!"

Mrs. Masters came in. She looked at him and said, "Yes, it is dishonorable. But Abby wants you."

"Ah, yes. Yes, yes. Quite so," the old gentleman stammered, confused. "Ah, if you will excuse me—"

Jed caught his wife's hand as she passed his chair. He held her a moment, listening to tired steps on the stairs. A door closed, muffling a faint sobbing.

"We must help them out," Jed said.

"She isn't your cousin. No reason they should be a burden on you."

"Why do you hate her?" Jed asked, looking up at his wife's face.

"Hate her! Why, Jed!"

He continued to look at her steadily and in a hard voice she said, "She has a son. Her baby lived. Let him take care of them."

"Clara!"

"Let me go," she said, choking. "I must get supper."

They rode to town next day in the buckboard. Huddled together on the back seat, Abby Lansing and her husband murmured to each other. They still cherished a little hope. Jed drove in silence, a clumsy bulk of fur coat; his wife sat beside him, straight and elegant in rich black.

Both lawyers, and the banker too, confirmed Jed's opinion. The Duxbury home was lost. "Better sign the quitclaim," the banker said. "You'll save twenty-five dollars, anyway."

Harvey Denning's office was beside the brick bank, in one of the old frame buildings not yet torn down.

Jed explained what was wanted. Harvey Denning adjusted his spectacles and began to fill out a quitclaim deed, copying from the contract. Abby Lansing wept softly and her husband sat close beside her, holding her hand. Jed stood by the battered desk and watched Harvey Denning's pen. His wife sat primly, her hands in the tiny muff on her lap. She had opened her coat a little, revealing shirred cashmere and a glint of gold pin. She was so still that the light hardly twinkled on the jet trimming of her velvet bonnet.

Harvey Denning read the description aloud: "From the corner of Appletree Lane, north-north-east to Shady Brook, thence. . . ." Abby Lansing's quivering breath was the only other sound. She wiped tears from her cheeks with a damp handkerchief. Her husband helplessly patted her hand. When Harvey Denning handed him the pen, he was hardly able to hold it steady enough to sign his name.

"Now, Mrs. Lansing," Harvey Denning said. "On this line, please. Your full name, Abigail Lewis Lansing."

She could not see. The wet handkerchief would not stop her tears. Her husband wiped her face with his handkerchief, and, drawing a shaking breath, she wrote her name. Her old mouth squared like a baby's, tears running into it. She drew its corners down and put one hand to her sobbing throat.

"It's gone—Perley, our home—" She looked up and touched Jed's fur sleeve. "Oh, Jed, what will we—"

"Take your hands off my husband, Abby Lewis!" Mrs. Masters said. It was like a snake striking from that quiet, unnoticed corner. They stared at her, petrified. She was on her feet, quivering with rage. For an instant some barrier in her held, then it broke.

"Keep your hands off him, you hear me? Liar! Thief! You crawling sneaking hypocrite! I own that farm, understand? I'm the one that bought it through Lawyer Stebbins. That's why I've been keeping you two out here. What did you think, you silly fool? Think I'd forgotten? Think I don't know what you did to me years ago? Oh, I heard you. I heard you two in Appletree Lane that night! You, with your baby face! Steal him, ha! Elope with him before our wedding day. 'Poor Clarinda. But oh, Abby, I love you so.' I'll show you who's jilted, Perley Lansing! Who's got the old Lansing place now, you sniveling two-faced—" She panted. "Stay out here in the West and root hog or die, like I did! And I hope you rot in—" Jed Masters' hand closed over her mouth.

His other arm lifted her off her feet. He carried her out of the office, set her on the sidewalk, walked her across the street to the buckboard. "Get in," he said, and helped her mount to the seat before he took the blankets from the black mares and untied them.

The buckboard rattled swiftly out of town, the blacks' oiled hoofs ringing on the frozen road.

Jed reached across his wife's lap and tucked the lap robe in more snugly. "Better button your coat," he said. "This wind's a norther."

"I don't repent," she told him. "Let them work and worry and fight and suffer, like we did. It won't be enough to pay for what she did! Think of it, Jed, all our hard times. And they living back East all the time. Drought, and grasshoppers, and that prairie fire and the Hard Winter, and the baby—"

"That's all past," he said steadily. "I don't hear but one word you said."

"What word?"

"'Our.' Our hard times."

He had to hold the lines with both hands. The blacks were going home, with the wind behind them.

"Where did you get the money?" he asked with simple curiosity.

"Aunt Abigail's legacy. I didn't tell you, but she left everything to me. I always thought Aunt Abigail suspected— And when he wrote me about it, Lawyer Stebbins said the Lansing place was for sale. The contract was his idea; he was sorry for them. But when I read it over, I got to thinking—" She was telling him everything, hiding nothing any more.

He said, "Well, here we are home." The new hired man looked out of the barn and Jed called to him, "Take the blacks and rub 'em down, will you?"

His wife had opened the heater's drafts and was taking off her coat. He threw it on a chair, cast his own on it, and put his arms around her.

"Kind of nice to have the place to ourselves again, mh?" He hesitated and tried to say carelessly, "Don't want to go back East to that farm of yours, do you?"

"Why, no!" she said, surprised.

"Well, then, why not let 'em live there? What's it to us?"

"All right. Let them live in my house, on my charity."

"You can sure hate when you put your mind to it," he said. Sitting down, he drew her onto his knees, into his arms.

"Look here, wife. You've been hating them for twenty years. Seems to me kind of a waste of energy. Hated 'em worse every time anything went wrong. It's a kind of habit you've got into. Put it that you married me in a hurry, that you'd've married any Tom, Dick, or Harry, just to jilt him before he jilted you. Take the both of us now: if you had a choice, would you take him?"

"Goodness, no!" she exclaimed. "I wouldn't have anybody but you."

"It's been a pretty hard twenty years, some ways," he said. "But this is worth it."


Rose Wilder Lane, interview with Almanzo Wilder

# Dakota Territory in the 1870s and around 1880

*In 1936, after having lived in the old family farmhouse on Rocky Ridge for eight years, Rose Wilder Lane left Mansfield. A publisher was pressing her to write a book on the background and history of Missouri—a project that would require extensive research. Rose settled into the Tiger Hotel in Columbia, where she would be close to the library facilities of the University of Missouri.*

*Almanzo and Laura longed to move back into their old home place; when Rose left it, they closed up the newer stone house and returned to what they had always considered home. Never again did they move from the white-painted farmhouse on the hill.*

In 1937 the Saturday Evening Post *ordered a pioneer serial from Rose. She titled the series (which later became a best-selling book) "Free Land." Her message, in fiction form, was that the free land of homesteading had never been free; those quarter sections of western land had been paid for with hardships, backbreaking labor, sacrifice, and slow success. Much of the "Free Land" story was similar to her own family's experience. Her father, Almanzo Wilder, served as Rose's chief protagonist, and her mother's family served as prototypes for supporting characters in the story.*

*Rose wrote "Free Land" while living in her suite at the Grosvenor Hotel in New York City. Most of her story she knew firsthand and could remember well from her early days on the Dakota prairie. But realistic details, so typical in her writing, sometimes escaped her. At home, on Rocky Ridge, Rose could easily quiz her parents for material, but her schedule was too crowded and deadlines were advancing too rapidly for her to travel to Mansfield. Instead, Rose typed an interview for Almanzo, which he completed for her before she gave her manuscript to editors at the* Saturday Evening Post.

*Rose's questions show her concern in supplying her readers with accurate Americana. Almanzo's responses demonstrate his keen memory and wit in recalling his days of homesteading nearly sixty years earlier.*

W HAT WAS THE price of lumber?

Common lumber 2 × 4 and 2 × 6 for $30.
Finished lumber about $50 per thousand.

About how much did it cost to build a frame claim shanty?

$25.

What were your wages on the railroad? The lowest wages you got?

I worked with a team at $3.50 per day. Men—$1.50, and feed your own team.

Did you get board also, in the railroad camps, or was the cost of it deducted from your wages?

Board yourself.

How many hours a day did you work on the railroad?

10.

What did the farmer get for wheat, the first years it was raised there?

Not sure but I think it was 80¢ [per bushel].

Was winter wheat known then at all? It was brought to this country by the Russians. Did you hear of it in the 1870s?

I don't think it was but I'm not sure. We took our claims in 1879. I don't know anything about Dakota in 1870.

What was a fair price for a good horse?

Average good work horse, $150.

A wagon?

$65.

A saddle?

$30 to $60; cowboy usually about $60.

A plow?

Breaking plows to break up the prairie sod was $20 to $30 according to size.

A harness?

$40 to $60.

What would seed wheat cost, shipped from the east?

I think it was $1.50 the first spring.

How much seed wheat would you get for $1.50, if shipped from the east?

A bushel and a half.

Were any other crops raised to sell? If so, what, and how much did they sell for, and how much was raised to the acre?

Oats. Seed was anywhere from 60¢. We sowed 3 bushels per acre.

The first crop was in 1881 and we got 90 bushels per acre and we got 40 bushels of wheat per acre.

Do you remember what year the first crops were raised around De Smet?

1881.

And whether that was a good crop year? And the next, and the next, and so on?

The 1881 crop was the best. We got nearly as good in 1885.

Could you give me a general idea of each year's weather conditions for a few consecutive years, with dates?

The winters were usually about the same. A few people would get lost in blizzards and freeze to death. The worst blizzard was January 8, 1888. It came up about 2 in the afternoon after a nice warm morning and lasted that day and two more days and three nights. Cleared about 4 in the morning on January 11. Several froze to death. Two men walked all the time during that blizzard and were 60 miles from where they started. Their hands and feet were frozen some but not bad. [Here Laura added this note: "Described in *First Three Years*" (now published by Harper and Row as *The First Four Years*).]

Do you remember prices of furniture? Bedstead, table, cookstove, etc.?

Cane-seat chairs $1.25 each. Bed and springs, bureau and commode $15.00. Cookstove about $25.00. Nails 3¢ per pound.

Dress goods?

Calico 7¢ per yard.

What did you usually wear at work?

Wore the suit after it got too old to wear for dress-up. Don't remember of seeing any overalls.

What did a window cost?

Cheap window for shanty $1.

Did you buy it complete, the glass in the sash?

Yes.

How much cash did it cost to prove up on a homestead?

About $10. Had to have 2 witnesses to prove you had lived on land for 5 years.

What kind of trees did you plant on a tree claim?

Willow, box elder, and cottonwood.

Did people want a slough on their land or not? Why?

Yes, slough grass was much larger, 3 or 4 tons per acre.

What papers did you have to have to prove up on a claim?

The papers you got when you took the claim.

Was there a land office in De Smet?

No—had to go to Watertown.

How deep did you dig for water for a well?

From 10 feet on down, usually 20 feet. Sometimes they dug clear down and did not get water.

What interest did you pay on mortgage?

Long-time 10 percent.

On personal notes?

Short-time 3 percent a month.

What newspapers and magazines were read?

*De Smet News, Chicago Inter-Ocean, Youth's Companion.*

What did a buggy cost?

From $65 to $85 depending on the make.

Did folks generally feel that free land, homesteading, was a *new* thing? Dating from only 1861? A kind of triumph of the poor man in America?

I don't think they did.

Do you remember any more of this song than:

> Come to this country and don't you feel alarm,
> For Uncle Sam is rich enough to give us all a farm.

No.

Do you remember what other songs were popular then? I already have "Little Old Sod Shanty on the Claim."

I can't remember any more except "There'll be a hot time in the old town tonight," but that is all I can remember of it.

Say a man's feet are so badly frozen that he is laid up, cannot walk on them, but later recovers. What do they look like at various stages of freezing and recovery?

I never saw any. They said they sweat badly. Turn black and blue like a bad bruise. The skin peels off. They are sore a very long time.

What were the ordinary extremes of winter and summer temperatures?

A nice day for a sleigh ride was zero. A cold day was anywhere from 20 to 40 below. I have been out with a team at 45 [below].

Ordinary wind velocity?

20 to 30 [MPH]. 60 for a day or two sometimes.

Do I remember correctly that you lighted a cigar in a high wind by holding the match against it and striking the match with the side of the matchbox?

No. I lit a cigar by striking the match on anything handy and got it to the cigar *quick*. [That's all.] 40- or 50-mile winds did not stop a smoke.

What slang do you remember? For instance, if asked "How are you?" in 1908, the reply was "Fine and dandy!" Now it is "Okey-dokey!" What was that kind of reply then? You said a man was "all wool and a yard wide." What other slang would you use to describe him? Or say he was no good, what would you say of him?

No good—he is a shiftless, no-account fellow. All wool—meaning he was honest and a good fellow. Sometimes nickname him lazy John, or whatever his name might be.

What was the price of coal?

Soft coal from $8 to $9 a ton.

How much did it take to heat through a winter? [I know] it was hard coal.

$15 to $18. About $80 whichever you burned.

What else was generally burned for fuel?

Hay.

Were buffalo chips and hay in fairly common use?

Yes.

What wild animals did you see after the claim shanties were built? Did you ever see buffalo? Antelope? Wolves, elk, in the late 1870s? I know there were coyotes.

No buffalo, quite a few antelope.

Did blanket Indians ever come into De Smet?

No.

Or Indians in white man's clothes?

No.

What kind of a gun did you have?

An old army musket.

Make? Caliber? I know nothing about guns; please tell me all you can about it. What did it cost? What did cartridges cost? Were pistols carried then? What make would they be, etc., etc.? Revolvers were later, weren't they? I remember Mama Bess had a revolver in Florida, but wasn't it a lady's weapon?

All the standard makes that are made now were made then. They did not carry guns. Some had the old colt revolvers that were loaded with powder and ball and cap. Revolvers were used but I don't think they had the automatic at that time. Cartridges cost 50¢ a box.

What was the attitude toward cigarettes?

Never heard of a cigarette at that time.

What groceries were luxuries, and do you remember their prices? Oranges, for instance?

50¢ a dozen.

What else? Figs? Dates?

Dried 20¢ a pound. Dried apples 10¢ a pound. Dried apricots 15¢ a pound. Dried peaches 12¢ a pound. Fresh peaches 3 for 10¢. Fresh apples 2 for 5¢.

Do you remember approximately the price of flour? Sugar? (Was white sugar the usual thing?) Beans, fat pork? Coffee? Tea?

Yes, sugar 10¢ a pound. Flour 4¢ a pound.

What other groceries were staple supplies?

Same as now except they did not have canned vegetables.

Were fancy vests still worn?

No.

Did bankers, etc., wear frock coats and tall silk hats?

Not there.

Remember what the political arguments were about at that time? Around town in stores and so on. I remember the Cleveland arguments but of course not the 1870s.

Populist-Democrats and Republicans. Mostly Populist and Republicans.

Did you carry a Barlow knife?

No.

Or a Bowie? Or know of any young men who did?

No.

Was a horse called a cayuse?

No, not there.

The jail, the calaboose?

Yes.

A dollar ever called a piastre, or a plaster?

No, that was earlier and it was paper 25–50–75¢ pieces called
plasters.

Did you say "two bits," etc.?

No.

What was the slang word for *dollar?*

Didn't have any.

What were the early saloons like?

Saloons.

Did they have mahogany bars and mirrors?

Yes.

Paintings behind the bar, swinging doors, frosted windows, or
anything like that?

Paintings, yes; swinging doors, no.

Brass rails? Brass cuspidors?

Yes.

Were they poolrooms or were poolrooms separate places?

Yes.

Did you shake dice for drinks?

Yes.

Did you get cigars in saloons and drugstores?

Yes. Groceries and drygoods stores had cigars and we shook dice for them, never bought one.

What did you pay for cigars? What kind of cigars?

Don't remember any brand of cigar; they were 5¢ or 10¢.

When people said "the East" and "easterners," did they mean New York and Washington, or Minnesota and Chicago? When they said "the West," did they mean California, or Wyoming and Montana?

New York or Ohio and California.

What was your attitude toward the local banker?

He was a whole fellow. We would say "Hello, Tom" [banker Tom Ruth, of De Smet], but when it came to borrowing money it was 3 percent a month.

Your father, as a farmer, looked down on townspeople and did not want you to be one of them. Was the feeling different in the Dakotas?

Yes.

Was there a feeling of difference between townspeople and farmers?

No.

Did homesteaders feel superior to merchants, or merchants feel superior to homesteaders?

No difference.

About how much could a man sell a homestead claim for? Say he had held it three years and had a shanty and a barn on it and half of it in cultivation. I just want a general idea of land prices.

About $300 or $400.

A man had to live 7 months of the year for 5 years on a homestead claim to prove up on it, didn't he? What other requirements were there? Roughly, how much cash money would required improvements cost a man?

6 months. He had to have at least 10 acres broke and in crop. A house and barn—no requirements as to size or quality.

Please tell me about the different kinds of wild grass: what they looked like, where they grew, what they were good for, did they make a difference in breaking sod, etc. Did you have all kinds on your homestead or tree claim?

Buffalo grass grew about 6 inches high, very thick, always looked like it was dead or very near it, but cattle would get fat on it. The bluestem, or as was sometimes called turkeyfoot, I suppose because the top spread out three ways like a turkey foot—it grew a thick pattern of leaves much like orchard grass and the stem had a bluish cast and branched out like this. The bottom was very thick and it made good hay. Slue [slough] grass was principally all blades of grass close to the ground; they would be in the round stem and seem to be all blades 1/4 inch wide at the bottom and run to a point from 3 to 5 feet high. It made very good hay but not quite as good as bluejoint because the leaves were a little tough. Made the best hay for fuel.

What kind of wild flowers and weeds do you remember? That would strike an eye looking at the country, and at what different times of year, and weeds that were pests to the farmer? (I can imagine the country in June when the wild roses were blooming, but what did it look like earlier or later? What masses and colors of wild flowers? Ozarks are white with daisies, but they came in later, didn't they?)

I am sorry but I can't remember any wild flowers except violets and wild roses. The violets came early in spring but did not show as they do here for the wild grass started early and the whole country looked green but you would find violets in a few places. Roses were everywhere. I don't remember of any weeds. They came in with horse feed oats and mill feed and seed grain but no weeds at first as I remember. The Russian thistle came later, first started in Russian settlements and spread all over. The worst pest there is. They grow round as large as a bushel basket and when the seed gets ripe it dies and the wind breaks it off and it will blow till it hits something like a fence or buildings and it scatters seed every time it rolls over and when the wind changes it comes back.

Just in general, driving out from town, how far across country would you look on a clear day?

About 5 or 6 miles, yet up on a ridge you could see farther.

Would you say the land is flat or rolling?

Rolling.

Why did you take a claim nearer town?

Because I like to live near town.

Did homesteaders usually move into town for the winters? Or only for the Hard Winter?

Nearly all were single men and boarded in town when there was no work to be done on claims. That was why they were in town for the Hard Winter. After that most of them got married and stayed on the claim or had so much stock they had to stay and take care of it.

What year did you take your first claim?

1879.

In the spring when you looked at the country, did you see a lot of activity, plowing, etc., or did it seem wild and lonely to look at?

Not lonely but wild enough.

How near were how many neighbors? In shanties or soddies? What nationalities were they? Which ones were married?

Almanzo as a young Dakota homesteader

We were only 1 mile from town. I think at the time they were all Americans. In the fall of 1879 when we built our sod shanties we were there for a month in October and November and did not see anyone but heard after that there was a man living 9 miles from where we built our shanties. We dug a well that fall and got good water in gravel at 7 feet deep. The next spring neighbors built on nearly every claim around us and all were married men.

Why did you pick out that particular piece of land? Were the others already taken that you would have preferred, and why? What was the most desirable in a claim, there and at that time, from the homesteaders' point of view?

I knew where the town was to be and wanted to get land close to town as I could and took it without ever seeing it and it was all good land, wasn't much difference in it.

What, in regard to your claim, gave you the most satisfaction during the first few years? I mean *moments* of satisfaction, such as finishing the shanty, putting up the team after the sod was broken, or seeing the wheat up, something like that. Those special times that one remembers of looking at something and feeling *good*. As, for instance, the day on Rocky Ridge when the first mortgage was paid off, and we said, "Now the place is *ours!*" It must have been a grand moment when you walked into the bank and handed that money to old man Freeman. Must have been moments like that, in homesteading.

To save me, I can't remember of anything except that when we thrashed the first crop that was the best crop we ever had, but it was before we had much land broke up. My life has been mostly disappointments.

Were the summers always dusty?

No, as long as we stayed there there was not land enough broke up to make dust storms.

Did people believe the trees would survive on tree claims? Were there arguments about it, and what was said?

They seemed to think willow and cottonwood would grow.

Did windbreaks survive? Are there trees around farmhouses now?

A very few. Most of them are dead.

Did people say "take a claim" or "take *up* a claim"?

"Take a claim."

Did you fence the land right away? Or raise wheat unfenced? What kind of fence? What did it cost? Where did you get fence posts?

It was several years before anyone fenced and then posts were 15¢ each. Barbed wire $3 a hundred pounds.

Remember when wire nails came out? And anything about the first time you saw them?

About 1884 when they first came out they would nail the boxes together good. They were shipped in with wire nails and you couldn't hardly get the cover off, and when you did there was a card with big letters: "This cover was nailed on with gliden steel wire nails, what do you think of their staying qualities?"

First threshing machine? What was it like?

They were the same as now, maybe not quite as large.

First binder?

Was before we went to Dakota.

Any other new machinery in the 1870s? Or striking invention of any kind?

Don't remember of any. Were some improvements on mowers and other machinery.

You used kerosene lamps; what did kerosene cost?

15¢ a gallon.

The kerosene cookstove came later, didn't it?

Yes.

Did most claim shanties or soddies have board floors?

Yes.

What did flooring cost for an 8' × 10' room?

Did not have floors in our shanties.

If I know you, you had a fit of extravagance now and then. What did you spend money on? When you had it in your pocket and just felt like spending it? Nowadays a man would buy a new car. Remember one time when you did something like that? And hardly dast face Mama Bess with whatever you'd bought? That would be in the 1880s, but it's all the same if it was something you could have bought in 1870s. Or maybe it was one time that Roy went on a spending spree, bought something you didn't *have* to have, but just wanted.

I bought a top buggy in 1882. I bought a $50 nickel-plated harness in spring 1882. I am sorry I could not remember more but it has been a long time and things did not impress me when they happened like they did some people.

# Laura's Book Fair Speech

*With her first four "Little House" books selling well, Laura's editors at Harper and Brothers were eager for her to meet her young readers and the educators who wholeheartedly encouraged the reading of her books. During the 1930s, publishers were organizing book fairs to bring authors and readers together, and Laura Ingalls Wilder was often requested for an appearance.*

*In the fall of 1937, Laura accepted an invitation to appear at a book fair sponsored by the J. L. Hudson department store in Detroit. She was jittery; years had passed since she had spoken before a crowd, and she admitted in a letter to Aubrey Sherwood of the* De Smet News, *"I have never lost my timidity with total strangers." But Almanzo promised to travel to Detroit with her, and Rose urged her to go, stressing the value of personal contact with editors, teachers, librarians, and other authors. "Everyone who meets or sees you will buy your books," Rose predicted in a letter to her mother (October 11, 1937).*

*Laura anxiously sought Rose's suggestions; she always relied heavily on her opinions about writing. Rose was lavish with encouragement and praise and gave her mother detailed advice. From New York City, she wrote to Laura at the Statler Hotel in Detroit:*

The chiffon velvet must be perfectly beautiful. . . . Wear your wine-colored hat with it for afternoons; it will be perfection. I bet you are the most dazzling woman at the whole show. . . . You will make a grand talk and be a lovely lion. . . . Remember, you like Harpers, and be sure to say so. Tell Ida Louise [Miss Raymond, Laura's editor] you like the looks of the books, you like the illustrations. . . . *Speak out and say* you like anything you do like. Praise from an author is high praise indeed, so do not deprive Ida Louise of any of it that you can sincerely give her. (October 11, 1937.)

*While Almanzo spent hours wandering through the Henry Ford Museum and marveling at the collections of antique implements and vehicles, Laura made "a lovely lion" at the book fair. She had prepared her speech at home on Rocky Ridge, drafting it in pencil on the same lined tablets she used for writing her books. On October 16, 1937, before an enthusiastic crowd of Michigan admirers, Laura explained her purposes, her goals, and the strong autobiographical nature of her works in progress, the "Little House" books. Over forty years later her speech was published in the September 1978 issue of the* Saturday Evening Post.

M ANY YEARS AGO, in the Little House in the Big Woods, Sister Mary and I listened to Father's stories.

There was no radio to amuse us then, no moving pictures to go see, so when the day's work was done, we sat in the twilight or by the evening lamp and listened to Pa's stories and the music of his violin. Our little family must be self sufficient for its own entertainment as well as its livelihood and there was no lack of either.

Mother was descended from an old Scotch family and inherited the Scotch thriftiness which helped with the livelihood.

Although born and raised on the frontier she was an educated, cultured, woman. She was very quiet and gentle, but proud and particular in all matters of good breeding.

Father's ancestors arrived in America on the Mayflower and he was born in N.Y. State. But he also was raised on the frontier. He was always jolly, inclined to be reckless and loved his violin.

So Ma taught us books and trained us in our manners, while Pa taught us other things and entertained us.

We had a busy happy childhood, but of it all, Sister Mary and I loved Pa's stories best. We never forgot them and I have always felt they were too good to be altogether lost. Children today could not have a childhood like mine in the Big Woods of Wisconsin but they could learn of it and hear the stories that Pa used to tell. But I put off writing them from year to year and was sixty when I wrote my first book, *Little House in the Big Woods*.

When to my surprise the book made such a success and children from all over the U.S. wrote to me begging for more stories, I began to think what a wonderful childhood I had had. How I had seen the whole frontier, the woods, the Indian country of the great plains, the frontier towns, the building of railroads in wild, unsettled country, homesteading and farmers coming in to take possession. I realized that I had seen and lived it all—all the successive phases of the frontier, first the frontiersman, then the pioneer, then the farmers, and the towns. Then I understood that in my own life I represented a whole period of American History. That the frontier was gone and agricultural settlements had taken its place when I married a farmer. It seemed to me that my childhood had been much richer and more interesting than that of children today even with all the modern inventions and improvements.

I wanted the children now to understand more about the beginnings of things, to know what is behind the things they see— what it is that made America as they know it. Then I thought of writing the story of my childhood in several volumes—an eight volume historical novel for children covering every aspect of the American frontier.

After the work was well started, I was told that such a thing had never been done before; that a novel of several volumes was only for grownups. My daughter, Rose Wilder Lane, a writer and novelist, said it would be unique, that an eight volume novel for children had never been written.

I hesitated. Perhaps my idea was all wrong.

But letters kept coming from children, individuals, whole classes

"I am so glad to have your picture," Rose wrote Laura in 1936, "but I do not think it flatters you at all. Indeed you are much prettier than it. I suppose the camera can not lie and to a machine you look so, especially as it sees you not changing at all, but when anyone is looking at you you seem much younger than this, for one thing. Your eyes are so lively and your in schools, mothers of children too small to write letters—all wanted to know what happened next, wanted me to go on with the story. I decided to do so. Someone has to do a thing first; I would be the first to write a multi-volume novel for children. So I wrote the second volume, *Farmer Boy*. This is the story of a farm boy in the east before he went west. It is the story of the childhood of my husband on his father's farm near Malone, N.Y.

The old house is still standing just as it was when his mother sat at her spinning wheel in the attic chamber. We got some wintergreen plants from the old place, a few years ago, to set out on our Ozark farm.

Almanzo still loves horses as well as when he was that Farmer Boy, but he doesn't drive them now. He drives a Chrysler sedan instead, at least he holds the wheel. Of course I do the driving with my tongue.

You may wonder that the name Almanzo, of Central-Asian origin as it is, should have been given to a Yankee farmer boy. The name Almanzo comes from *El Mansur* and was brought into England from Asia during the crusades and from England to America by the Wilders when they came to Plymouth in 1631.

The third volume of my children's novel goes back again to Laura in the *Little House on the Prairie* and [Laura appears again] in the fourth volume, *On the Banks of Plum Creek*, just published.

Almanzo, the Farmer Boy, appears again in the fifth volume, on which I am now working. He goes with Laura the rest of the way through the three more volumes it will take to make the eight and complete the novel. But these are still to be written so I'll not give any details now.

*On the Banks of Plum Creek* shows Laura and her family in Western Minnesota where Ma thought they were all safe in a civilized

---

expression changes so, and though if one stops to think of it your hair is white, still the effect is really of blonde hair, of light hair that contrasts so with your dark eyes and dark lashes, and is always so wavy and pretty. You look much older in the picture than you really do, so that the first sight of the picture was a shock to me. Still it is a very attractive picture and even people who do not know you will like to look at it."

country where nothing could happen to them. When you read the book you will see how wrong she was. There were runaways and fires and storms—such terrible storms—and the grasshoppers— the grasshopper plague of 1874, the worst ever known since the plagues of Egypt.

I read recently of a grasshopper invasion where, so the author said, the grasshoppers' breaths smelled strongly of onions from eating so many of those vegetables.

Now I never smelled a grasshopper's breath, but I have lived among uncounted millions of them. I have seen clouds of them darken the noonday sun. I saw their bodies choke the waters of Plum Creek, I saw them destroy every green thing on the face of the earth, so far as a child would know. There are unforgettable pictures of those grasshoppers in my mind that I have tried to draw plainly in *On the Banks of Plum Creek*.

Even so, Plum Creek was too civilized for Pa and we went west again to Dakota Territory where Almanzo was homesteading, where he helped save Laura, and the other people of the new settlement, from starving during the Hard Winter. And where he and Laura thought zero weather fine for sleighing and decided 40 below was just a little too cold.

But that will all be told in the remaining volumes of my children's novel which ends happily (as all good novels should) when Laura of the *Little Houses* and Almanzo of *Farmer Boy* were married.

Every story in this novel, all the circumstances, each incident are true. All I have told is true but it is not the whole truth. There were some stories I wanted to tell but would not be responsible for putting in a book for children, even though I knew them as a child.

There was the story of the Bender family that belonged in the third volume, *Little House on the Prairie*. The Benders lived half way between it and Independence, Kansas. We stopped there, on our way in to the Little House, while Pa watered the horses and brought us all a drink from the well near the door of the house. I saw Kate Bender standing in the doorway. We did not go in because we could not afford to stop at a tavern.

On his trip to Independence to sell his furs, Pa stopped again for water, but did not go in for the same reason as before.

There were Kate Bender and two men, her brothers, in the family and their tavern was the only place for travelers to stop on the road south from Independence. People disappeared on that road. Leaving Independence and going south they were never heard of again. It was thought they were killed by Indians but no bodies were ever found.

Then it was noticed that the Benders' garden was always freshly plowed but never planted. People wondered. And then a man came from the east looking for his brother, who was missing.

He made up a party in Independence and they followed the road south, but when they came to the Bender place there was no one there. There were signs of hurried departure and they searched the place.

The front room was divided by a calico curtain against which the dining table stood. On the curtain back of the table were stains about as high as the head of a man when seated. Behind the curtain was a trap door in the floor and beside it lay a heavy hammer.

In the cellar underneath was the body of a man whose head had been crushed by the hammer. It appeared that he had been seated at the table back to the curtain and had been struck from behind it. A grave was partly dug in the garden with a shovel close by. The posse searched the garden and dug up human bones and bodies. One body was that of a little girl who had been buried alive with her murdered parents. The garden was truly a grave-yard kept plowed so it would show no signs. The night of the day the bodies were found a neighbor rode up to our house and talked earnestly with Pa. Pa took his rifle down from its place over the door and said to Ma, "The vigilantes are called out." Then he saddled a horse and rode away with the neighbor.

It was late the next day when he came back and he never told us where he had been.

For several years there was more or less a hunt for the Benders and reports that they had been seen here or there. At such times Pa always said in a strange tone of finality, "They will never be found." They never were found and later I formed my own conclusions why.

You will agree it is not a fit story for a children's book. But it shows there were other dangers on the frontier besides wild Indians.

Then there was the family of children frozen in the terrible blizzard on Plum Creek. I couldn't tell that either.

Sister Mary and I knew of these things but someway were shielded from the full terror of them. Although we knew them true they seemed unreal to us for Ma was always there serene and quiet and Pa with his fiddle and his songs.

The spirit of the frontier was one of humor and cheerfulness no matter what happened and whether the joke was on oneself or the other fellow. Strangers coming west possessed or acquired this spirit if they survived as westerners.

There was the man from the east who knew nothing of Dakota mirages. The first morning after stopping at a little frontier town, he saw from the hotel a large lake and trees nearby. He said to the hotel keeper, "I always like a short walk before breakfast. I am going to the lake. Will breakfast be ready when I come back?"

The hotel man looked at the lake that appeared so near and knew it was a mirage and that the real lake was over forty miles distant.

He said, "Your breakfast will be ready by the time you get back," and watched the stranger walk away.

At noon a teamster coming in met the easterner away out on the prairie on the bank of a tiny creek. He had taken off all his clothes and was rolling them into a tight bundle.

"What in the world are you doing?" the teamster asked.

Looking up from his bundle the man answered, "I don't want to get my clothes wet and I'm going to carry them on my head when I swim across this water." And seeing how astonished the teamster looked he added, "Oh, I know it looks only a step across, but judging from how near the lake looked this morning and how far I have walked without finding it there is no telling how far I will have to swim before I get to the other bank of this creek."

Then there was the settler leaving the country after one of its periodic droughts. All his worldly goods were in the covered wagon with the family. A cow was tied behind and several scrawny colts and horses followed. The kind of horses that in that place at that time sold for $1 a head. He stopped at a little windblown town to water his horses before camping on the prairie beyond.

The hotel keeper at that place had a great curiosity and was noted all over that country for asking questions.

He asked the traveler where he was from and then, "Own a farm out there?"

"Yes!" the man answered.

"How much land?" the hotel keeper wanted to know.

"160 acres," the man told him.

"And what did you do with it?" the hotel man asked.

The man turned on the wagon seat and pointed to the poorest, most worthless colt among the horses.

"See that colt back there?" he asked. "Well, I traded 80 acres of land for that colt."

The hotel keeper looked at the colt but he wasn't satisfied. "What did you do with the other 80?" he persisted.

"Oh!" was the reply. "The man I traded with was a poor, ignorant fellow from the east. I slipped the other 80 in on the deed and he never noticed it."

My parents possessed this frontier spirit to a marked degree. It shines through all the volumes of my children's novel.

Whether it was the Indian troubles in *Little House on the Prairie* or the terrible storms and the grasshoppers in *Plum Creek*, once past they refused to dwell on them but looked ahead to better things.

When times were hard the fiddle and Pa sang:

Oh drive dull care away
For weeping is but sorrow.
If things are wrong today
There's another day tomorrow.

So drive dull care away
And do the best you can.
Put your shoulder to the wheel
Is the motto for every man.

If our fare was scanty at times still it never lacked variety for as Pa and the fiddle sang:

One day we had greens
And a dish full of bacon.
The next day we had bacon
And a dish full of greens.

Laura Ingalls Wilder

# The Land of Used-to-Be

*Laura's confidence in her writing was bolstered when she appeared at the 1937 Detroit Children's Book Fair. In a letter to Rose she told about the enthusiastic children at the fair: [they] "all seem wildly interested and want to know how, when and where Laura met Almanzo and about their getting married. . . . You should have seen the interest in their faces when I spoke of it. . . . And lots of their letters want me to hurry up and write about it" (January 26, 1938).*

*The trip to Detroit also kindled the Wilders' old wanderlust. Before Laura started her last books about her Dakota years, she wanted to see the shores of Silver Lake, the big slough, the town of De Smet, and the surrounding prairies. She felt a need to clarify in her mind the great sweeps of land she would use as her setting and to check into details that neither she nor Almanzo could precisely recall. Through the winter months of 1938, Laura and Almanzo planned a return trip to South Dakota. "Now is the time to snort," Laura wrote Rose. "We will spend our money for gasoline and our time burning it!" (December 29, 1937).*

*When the Wilders left Rocky Ridge in May of 1938, they were accompanied by a young Mansfield couple, Silas and Neta Seal. Silas drove for eighty-one-year-old Almanzo, and his wife was a cheerful companion. The four traveled west to Oregon and California and then back east to South Dakota.*

*In the Black Hills the travelers stopped to visit Laura's recently wid-*

owed sister, Carrie Ingalls Swanzey, at Keystone. Along with many other tourists they looked with awe at Mount Rushmore, just up the road from Carrie's house, where the Borglum presidential sculptures were emerging from the granite.

As the Missourians drove on Highway 14 through South Dakota, the land stretched into the familiar prairie that Almanzo and Laura knew so well. In the village of Manchester, seven miles west of De Smet, they visited Laura's sister Grace and her husband, Nate Dow.

The Wilders were in De Smet for the 1938 Old Settler's Day celebration. The annual gala was actively promoted by the community and by Aubrey Sherwood, whose De Smet News office was a meeting place for old friends to congregate and to pin on their appropriate badges showing their length of association with the town.

Laura and Almanzo proudly wore their "Hard Winter" badges; the couple represented a dwindling breed of pioneer. Much had changed in the town of their memories. "Many of the old buildings had been replaced," Laura observed, and "everywhere we went we recognized faces, but we were always surprised to find them old and gray like ourselves, instead of being young as in our memories" (from a composite letter prepared by Harper and Brothers, n.d.).

Rose's "Free Land" had gained much attention in its recent Saturday Evening Post serialization, and De Smet residents were intensely interested in the use of their area as the setting for the homesteading saga. Everywhere the Wilders went they were feted and introduced as the parents of the famous Rose Wilder Lane.

When Laura and Almanzo returned to Rocky Ridge, Laura earnestly started on the final stretch of her "Little House" series. She completed the final editing and preparation of By the Shores of Silver Lake, the story of the Ingalls family's first year in Dakota Territory; and she planned to finish her writing with two more titles, "The Hard Winter" and "Prairie Girl."

As the 1939 Old Settler's Day festivities approached, the Wilders longed to travel again to De Smet. They decided to travel alone and were staunchly confident in Almanzo's driving their Chrysler. Rose was concerned; she preferred that her parents hire a driver. But Laura assured her, writing, "We have planned to take our driving easily, stop early and lay over if we are tired. And not drive at all on Sunday. . . . If we find it too hard, we *can come home any time. . . . We will be very careful, drive slowly and stop when we please" (May 23, 1939).*

*So they went journeying again, repeating the pleasant pattern of visiting friends and scenes in De Smet. They again dropped in at the De Smet News to register as "Hard Winter" pioneers, and vibrant Aubrey Sherwood asked the distinguished visitors to pose for his camera for a newspaper photo. Wearing their badges, the Wilders sat for the camera in front of a historic array of photographs of early people and places in De Smet. Prominently displayed was the Ingalls family portrait.*

*From De Smet Laura and Almanzo drove west again, visited Grace and Carrie, then returned to the shady coolness of Rocky Ridge before the summer heat bore down. Back in her quiet writing study, Laura mused over their return to the prairies. She called up images of the Dakota pioneering days for "The Hard Winter," but she also wrote about her visit to De Smet. This article, "In the Land of Used-to-Be," appeared in the children's section of the* Christian Science Monitor *on April 4, 1940. In payment for her submission, the* Monitor *sent Laura a check for fifteen dollars.*

I T WAS THE first of June. The days were lovely, warm, going-somewhere-days and one morning when the blue haze hung over the Ozark hills, Almanzo said, "Let's go back to De Smet for the Old Settler's Day celebration. I would like to see the old place and the folks we used to know."

"Let's do," I agreed eagerly, for I had just finished writing *By the Shores of Silver Lake.* "We could see the homestead Pa took so long ago and Carrie and Grace."

Friends thought we should not take such a trip by ourselves. We ought anyway to have a driver. They were very tactful but their idea was that we should not go so far from home alone.

We don't think that seventy-two or eighty-two is old and we object to being taken care of.

Almanzo said, "I have driven horses all over that country and the roads to it and I can drive a car there."

"I rode behind those horses with you and I can still ride wherever you can drive," I said.

So we told the man who lives on our farm that we were leaving

Almanzo and Laura pose for Aubrey Sherwood's camera at the *De Smet News* office during the 1939 Old Settler's Day celebration.

and didn't know when we would be back. He was very kind and promised to take care of everything while we were away.

## Off for South Dakota

Then, one early morning, we packed our bags, put them in the trunk of the Chrysler, said good-bye to our pet bulldog and started to South Dakota and the Land of Used-to-Be.

It was still early in the morning when we came to Springfield, fifty miles away.

Going into Springfield we took the wrong turn and were some time finding the street that lead to the highway we must take. A little way and the street detoured. We took the detour and went on and on.

"Haven't we gone far enough to come to the highway?" Almanzo asked at last.

"It seems like it," I said, "but going East we are bound to find the highway running North." Instead we found ourselves on a country road.

A friendly stranger directed us and soon we saw the highway signs and were on our way.

"This is a good start," I grouched, "lost twice this early in the morning and our first day out. Do you suppose we will get lost coming and going in every city on our way?"

"It wasn't we were lost. It was the highway," Almanzo said earnestly.

We stopped for lunch at a little eating place beside the road, then went on again in the pleasant afternoon.

When we came to a junction of our highway with one crossing it, we took the wrong end of the new highway. After going a few miles we discovered our mistake, retraced our way and followed the highway on in the right direction.

"That is three times lost in one day," Almanzo said.

"I think it is the limit," I added.

"We will make it the limit," Almanzo declared. "Three times is enough to be lost in one day."

On the Prairie

We drove happily on across the level land of North Missouri and Southwestern Iowa. Then out on the Dakota prairie where meadow larks sang beside the road. The sun shone into the car and the soft Spring wind blew in my face. Almost I seemed to hear Ma say, "Laura, put your sunbonnet on! You'll look like an Indian." So I tilted my wide hat brim to shield my face from sun and wind.

Late one afternoon we came to De Smet.

The little town we used to know was gone. In its place was a town that spread North beyond the railroad tracks, East to the lake

The Ingalls homestead south of De Smet as it appeared eight years after Laura last saw it in 1939. This photograph was taken by Garth Williams, who sought out the homestead before illustrating a new edition of the "Little House" books.

shore, South where the big slough used to be and far to the West. The old schoolhouse was gone. Its place was taken by a large brick school building.

Along Main street were fine business houses in place of the one story with a two story false front, stores of the old days.

A large brick bank with offices above stood on the corner where Pa had built his small office building. We took rooms in a hotel a little way from it.

Next morning at breakfast, two men looked sharply at us as they passed our table, then came back and stopped.

"Hello, Laura," one of them said.

I looked up in surprise into the laughing black eyes of a tall man.

"I am Laura, but who are you?" I answered him.

"I am Sam," he said, "I would know you anywhere." And then

I remembered him for an old schoolmate, one of the younger boys in our crowd.

## Talk of Old Times

The other man had known Almanzo well. They joined us at the table and we recalled old times together.

Main street was full of street fair and it rained. It rained all day but nobody cared. After so many dry years people were happy to be rained on. When a hard shower came they ducked under awnings and into doorways. Between showers they splashed smilingly up and down and across the street where water was running.

Almanzo and I were crossing the street when I heard someone calling, "Oh, Laura, Laura!" I looked back. Running after us was a little woman.

"I knew you!" she exclaimed. "I knew you!"

"You are Maggie," I said. We stood in the middle of the street— we who had last seen each other as girls in school—and the rain poured down.

Wherever I went someone called, "Laura." It makes me feel quite young again. Then I met an old schoolmate with her grandchildren.

We drove out to see Pa's old homestead. There is a nice farm house in place of the little claim shanty, but the Cotton Wood trees we set that long ago day when Grace was lost among the violets are still growing—big trees now.

We drove to a near-by town to see Grace and her husband (Manchester, South Dakota). From there we drove across the plains to the Black Hills.

Sister Carrie lives in the Black Hills at the foot of Mt. Rushmore, where the great stone faces are carved in the living granite of the mountain top. As we drove the winding roads, these stone likenesses of Washington, Jefferson, Lincoln and Theodore Roosevelt looked down on us.

Carrie and Grace who used to be my little sisters are now taller than I am. We talked together of childhood days and Pa and Ma and Mary.

When we talked of our return journey, we decided not to go back the way we came. Instead, we drove on to further adventures. But that is another story, for as we drove away from sister Carrie's home, our visit to the Land of Used-to-Be was ended.*

Laura Ingalls Wilder

# The Dakota Prairies

*"Almanzo and I were speaking of De Smet the other day, and of how we were still homesick for Dakota," Laura confided to a reader-friend in 1948 (letter to Frances Mason, October 20, 1948). She admitted that even though she and her husband had returned to De Smet three times during the 1930s, they had not left wholly satisfied. Perhaps, Laura reasoned, they had somehow hoped to find their lost youth on the prairies of their early days. But as Laura had mused in* Little House in the Big Woods, *"Now is now; it can never be a long time ago" (p. 238).*

*Her prose included five books that recalled the days on the Dakota prairies:* By the Shores of Silver Lake, The Long Winter, Little Town on the Prairie, These Happy Golden Years, *and* The First Three Years and a Year of Grace *(now published as* The First Four Years*). Occasionally, however, Laura slipped into verse as she expressed her affinity with the wide-open spaces, the level lands, and the mystical sunrise and sunset of the Dakota Territory of her girlhood.*

E VER I SEE them in my memories' vision
As first my eyes beheld them years agone,
Clad all in brown with russet shades and golden
Stretching away into the far unknown;

---

*Pa Ingalls died in 1902. After his death, Ma and Mary lived together until Ma's death in 1924. Mary died in 1928 while visiting Carrie in Keystone.

Never a break to mar their sweep of grandeur,
From North to South, from East to West the same,
Save that the East was full of purple shadows,
The West with setting sun was all aflame.

Never a sign of human habitation
To show that man's dominion was begun;
The only marks the foot-paths of the bison
Made by herds before their day was done.

The sky downturned a brazen bowl above me
And clanging with the calls of wild gray geese,
Winging their way into the distant southland
To 'scape the coming storms in rest and peace.

Ever the winds went whispering o're the prairies,
Ever the grasses whispered back again
And then the sun dipped down below the skyline
And stars lit just the outline of the plain.*

Remembering the thrill of the birds that filled the blue-bowl
prairie skies and sounded in the grassy, marshy sloughs, Laura
wrote this short poem in an autographed copy of *By the Shores of
Silver Lake* (Kerlan Collection, University of Minnesota Library):

At evening still my fancy sees
The flash of snowy wings,
And in my heart
The meadow lark,
Still gaily, sweetly sings.

Laura's sisters Carrie Swanzey and Grace Dow both lived to see
"Little House" books published and realize the fame of their family. Grace died in 1941, but Carrie lived to read all eight of Laura's
books and show them proudly to friends. When the final volume,
*These Happy Golden Years*, appeared, Laura mentioned to a reader,

---

*This poem was first published by Aubrey Sherwood in his *De Smet News* on
June 20, 1930.

"Sister Carrie writes me that after she read the book it seemed she was back in those times and all that had happened since was a dream. I considered it a great tribute to the truth of the picture I had drawn" (quoted in Mary Phraner Warren, *Cobblestone* magazine, February 1986).

Laura's affection for Carrie is evident in a poem she composed and penned into the flyleaf of her sister's copy of *The Long Winter:*

> Here is a true story of the long ago,
> To bring to your mind once more
> The dangers and strife and the joy of life
> We shared in the days of yore.
> When toil and hardships were gaily met
> With a word of cheer or a song
> When our eyes were bright and our feet were light
> And our hearts were brave and strong.
> As you read this tale of long ago
> You may be sure today
> The love of our early childhood
> Has followed you all the way.

---

*Carrie Ingalls Swanzey died in 1946, leaving Laura the sole survivor of her family.

# Epilogue

When Laura and Almanzo Wilder returned to Rocky Ridge after their trip to South Dakota in 1939, their traveling days were over. They settled contentedly into the quiet pattern of seasons on their beloved Ozark farm, watching the world around them with keen interest but seldom venturing into it.

Laura completed the last "Little House" books in quick succession. *By the Shores of Silver Lake* appeared in 1939 and was followed by *The Long Winter* in 1940. Her working title, "The Hard Winter," had been rejected strenuously by the editors at Harper and Brothers; nothing, they believed, should be presented as "hard" to children.

Laura's original plan was to round out the story of her teen years in Dakota with a single volume entitled "Prairie Girl." But her school days, teaching stints, courtship, and marriage stretched into two additional books: *Little Town on the Prairie* was published in 1941, and *These Happy Golden Years* was introduced with bittersweet fanfare in the spring of 1943. Readers read eagerly of the Wilders' happy marriage and first prairie home, but they mourned when the last page of the book proclaimed it "The End of the Little House Books."

*These Happy Golden Years* won the *New York Herald–Tribune's* Spring Book Festival Prize. The *Horn Book Magazine* also paid tribute to Laura, calling her "our most living heroine," but she could not be induced to write any more stories. "I have thought that Golden Years is my last," Laura firmly told George Bye, her agent, "and that I would spend what is left of my life in living, not writing about it" (letter dated May 10, 1943, George Bye Papers, Butler Library, Columbia University, N.Y.).

Almanzo and Laura at Rocky Ridge in 1948

An interviewer sought out the Wilders in Mansfield and suggested that another book would certainly bring in more money. "Why! We don't need it here!" Laura exclaimed, and she explained that she had been "hit by income tax" from the royalties on her eight books (Lucile Morris Upton, *Springfield News and Leader*, May 22, 1949).

On Rocky Ridge there was the solitude the Wilders had always enjoyed, enlivened by the simple pleasures of gardening, caring for the goat herd, churning butter, and watching the antics of Jack, the donkey, and the spoiled bulldog, Old Ben. "The Ozarks are beautiful now," Laura wrote as news of D-Day dominated the radio in June 1944, "and in our quiet home it seems impossible that such terrible things are happening in the world" (letter to Bye, June 10, George Bye Papers).

Rocky Ridge routines varied little. Laura cooked the seven o'clock breakfast while Almanzo fed the stock. Then he tended the garden, split wood for the range, or tinkered in his workshop while Laura did her housework. "To care for a ten-room farmhouse is no small job," she said (William Anderson, ed., *Horn Book's Laura Ingalls Wilder*, Laura Ingalls Wilder Memorial Society, 1987).

When the mailman had stopped at their lane, Laura and the brown bulldog left for a half-mile walk and usually returned with Laura bearing handfuls of letters. She often received fifty letters a day from her readers, and she answered each one.

"And when the day is over and evening comes we read our papers and magazines or play a game of cribbage," Laura wrote. "If we want music, we turn on the radio" (Anderson).

In her seventies, Laura was still pretty. Rose combined her impressions of her mother to provide this portrait of Laura for readers:

> She's the serious, wide-eyed girl now almost shyly hidden under a surface quickness and sparkle. She's little, about five feet tall; has very small hands and feet, and large violet-blue eyes; I have seen them purple. Baby-fine, pure-white hair. She wears it short and well-groomed, and moves and speaks quickly, sometimes vivaciously. But her character is Scotch; she holds a purpose or opinion like granite. . . . She has a charming voice, with changing tones and colors in it, and is sometimes witty or fanciful, but this is always a little startling; she is never talkative and usually speaks in a matter-of-fact way. Often she is silent nearly all day long; she is

completely self-reliant, is never lonely, has no need of companionship. She speaks only when she has something to say. (Anderson.)

The Wilders' admirers—teachers, librarians, and families all familiar with the "Little House" books—visited Rocky Ridge, and the hero and heroine of the stories were congenial hosts. Tongue-tied children—and adults—were invited to explore the big farmhouse or to sit on the front-porch swing to visit. Almanzo and Laura marveled at the diverse license plates on the cars arriving just to visit *them!*

The six years following the publication of Laura's last book were indeed golden for the Wilders. This pleasant time continued until Almanzo's heart attack and slow recuperation during the summer of 1949. He was ninety-two when he died suddenly one Sunday morning, October 23, 1949, with Laura beside him.

Without Almanzo, her constant companion for sixty-four years, Laura was bereft. "It is so lonely without Mr. Wilder that at times I can hardly bear it," Laura mourned. But there were happy moments. Libraries were named for her in Detroit, in Pomona, California, and right in Mansfield. The American Library Association established the Laura Ingalls Wilder Award in 1954 and presented their first medal to Laura herself. Her birthdays became red-letter days at the Mansfield post office; on February 7, 1951, nine hundred greetings arrived for Laura. "There is some advantage in being my age," she wrote to George Bye three years later. "Everyone is so glad I am 87 years old. I have had two birthday dinners in celebration while cards and gifts are still overloading my mail" (February 16, 1954, George Bye Papers).

Laura stayed on Rocky Ridge Farm. She was alone, but friends telephoned and often stopped in to chat. Rose made long visits from Danbury, Connecticut, and once Laura went to visit her daughter at her Connecticut home—traveling by airplane!

The love and recognition of her work constantly warmed Laura during her last years. "Thank you!" she exclaimed. "I appreciate very much the honor given me and my 'Little House' books. It is especially gratifying that through the books I have been acquainted with so many whom I regard as personal friends."

Laura's last public appearance, at Brown's Bookstore in Springfield, Missouri, in October 1952. The famous author, nearly eighty-six years old, autographed her books for lines of admiring fans. "She was adored that day," remarked Irene Lichty (the woman facing the camera), who drove Laura from Mansfield to Springfield for the occasion.

Each year, that circle of friendship widened. Children in America—and increasingly in countries where the books were translated—discovered and loved Laura's stories. She hoped that her books had shown her young friends that "courage and kindliness and helping each other and just plain being good are always the same and always needed." To the children Laura wrote earnestly:

The "Little House" Books are stories of long ago. Today our way of living and our schools are much different. It has been many years since I beat eggs with a fork, or cleaned a kerosene lamp; many things have made living and learning easier. But the real things haven't changed; they can never change. It is still best to be honest and truthful; to make the most of what we have; to be happy with simple pleasures and to be cheerful and have courage when things go wrong. Great improvements in living have been made because every American has been free to pursue his happiness, and so long as Americans are free they will continue to make our country ever more wonderful. (From a composite letter prepared by Harper and Brothers, n.d.)

In her last message to Rose, Laura wrote this assurance: "My love will be with you always" (letter dated July 30, 1952, to be opened after Laura's death). When Laura Ingalls Wilder died on February 10, 1957, three days after her ninetieth birthday, Rose knew, along with thousands of friends, known and unknown, that Laura's love would remain.

Rose Wilder Lane never returned to Mansfield to live following her long stretch of working on "Free Land" in New York City. The pioneer homesteading tale—first a serialization—became a best-selling book in 1938, and the *Saturday Evening Post* paid Rose thirty thousand dollars to print it. At the height of this success, Rose was intrigued with the romanticism of living in a five-story, cold-water, walk-up slum apartment in New York. She rented the place for twelve dollars a month and had it renovated and furnished for two hundred dollars. Her neighbors and close friends were the new-lyweds Norma Lee Browning, a writer, and Russell Ogg, a photographer; they bedecked her fire escape with colorful flowering plants, and Rose exclaimed that it all reminded her of Paris.

Rose kept the slum apartment for business and writing in the city. Writer friends, her agent George Bye, and editors often crowded in to visit, and Rose would send out for a dozen of Schrafft's special tea cookies for twelve dollars—the same amount that paid her month's rent. For the summers Rose bought a country home along a quiet lane in Danbury, Connecticut. It was a simple farmhouse, with a stone wall separating it from King Street. Rose loved the place and eventually made it her permanent home. Over the years she remodeled the house and added to it extensively, and on her small acreage she gardened and canned and stowed away jars that glowed like jewels in the cellar. The preserved produce fed her lavishly—she even had crates to share with

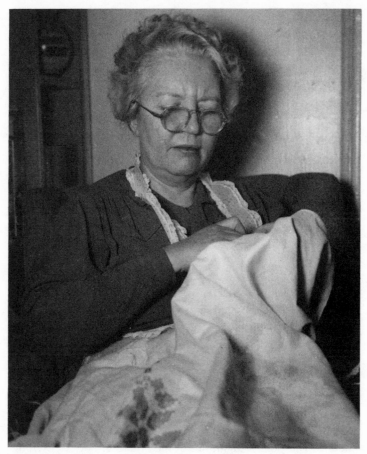

Rose in her New York slum apartment, photographed by Russell Ogg

friends—during the food-rationed years of World War II. Rose herself would not accept a ration card from the government.

With the onset of the war, Rose's writing for publication had diminished to an occasional piece for *Woman's Day*. Mama Bess was still preparing the last of the "Little House" books, and Rose helped her mother with these, but she produced no more of her own fiction. Her interests were firmly rooted in exploring history, economics, and political philosophies. She was most interested in man's dealings with authority and in the mystical, marvelous concept of individual liberty.

In 1943 Rose published what she considered her most important book: *The Discovery of Freedom*. It traced humankind's struggle for individual self-rule since the time of Adam. Her treatise championed the tenets of personal freedom that had touched off the American Revolution, and she challenged every American to remain vigilant of that freedom. "Ideas move the world," Rose stated. "False ideas bring on dark ages. True ideas caused America."

For the rest of her life, Rose Wilder Lane explored individualist thought. She was influential in advancing education and discussion of American principles. She was proud that the "Little House" books helped to show children the values of self-reliance, ingenuity, and courageous living.

After Mama Bess had died, readers begged Rose to write more about the family. "What happened next?" demanded thousands of letters. So Rose decided to provide an answer. In her mother's papers was the five-cent oblong memo pad in which Laura had recorded the daily happenings on the journey from De Smet to Mansfield in 1894. Rose typed Laura's penciled entries, added her own comments, and wrote an introduction and a conclusion for the diary. *On the Way Home* was published in 1962, but thereafter Rose would write no more of Mama Bess; she left her, as she remembered her in the last lines of *On the Way Home*, whistling cheerfully as she fixed supper in the little cabin on Rocky Ridge Farm.

In 1965 *Woman's Day* sent Rose to Viet Nam to report on the war; they wanted a woman's viewpoint. Rose was in her seventy-ninth year, and the State Department attempted to block her trip because of her age. Rose was stubborn; she had dusted off her dispatch case and intended to go, even if she had to swim to Saigon. She made the trip and was America's oldest active war correspondent.

After the Viet Nam assignment, Rose intended to retire. She bought a winter home in Harlingen, Texas, and lived there with her two dogs; she was a happy woman, full of memories and stories of an exciting life and loved by friends and neighbors. But that same restless wanderlust of her Grandpa Ingalls, her father, and her mother worked on Rose. When she was eighty-one, she decided to travel around the world. Just before she was to depart, however, Rose Wilder Lane died in her sleep in her Danbury home on October 30, 1968.

Rose was the last of the pioneering Ingalls and Wilder families. Like them, she had lived long and well. "The longest lives are short," she had once said. "It is our work that lasts longer."